Feminist Sport Studies

SUNY series on Sport, Culture, and Social Relations
CL Cole and Michael A. Messner, editors

Feminist Sport Studies
Sharing Experiences of Joy and Pain

Edited by
Pirkko Markula

State University of New York Press

Published by
State University of New York Press, Albany

For information, address State University of New York Press,
194 Washington Avenue, Suite 305, Albany, NY 12210-2384

Production by Diane Ganeles
Marketing by Susan M. Petrie

Library of Congress Cataloging-in-Publication Data

Feminist sport studies : sharing experiences of joy and pain / edited by Pirkko Markula.
    p. cm. — (SUNY series on sport, culture, and social relations)
  Includes bibliographical references and index.
   ISBN 0-7914-6529-2 (hardcover : alk. paper) — ISBN 0-7914-6530-6 (pbk. : alk. paper)
  1. Feminism and sports—Congresses.   2. Women's studies—Congresses.   3. Feminist
theory—Congresses.   I. Markula, Pirkko, 1961-   II. Series.

GV709.F34 2005
796'.082—dc22   2004021534

10 9 8 7 6 5 4 3 2 1

Arja Laitinen 1992

In Memory of Arja Laitinen
(1949—1999)

Arja Laitinen was an academic and a teacher. She was a consultant in the Arinna Institute, and a mother of two sons. She pioneered feminist sport research in Finland by becoming a founding member of the first Finnish feminist sport research project titled, "Movement Culture and Women" at the University of Jyväskylä, Finland. She was a feminist who preferred collaboration to heated arguments and as a result created a community of researchers who believed in similar ideas. She was soft spoken, modest, and brave. She was not afraid to confront difficult challenges in both her personal and professional lives. This she always did with extraordinary grace.

Arja strongly advocated new ways of studying sport in Finland. As a researcher, she problematized many taken-for-granted research conventions, adopted innovative qualitative research methodologies, and was among the first ones to critically apply these new ideas into practice. Central to Arja's research were the notion of "difference" and experiences of difference among women. In addition, she was a passionate advocate for feminism and the peace movement. The quest for "truthful" research was a lifelong inspiration for Arja. All of us who have contributed to this book have kind memories of Arja as a sincere, warm, and loving human being. With this book, we wish to continue the legacy of her work and celebrate her life as a feminist sport researcher.

Contents

Acknowledgments

This book would not have been possible without the help of a number of people. I want to specifically thank Leena Laine for initiating this project. Many grateful thanks to the contributors who have been extremely supportive and positive about this book. Without the enthusiastic support of the series editors, Michael Messner and CL Cole, our proposed book would never have materialized into a publication. Thank you for your efficiency in pushing this book through the stages required to complete it. I wish also to thank the reviewers whose detailed and constructive comments helped to develop this book further. Finally, I would like to thank Jim Denison for his emotional and intellectual support, his assistance and advice with editing, and his friendship during this project.

Introduction

Pirkko Markula

In the summer of 2000, a group of women academics met at the European Congress on Women and Sport in Helsinki, Finland. We were there to discuss the possibility of editing a book together. This proposed book carried a special meaning to us. Namely, it was planned to commemorate the death of a Finnish feminist sport scholar, Arja Laitinen, of breast cancer in 1999. From the discussion we realized that Arja, like several of her international colleagues, represented the first generation of feminist sport studies. Therefore, we decided to record the history of feminist work in this area, but instead of writing a collection of research essays, it seemed more valid to map this development through the vivid lived experiences of the first generation sport feminists. Consequently, this book, through feminist sport researchers' personal narratives, highlights the achievements of the first generation of feminist sport researchers and the pioneering role they played in the establishment of feminist sport studies as a legitimate academic subject area. The contributors come from Europe, New Zealand, and North America and specialize in subfields as diverse as sport literature, sport history, sport psychology, and sport sociology and are able to provide a broad international account of feminist sport studies. In addition, as this book features each contributor's personal research experiences, it aims to answer the call for more narrative, vital texts on sport that "make visible the complex, historically specific, matrices of social inequalities that surround us" (McDonald & Birrell, 1999, p. 295). Therefore, the purpose of this book is, through the critical personal narratives of prominent women researchers in this field, to examine the construction of feminist knowledge on sport and physical activity. These reflections cross disciplinary boundaries to discuss how feminists within sport studies understand the construction and control of knowledge in academia and in society.

This book embraces three key themes: the history of feminist sport studies, personal experience as a source for feminist sport inquiry, and narratives of the self by feminist sport scholars. To locate these personal narratives in their sociohistorical context, I will first outline the development of feminist sport studies as a field of inquiry. I will then discuss personal experience, and particularly feminist academics' personal experiences as a meaningful source for knowing about sport.

DEVELOPMENT OF FEMINIST SPORT STUDIES

Feminist sport studies can been seen to stretch across several subdisciplines such as sport literature (Bandy & Darden, 1999), sport history (e.g., Struna, 2000; Vertinsky, 1994), sport psychology (e.g., Gill, 2001; Oglesby, 2001), physical education (e.g., Scraton, 1992), and sport sociology (e.g., Birrell, 1988; Birrell, 2000; Birrell & Theberge, 1994; Bolin & Granskog, 2003; Dewar, 1993; Hall, 1988, 1996; Hargreaves, 1993; Scraton & Flintoff, 2001; Theberge, 2000). While this development has been recorded by several writers, the prevalence of feminist inquiry differs quite significantly between the different subdisciplines. For example, Dianne Gill (2001) notes that "sport psychology does not have well-developed feminist theories or models" (p. 364) while in sport sociology feminist scholarship has evolved into a well established field of research (see also Duda in this volume). This is due primarily to a number of influential North American feminist sport scholars such as Susan Birrell, Ann Hall, Carole Oglesby, and Nancy Theberge, several of whom trace their experiences in this book. Because of the substantial development of feminist research within sport sociology, I will outline the history of feminist research within sport studies mainly through the lens of sport sociology.

As several authors in this book recall, sport studies, particularly in North America, originated from physical education (see Bandy, Hall, and Thompson in this volume) where women's sport was addressed in relation to education (see Bandy in this volume, Rintala, 1991). In their chapters, Susan Bandy and Ann Hall for example, credit such physical educators as Ellen Gerber and Eleanor Metheny for their groundbreaking work on women and sport. With the increased emphasis on science in the 1960s, the physical education curricula were fragmented into various sport science subdisciplines. At this time, according to Susan Birrell (2000), research on women's sport appeared to increase.

While the initial studies into women's sport assumed a rather atheoretical premise, they nevertheless served as a first stage for feminist sport research. Birrell (2000) describes that at this early stage investigations into women and sport were "dominated by psychological topics focused on sex and gender roles, traits and motives, and role conflict" (p. 63–64). Several feminist sport scholars (e.g., Birrell, 2000; Dewar, 1991; Hall, 1996) label this research as distributive or categoric research because gender (or sex) was "conceived as a variable or distributive category" (Birrell, 2000, p. 64). This research attempted mainly to document "sex differences in sporting performance" and then attempted to explain them in terms of biology and socialization (Dewar, 1991, p. 151). Some of the major early contributors to research on women and sport were Jan Felshin, Susan Greendorfer, and Marie Hart. This early research might now appear to be simplistic and a naïve attempt to understand women's (non)participation in sport (see Hall and Thompson in this volume) and it is currently criticized for its focus on individual traits and behaviors. However, this is the stage where the authors in this book were introduced to the possibility of investigating women's issues and several report what a discovery it originally was to be able to study women's sport in the first place!

Feminist research of women's sport came to a full existence in the 1980s, when it moved from psychological considerations of sex differences and sex roles in sport to gender differences and gender roles, to the sex/gender system and to patriarchy and gender relations (e.g., Birrell, 2000; Hall, 1996). This stage, labeled by North American feminist sport scholars as feminist cultural studies (e.g., Birrell, 2000; Hall, 1988) is characterized by relational research where gender is seen as structured through hegemonic power relations that prevail in sport. With this shift, feminist sport studies became "a theoretically informed, critical analysis of the cultural forces that work to produce the ideological practices that influence the relations of sport and gender" (Birrell, 1988, p. 492). Susan Birrell and Nancy Theberge (1994) maintain that in the 1990s feminist researchers continued to establish sport as a site of production of the ideology of male superiority, but also expanded their analyses into media representations of physically active women. These images emphasized the difference between women and men by trivializing, marginalizing, and sexualizing women athletes and were thus a major factor that contributed to women's oppression in sport. In addition, issues such as homophobia, compulsory heterosexuality, and women's physicality became more central to feminist analyses. Birrell and Theberge also note that examinations of women's resistance to male dominance in and through sport became a major feature of feminist scholarship. Several chapters in this book focus on the researchers' experiences of conducting this type of relational research in the patriarchal world of sport (see chapters by Brackenridge, Fasting, Theberge, and Thompson).

While the authors in this book were major contributors to the critical feminist theorizing in sport studies, their work continues to evolve with the advances of feminist theorizing. The current stage of theorizing gender and sport is characterized by such labels as postmodernism (e.g., Birrell, 2000; Rail, 2002) or poststructuralism (e.g., Scraton & Flintoff; Rail, 2002). Such theorizing is eclectic, and Genevieve Rail (2002), for example, suggests referring to postmodernisms instead of a singular label of postmodern feminism. Although much of the scholarly work discussed in this book can be located within the critical feminist stage (see Hall's chapter in this book), the focus on writing about personal experience bridges it with some features of postmodern feminist scholarship. In this sense, the chapters in this book assume some characteristics of so-called third wave feminism (see Hall's chapter in this book).

The chapters in this book, then, bring the reader's attention to the achievements of the first generation of feminist sport researchers and the integral, pioneering role they played in the establishment of feminist sport studies as a legitimate academic subject area. In addition, it addresses the life of feminist academics beyond the boundaries of their research articles and results. Through their personal experiences, as academics, the contributors provide an understanding of the research context of academia and illuminate the everyday politics of being a feminist within sport studies. To further contextualize these experiences, I will examine the role of personal experiences as a legitimate area of study for feminist researchers.

PERSONAL EXPERIENCE AS FEMINIST RESEARCH

Within feminist scholarship, there has always been an acknowledgement of women's personal experience as an important source for academic knowledge. The premise of feminist theorizing is the acknowledgement that all knowledge is historically, culturally, and politically constructed. Consequently, feminists have demonstrated that academic knowledge, instead of being an objective, normative truth, is constructed based on the researcher's background and the ideological context of this background. This notion of knowledge as a social construct has guided feminists to challenge the prevailing, dominant notions of what constitutes valid academic research and consequently, encouraged new ways of understanding the nature of reality, knowledge, research, and research writing. Through feminist research, women's knowledge and their experiences have been lifted to the center of inquiry. For example, Barbara Laslett and Barrie Thorne (1997) argue that examining women's life experiences resonates with a feminist perspective in several ways. First, including individual women's voices enables the researcher to link the personal and political and the private and public spheres in her research. Second, personal experience can reveal categories of meaning that may have been submerged in more traditional social science practices. Third, personal experiences can illuminate the contradiction and ambivalence of women's lives in this global, commercial society. They can simultaneously draw attention to the structural oppression women face in this cultural condition and their agency—women's attempts to resist the societal notions of femininity imposed upon them. One of the most influential feminist theoretical approaches for understanding women's experiences has been standpoint feminism.

The main premise of standpoint feminism as advocated by Sandra Harding (1990, 1998), Nancy Hartsock (1990), and Dorothy Smith (1987), is the focus on the social construction of women's everyday experiences. Central to this feminist epistemology is the idea that reality, as we know it, is constructed through men's eyes and consequently, the knowledge that we have about women is also constructed through the same falsifying lens. In actuality, women's experiences differ considerably from men's experiences and therefore, there is a need for a feminist standpoint that takes women's experiences as primary and constitutive of a different world to the present, male dominated system. Nancy Hartsock (1990), for example, argues that women are alienated from their "real" experiences because they are forced to use dominant male, conceptual schemes. Consequently, women's experiences are a result of "bifurcated" knowledge; a result of living in both the dominated, men's world and in the separate, subordinate women's world. This dual experience, however, opens up the possibility for changing dominant social relations. It offers a more adequate and complete knowledge of women's conditions than just looking at women's lives through male created concepts.

Because women's experiences are central to defining alternatives to dominant structures, they have the potential to reveal several structures of oppression. Social order, and women's positions in this order, is made through several overlapping and conflicting structures such as androcentrism, racism, class oppression, and homophobia (Harding, 1990). Therefore, it is obvious that women's experiences are structured differently depending on their background. Women's oppression will also take different forms, and their resistance will differ depending on the specific structure of their gender identities. To fully understand women's cultural condition, it is imperative that women of color, working class women, and lesbians are present among the women whose experiences we examine. For Hartsock (1990), the analyses of the experiences of marginalized women provide the best shield against the dangers of the universalization of the category "woman." She argues that marginalized groups are far less likely to mistake themselves for a universal experience, because they are not the dominant who can afford to assume that their experiences are the experiences of all.[1] Consequently, understanding the oppressed exposes the "inhuman" relations that exist among people in general and that can create a base for feminist political action. Hartsock (1990) concludes:

> When various "minority" experiences have been described and when the significance of these experiences as a ground for critique of the dominant institutions and ideologies of society is better recognized, we will have at least the tools to begin to

construct an account of the world sensitive to the realities of race and gender as well as class. (p. 172)

In sport studies, standpoint feminism has been advocated openly only by few feminist sport scholars (e.g., Dewar, 1993; Krane, 2001) and some feminists conclude that "that dominant sociological approaches to the investigation of women in sport . . . have placed primary emphasis upon the institutional framework within which individuals operate rather than on the variable and more subjective qualitative experiences of women themselves" (Bolin & Granskog, 2003, p. 349). Despite this observation, the standpoint epistemology that recognizes differences particularly between marginalized groups' experiences has strongly influenced our scholarship. The focus has been on, first, how women's sporting experience expose the patriarchal premise of sport and second, how they create more women centered alternatives to masculine power relations.[2] Susan Birrell and Diana Richter (1987), for example, argue that feminist theorizing of sport should be "grounded in women's unique experiences" of the world. They continue that it is important that "feminist analysis entertains interpretations of findings that are informed by and consistent with women's experiences of the world" (p. 296), because only through their experiences can women turn sport from a hegemonic and alienating practice into a practice that has relevance within their lives. Similarly, Jennifer Hargreaves (1990) argues that the "most dynamic feminism arises from personal experience" (p. 180). Many researchers have since followed the call for feminist work deriving from women's personal sporting experiences. These studies have examined, through ethnographies and interview studies, the meanings individual women have placed on physical activity and how these meanings have been shaped by societal power relations (e.g., Bolin, 2003; Bruce, 1998; Granskog, 2003; Haravon, 2001; McDermott, 2000; Markula, 2003; Miller & Penz, 1991; Scraton, 1992; Theberge, 1995, 1997, 2000; Thompson, 1988, 1999; Wachs, 2003; Wright & Dewar, 1997). In addition, they have highlighted the possibilities for the transformation of dominance through women's resistant sport experiences. There has also been an increased focus on lesbian sport experiences (e.g., Broad, 2001; Clarke, 1997; Fusco, 1998; Griffin, 1998; Hargreaves, 2000; Krane, 1996, 1997; Lenskyj, 1994; Sykes, 1998; Wheaton & Tomlinson, 1998), sport experiences of women from different ethnic backgrounds (e.g., Hargreaves, 2000; Smith, 1992; Stratta, 2003; Wray, 2001) and experiences of women with disabilities (Guthrie & Castelnuovo, 2001; Hargreaves, 2000). In addition, women athletes' personal experiences have been collected in two recent anthologies of women's literature on women's sport (Bandy & Darden, 1999; Sandoz, 1997) and in one collection of women's nonfiction on sport (Sandoz & Winans,1999). Many of the authors in this book have contributed to this body of literature on women's sporting experiences and highlight some of their projects in more detail in this book.

However, despite the increase in personal experience texts within sport studies, feminist scholars have not commonly reflected on their own experiences within academia, or on the importance of these experiences to the accumulation of knowledge on sport. Because the accumulation of feminist knowledge within sport studies is highlighted through researchers' personal experiences in this book, it is necessary to ask at this point why there is an abundance of literature on women's experiences, meanings, and identities in different sporting contexts, yet writings about the researchers' own experiences are relatively rare?

EMOTIONALITY, SUBJECTIVITY, AND THE RESEARCHER'S SELF

It appears that feminist sport researchers are not afraid of politicizing and theorizing other women's experiences, but their own research experiences rarely become the subject of this same process of politicization. This seems rather odd considering that women's personal experiences occupy a central role in feminist research. Do we feel uncomfortable writing about ourselves? It is also notable that when sport women's experiences become feminist research, they often turn into objective, theoretical accounts of oppression or resistance. Participants speak through interview quotations and the researcher's voice remains hidden. Why is the feminist researcher's self so excluded from the research text? Elspeth Probyn (1993) writes about the problems that the inclusion of a researcher's personal experiences presents for feminist research.

Probyn (1993) finds that many feminists are troubled by the inclusion of their own voices within their investigations because it seems to connect their research with emotionality. While emotionality is often considered an important aspect of women's lives, for a feminist researcher, Probyn argues, it often connotes not being taken seriously. Being emotional or recording one's own personal experiences seems to equal "hysterical" (p. 83); a charge that many feminists are all too familiar with even when involved in rigorous theoretical work. Therefore, to gain academic credibility many feminists favor current trends in feminism that "as a body of theories, flees emotionality" (p. 83). Ridiculed and troubled with private experience and emotionality, Probyn concludes, feminism has resorted to overjargonized, theoretical writing. The problem with this is that, as writing is a way of using power and imposing dominance, feminists unquestioningly adopt and advance the values of "science" when opting for a "scientific" writing style. Therefore, it seems that feminism, while eager to challenge women's condition in contemporary society, is complying with, rather than contesting, the dominance of the mainstream academic research tradition. Mary Evans (1995) points to this contradictory situation when she argues that in concert with the development of its groundbreaking, innovating theorizing, feminist work has turned inaccessible and as a matter of fact, has became "a mirror image of some male scholarship" that has maintained its power position by being accessible to only a few "sophisticated intellectuals" (pp. 81–82). Furthermore, when we choose to theorize and write objectively we align ourselves with the dominant mode of scientific knowledge production. While it is, naturally, sometimes necessary to opt for a theoretical, objective writing style in feminist research, it is important to emphasize that such writing should be a choice among other ways of writing, not a precondition for "serious" scholarship. Therefore, feminist scholars should aim to contest the dominance, not the usefulness, of "scientific" ways of writing that exclude the researcher's voice.

One way of revealing the dominance embedded in objective research writing is to demonstrate the emotional dimensions of knowledge production by writing about the relationships and contexts influencing the research process. Writing about academic women's personal experiences, therefore, potentially reveals knowledge, not as an objective truth, but as being subjectively constructed. As Laurel Richardson (1997) points out: "how one writes one's theory is not simply a theoretical matter. The theoretical inscribes a social order, power relationships, and the subjective state of the theorist" (p. 49). In this way, personal accounts can contribute to contemporary theoretical debates about the nature of knowledge and pave the way for the potential deconstruction of the social sciences to include more than one dominant voice. As Louise Morley and Val Walsh (1995) write:

> Feminist analysis of the micropolitics of the academy in terms of power, policies, discourses, curriculum, pedagogy and intra- and interpersonal relationships, provides a framework for deprivatizing women's experiences and influencing change. (p. 1)

However, although a necessary facet of knowledge construction, recording one's experience does not alone advance feminist scholarship.

RESEARCHER'S VOICE AND CONSTRUCTING FEMINIST THEORY

To become a meaningful aspect of feminist scholarship, women academics' experiences, like all personal experiences, need to be located within theory—only through the process of speaking theoretically can we become creative agents for change. Feminist academics' personal experience narratives when embedded in theory can lead the way to a large scale change in women's cultural condition:

> Using theoretical constructs, our own biographies and experiences, as impetus, example and frame, women map present predicaments and inequalities, and identify sites and opportunities for strategic interventions. (Morley & Walsh, 1995, p. 1)

When merged with theory, personal experience, while always providing an access to unique human experience, also becomes a political tool to create sociological consciousness, and empower others toward collective action. As Probyn (1993) advocates: "The self here is both an object of inquiry and the means of analysing where and how the self is lodged within the social formation" (p. 105). For Richardson (2000), writing about personal experience becomes meaningful as "a collective story" that "tells the experience of sociologically constructed category of people in the context of larger socio-cultural and historical forces" (p. 14). As a collective, feminist academics can deconstruct the academy by revealing "the social and psychic labour involved in the daily negotiation of patriarchal power in the academy" (Morley & Walsh, 1995, p. 2). Therefore, the emotions and experiences of feminist academics can direct our research in new theoretical directions. Probyn (1993), for example, wants to

> examine an emotional foregrounding of the self as a way of critically acknowledging the ontological and epistemological bases of knowledge transformation. My interest here is in feminist uses of the auto-biographical as a tactic within the production of theory, or more precisely within the process of speaking theoretically. (p. 83)

In addition, Barbara Laslett and Barrie Thorne (1997) argue that writing about our experiences in academia might provide one way of constructing more readable and effective feminist texts, because engaging with personal experiences will expand the narrative and discursive repertoire of feminism. Such feminist writing can simultaneously draw attention to the structural oppression women face in this cultural condition and their agency—women's attempts to resist the societal notions of femininity imposed upon them. Several chapters in this book (by Kosonen, Kröner, Oglesby, Thompson) highlight how feminists within sport studies have experienced the structural constraints within academia and their negotiation with these pressures. Writing about one's own experiences to evoke a collective story embedded in feminist theory, is not, of course, a simple matter. There is always the recurring issue about how to represent the self, "the autobiographical I" as Liz Stanley (1992) labels it, without falling into the pitfalls of self-indulgence.

RESEARCHER'S VOICE AND SELF-INDULGENCE

It is commonly argued that the concern with one's self, such as including personal experience into one's research, or reflecting on one's own writing process, is merely narcissistic navel gazing that does not contribute to meaningful knowledge construction or create change in social conditions. Contrary to this claim, Richardson (1997) asserts that when a researcher's sense of self is diminished into a homogenized, detached professional voice, qualitative (feminist) texts can become boring and meaningless to all but the most devoted academics. Stanley (1992) adds that it is odd that the writer's self is actively left unproblematized in scientific texts when "the major epistemological issues for our time are raised in connection with the nature of 'selves', how to understand and how to study them under what kind of intellectual conditions and limitations" (p. 5). Stanley (1995) elaborates that the reason for the exclusion of the author's self stems from the fear that the "I" will deeply shake the foundations of what constitutes academic knowledge. But why should feminism, that already has challenged the scientific construction of knowledge, be worried about the effects of the "I" in its own research canon? Because it brings academic women's feelings, emotions, and subjective involvement into the analysis and evokes the humiliating charge of the feminist researcher, if not quite as hysterical, then definitely as narcissistic, self-indulgent, and atheoretical. Stanley (1995) argues, however, that excluding our academic selves from the writing process creates a hierarchical division between us, the researchers, and the women we study:

> "we" research and theorize "them," and through the practices of science we become detached . . . Insofar as any feminist academic speaks and writes "for the" women and not "as a" woman . . . , she takes up the speaking and writing position of men. (p. 184)

Therefore, instead of aligning with such a dominant stance, feminists should embrace their unique access to women's voices without repeating the hierarchical structure of "male" scientific inquiry. Including the researcher's own voice is not self-indulgent, but a necessary tool to reduce the authoritative power of an academic over her participants. While the researcher's self is an essential part of the feminist research process, Stanley does not promote an uncritical inclusion of the author's voice. Her point is to diminish the binary between the women researched and women researchers, and her concept "intellectual auto/biography" aims for the production of critically aware, reflexively constituted, and analytical feminist texts:

> This is an approach which recognizes that the academic feminist's account of her life and work (her "autobiography") necessarily includes her descriptions, interpretations and analyses of the lives and activities (thus "biography") of others, and theirs hers of course . . . ; and also that this is not merely a narrative—the story of the life of—but rather a critical and analytic account that looks rigorously at the grounds of its own knowledge-claims. (p. 185)

Through critical self-reflexivity, feminist auto/biographical writing shows that the "self" is fabricated: "not necessarily a lie but certainly a highly complex truth: a fictive truth reliant on cultural convention concerning what 'a life' consists of and how its story can be told both in speech and, somewhat differently, in writing" (Stanley, 1992, pp. 242–243). Therefore, the feminist researcher's "I" reveals itself also as a "self" that is socially constructed within a network of others. This way, Stanley (1992) reiterates, a feminist auto/biography that is characterized by its self-conscious traversing of conventional boundaries between different genres of writing is far from self-indulgent as it can open new exciting and challenging ways for conducting interesting and meaningful feminist analyses. While an inclusion of the researcher's self services the goals of feminism in several ways, a simple acknowledgement of the researcher's subjectivity does not collapse the boundaries between us and other women, and between objective and subjective knowledge construction. We need a commitment to ways of writing that allow the researcher's self to become an active part of the text. Here we are required to take the difficult step from the safety and familiarity of realist, scientific ways of writing to narrative ways of writing. But how can we, feminist academics raised on realist texts, suddenly enter a new genre of writing?

THE RESEARCHER'S VOICE AND RESEARCH WRITING

It is obvious that the researcher plays a major role in the construction of social science knowledge, but how is her voice to become explicit in the text? While the researcher's self can enter the text in multiple ways, some commonly used terms for these texts within social science are autobiography (Stanley, 1992), autobiographical narrative (Richardson, 1997), and autoethnography (Bochner & Ellis, 2002; Richardson, 2000). How do we distinguish between these different terms, or are distinctions even needed? Often these terms are used interchangeably and there is no need to insist on clearly defined categories here. Gertrud Pfister's chapter in this book, for example, blurs such categorical boundaries as she discusses her own development as a feminist researcher (autobiolographical narrative) through her research of an autobiography of a famous female athlete. However, as narrative ways of writing have evolved, there has been an increased emphasis on their literary qualities and presently, some types of narratives require advanced literary skills. While all research texts should be well written, it might be useful to describe some qualities attached to these different types of narrative writing. Awareness of different narrative genres can serve as a starting point for researchers, whose background is in realist writing, but are, nevertheless, interested in exploring the possibilities provided by narrative writing. Richardson's (2000) recent term "evocative representation" is an excellent guide for anyone embarking on this journey.

Richardson (2000) characterizes evocative representations as writing genres that "deploy literary devices to recreate lived experiences and evoke emotional responses" (p. 11). Evocative presentations, open to experience and emotionality, allow for self-reflection and encourage a process of self-transformation as we struggle to find "a textual place for ourselves" (p. 11). According to Richardson, such forms of writing as autoethnography, writing stories, ethnographic fiction, poetic representation, and ethnographic drama are forms of evocative representation. Ethnographic fiction and drama as well as poetic representation derive heavily from literary techniques and require an advanced understanding of different fiction-writing techniques. Therefore, writing stories and autoethnography seem safer starting points for feminist academics who want to enter the world of evocative representations.

Richardson defines writing stories as "narratives about the writing process itself" (p. 11). Writing stories are narratives that account for the context of the writing process by critically reflecting on the writing-self:

> They [writing stories] situate one's own writing in other parts of one's life, such as disciplinary constraints, academic debates, departmental politics, social movements, community structures, research interests, familial ties, and personal history. (Richardson, 2000, p. 11)

Most of the authors in this book could be described as writing feminist research stories whereas some have presented their chapters more as autoethnographies. What distinguishes story writing from autoethnography is the employment of specific literary techniques. Autoethnographies, according to Richardson, are "highly personalized, revealing texts in which authors tell stories about their own lived experiences, relating the personal to the cultural" (p. 11). Personal experiences become evocative when the author uses different fiction-writing techniques to hold back the interpretation; or in literary terms, aims to "show" the meaning of an experience as culturally constructed instead of directly stating, or "telling," how the events took place. Therefore, autoethnography is always open to multiple interpretations inviting "the reader to emotionally 'relive' the events with the writer" (p. 11). In Richardson's classification, memories or personal experiences told in the first person, in a realist manner, are not autoethnographic texts, but can be used as preliminary tools for constructing evocative tales.

Whatever evocative representation genre we choose, or how ever deeply we aim to blur the boundaries of literary and scholarly writing, Richardson reminds us that there is no one single way of writing. While theoretical, "realist" texts continue to offer a good alternative when we target academic audiences, evocative writing provides a chance to write differently to different audiences, and tell different women's stories in a variety of ways. As Richardson points out: "Learning alternative ways of writing increases your repertoire and increases the number and kinds of audiences you might reach" (p. 15)—a particularly pertinent goal for feminists who aim to speak to a large number of women and reach outside the academic audience. Richardson (2000) presents a serious challenge for feminist sport scholars who are used to the criteria of traditional, realist science writing. However, evocative representations can vitally expand the ways we look to expose, challenge, and create change in sporting women's lives in today's cultural climate. In addition, they provide a way to challenge our own academic realities: the ways knowledge is constructed, the ways research is evaluated, and the ways feminism's own categories of academic/political, detached/emotional, theoretical/personal, researcher/other enter into our everyday practices. For example, Linda Christian-Smith and Kristine Kellor (1999) conclude that narrative representation

> can surprise, disrupt, and create crises which have the potential to transform previously held assumptions and beliefs about self and others and foster agency and activism as well . . . Within this politicization lie possibilities for imagining alternative constructions of experience for women inside and outside the academy. (p. xiv)

In sum, to succeed, feminist evocative writing needs to be contextualized with theory to convey how women's, including academic women's, personal experiences are historically, politically, and culturally constructed. Only by merging the personal, the political, and the theoretical, can our stories show how academic women's everyday actions are not just shaped by domination, but how this domination can be resisted by individual women. Through stories we can share the pain and the joy of being an academic, a woman, an activist, a survivor, a creative agent for change. In this light, politicizing the experiences of female researchers who study physical activity can create a further understanding of the nature of domination within academia; the impact of power relations on the lives of women researchers; and on the construction of feminist knowledge on sport and physical activity.

ACADEMIC EXPERIENCES AND FEMINIST SPORT SOCIOLOGY

Despite the relative scarcity of texts that map feminist researchers' personal experiences, there are some such collections, for example, in sociology (Lasslett & Thorne, 1997; Orlans & Wallace, 1994), in education (Christian-Smith & Kellor, 1999), and in British academia (Morley & Walsh, 1995). While this book is the first of its type in sport studies, there have been some previous personal experience narratives written by feminist sport scholars.

CL Cole (1991) and Toni Bruce (1998) both appeal for a problematization of the authority of the feminist researcher's voice in sport research and urge us to consider using narrative strategies in sport studies. Since these calls, a few feminists in sport studies have followed this path. Some of the earliest examinations of women's personal sport experiences come from Finland. For example, Ulla Kosonen (1993a) traces her personal body history through memory work. Kosonen is also one of the earliest advocates of life story and subjective experience as legitimate forms of sport research (1993b). In this book, Kosonen tells the story of her feminist colleague and friend Arja Laitinen (Chapter 1). Closely following Kosonen's work, other Finnish women reflected on their physical activity experiences (Kaskisaari, 1994; Veijola, 1994) in a special issue of the *International Review of Sociology of Sport* titled Narrative Sociology edited by Henning Eichberg (1994). In another special issue on new ways of writing titled, Sociological Imaginings, Sociological Narratives, also edited by men (Denison & Rinehart, 2000) in the *Sociology of Sport Journal*, three women, Margaret Duncan (2000), Eleanor Miller (2000), and Tosha Tsang (2000) were among the contributors who examined their physical activity experiences from a feminist perspective. While these personal experience narratives are evocative by providing us with self-reflexive accounts of women's physical activity experience, the authors do not explicitly relate their recollections to their working lives as feminist academics. There are other feminist sport researchers who do reflect on their professional careers.

In her book, *Feminism and Sporting Bodies* Ann Hall (1996) critically reviewed her own development from a positivist researcher to a critical feminist. Similarly, Celia Brackenridge (1999) offered a story of her personal and professional struggles as a feminist researcher of sport. Both of these texts appear in revised form in this book. In addition, in her presidential address to the North American Society for Sociology of Sport, Margaret Duncan (1998) used personal experience to illustrate the meaning of stigmatized bodies in physical activity and how she, as a feminist academic, began to understand these issues through her scholarship. In her text, then, Duncan blurs the boundary between her personal and professional selves.

The impact of personal accounts shared publicly with other colleagues can be significant. For example, the impetus for this book derived directly from one such occasion. The original idea for this book stemmed from the death of Finnish feminist sport sociologist, Arja Laitinen, to cancer in 1999. While it was agreed that a book would be the best way to commemorate her work, it was not immediately clear what topic the book would cover. However, all the contacted contributors instantly remembered Arja's talk at the The International Congress of Movement and Sport in Women's Life in 1987. In this talk she, through her personal experience, examined the role of feminism, the role of the feminist researcher, and the role of research on women's sport within sport studies. Her experiences of the obstacles and resistance to her research resonated with the other feminist sport researchers who found her attempt to openly address the domination of women in academia incredibly brave. This book offers an opportunity to share the joys and pains Arja experienced in her career as a feminist within sport studies. Through their stories and autoethnographies, the authors aim to contextualize the development of feminist research in sport. They tell their research stories, the joy they have experienced when opening the secrets of sport for women, and the pain they, as feminists, have shared while on this path. In the following chapters they discuss their feelings, emotions, and experiences of being women researchers in the male dominated field of sport.

This book is divided into three parts. Part One, Feminist Sport Studies: Stories of Discovery and Dismissal, focuses on the development of feminist sport studies through the personal research histories of the authors. This section opens with a chapter tracing the life of Arja Laitinen written by Ulla Kosonen as it was important to set off the rest of the chapters from Arja's life. In a sense, this book is part of the mourning for the loss of a dear colleague that we still go through. The contributors have warm memories of Arja who, with her endless enthusiasm for things novel, her openness to ideas, and her unceasing faith for the feminist cause, was an integral part of our inspiration and optimism. Based on her life experiences within sport feminism, Ann Hall takes us on a journey through the early years of liberal feminist sport research through socialist and critical feminism all the way to "third wave" feminist sport research in Chapter 2. In Chapter 3, Joan Duda looks at the development of sport psychology through the lens of her own career as a researcher of motivation. In her narrative of self-discovery Duda reflects on her personal enthusiasm for engaging in sport psychology and how this influences the ways in which she approaches the major issues and controversies in her area of study.

Part Two, Personal Experiences as a Source for Feminist Inquiry in Sport, accounts the accumulation of feminist knowledge in the sport sciences and the joy recognized in that, despite the bumpy ride, we are moving forward. Nancy Theberge, in Chapter 4, tells her story as a feminist sport researcher and particularly as an ethnographer studying women's ice hockey. Theberge highlights issues that confront many ethnographers who enter the field. For example, she discusses how she, as a nonskating "outsider," gained access to the elite women's hockey culture; how she created rapport with the team members, coaches, and the management of the team; and how she negotiated her role as an observer, rather than a member, of women's ice-hockey culture. While Theberge's research focuses on sporting women's experiences, Carole Oglesby highlights how academic experiences inform the feminist researcher's inquiry. In Chapter 5, Oglesby, one of the major contributors to the field of feminist sport studies, examines how structural difficulties in academia can turn into traumatic experiences that have a deep felt impact on the feminist researcher's life. Based on her own experiences, Oglesby also offers advice on how, despite the trials and tribulations, a feminist researcher can stay in her chosen research course and thus, by using her agency to continue her feminist work. Sabine Kröner's resistance to the male-dominated field of sport studies materializes in a quite different form from Oglesby. In Chapter 6, Kröner takes the readers outside of the male-dominated environments to reflect on how her dream of creating a physical activity environment for women by women worked in practice. Kröner accounts both the disappointments and successes she experienced as the leader of such a feminist project. Kari Fasting, in chapter 7, discusses her research on sexual harassment among female athletes. She then continues to discuss how this research can inform the lives of women academics as well. She aims to shed light into situations that can be regarded as sexual harassment in sport and calls for more attention to the similarities between sport academia and elite sport as male-dominated environments.

Part Three, The Feminist Sport Researcher: Multiple Selves, highlights the idea that our research experiences are shaped by the multiple identities that construct what we identify as our "selves." In Chapter 8, Celia Brackenridge offers a story of her personal and professional struggles as a feminist researcher investigating a sensitive research topic, sexual harassment in sport. Brackenridge reflects on what it means for a middle-class, lesbian, political activist and advocate to engage in a gendered research process. Furthermore, she explores how her research project required several selves—the personal, the political, and the scientific—to act and react simultaneously. In Chapter 9, Gertrud Pfister weaves together her autobiography as a sport historian with a biography of a famous female pilot, Sophie Peirce-Evans. The selves of the researcher and the researched meet as Pfister reflects on her contradictory fascination with Sophie's exceptional and often glamorous life against her own identity as a feminist. Susan Bandy, in Chapter 10, explores her identity as a "transnational" feminist who, originally from the state of Georgia in the United States, has traveled in her career through several departments, several subdisciplines, and several countries. Her story is a story of negotiating different cultures, different cities, different jobs, and different feminisms as she crosses academic boundaries in the United States, France, Hungary, and Denmark. Shona Thompson, similarly, takes us through her travels across New Zealand, Canada, and Australia in Chapter 11. Her autoethnography moves between different time periods, different continents, and different research projects to trace her career as a woman studying sport to a sport feminist. Thompson's multiple selves are blurred into one identity when the story advances to show the context for her feminist path.

NOTES

1. The concept "experience" has been problematized by some poststructuralist feminist scholars. For example, Joan Scott (1992) points out that experience, like any concept, is a socially and linguistically produced category, not a guarantee of "authentic" link to women's "reality." When taken for granted as a research category, experience can result in individualism and essentialism. Scott argues that talking about experience as externally structured, yet offering "internal" agency leads us to take the existence of individuals for granted (experience is something people have) rather than to ask how conceptions of selves (of subjects and their identities) are produced. It operates within an ideological construction that not only makes individuals the starting point of knowledge, but that also "naturalizes categories such as man, woman, black, white, heterosexual, or homosexual by treating them as given characteristics of individuals" (p. 27). While Scott does not support abandoning research based on experiences, she calls for careful analysis and redefinition of the meaning of experience through understanding "complex and changing discursive processes by which identities are ascribed, resisted, or embraced and which processes themselves are unremarked, indeed achieve their effect because they aren't noticed" (p. 33). In sport studies, poststructuralist redefinition of identity has also been promoted by several feminist scholars (e.g., Cole, 1993; Markula, 2003; Rail, 2002).

2. Nancy Theberge (1985, 1987) was one of the first sport feminists to theorize resistance within this framework. Based on Hartsock's theory of liberatory possibilities embedded in women's experiences, Theberge (1987) asserted that feminist change in sport requires action at the personal, group, and institutional level with each level being a precondition of the other. In a later work, Birrell and Theberge (1994) theorize that sport can serve, in addition to personal and group transformation, as a vehicle for institutional change. In this work, they distinguish among empowerment, resistance, and transformation: resistance, refers to personal and group-level empowerment whereas transformation constitutes social, institutional change. Furthermore, for social change to occur, resistant acts should be conscious, collective, political, and public.

REFERENCES

Birrell, S. (1988). Discourses on the gender/sport relationship: From women in sport to gender relations. *Exercise and Sport Sciences Review*, 16, 459–502

Birrell, S. (2000). Feminist theories in sport. In J. Coakley & E. Dunning (Eds.), *Handbook of sport studies* (pp. 61–76). London: Sage.

Birrell, S., & Theberge, N. (1994). Ideological control of women in sport. In M. Costa & S. Guthrie (Eds.), *Women and sport* (pp. 341–359). Champaign, IL: Human Kinetics.

Bolin, A. (2003). Beauty or the beast: The subversive soma. In A. Bolin & J. Granskog (Eds.), *Athletic intruders: Ethnographic research on women, culture, and exercise* (pp. 107–130). Albany: State University of New York Press.

Bolin, A., & Granskog, J. (2003). Pastimes and presentimes: Theoretical issues in research on women in action. In A. Bolin & J. Granskog (Eds.), *Athletic intruders: Ethnographic research on women, culture, and exercise* (pp. 247–260). Albany: State University of New York Press.

Bruce, T. (1998). Audience frustration and pleasure: Women viewers confront televised women's basketball. *Journal of Sport & Social Issues*, 22, 373–397.

Bruce, T. (1998). Postmodernism and the possibilities for writing "vital" sports texts. In G. Rail (Ed.), *Sport and postmodern times* (pp. 3–19). Albany: State University of New York Press.

Christian-Smith, L. K., & Kellor, K. S. (1999). *Everyday knowledge and uncommon truths: Women of the academy*. Boulder, CO: Westview Press.

Cole, C L (1991). The politics of cultural representation: Vision of fields/fields of vision. *International Review for Sociology of Sport*, 26(1), 37–49.

Cole, C L (1993). Resisting the canon: Feminist cultural studies, sport, and technologies of the body. *Journal of Sport and Social Issues*, 17(2), 77–97.

Denison, J., & Rinehart, R. (2000). Imaging sociological narratives. *Sociology of Sport Journal*, 17.

Dewar, A. (1993). Sexual oppression in sport: Past, present, and future alternatives. In A. G. Ingham & J. W. Loy (Eds.), *Sport in social development* (pp. 147–166). Champaign, IL: Human Kinetics.

Duncan, M. C. (1998). Stories we tell ourselves about ourselves. *Sociology of Sport Journal*, 15, 95–108.

Duncan, M. C. (2000). Reflex: Body as Memory. *Sociology of Sport Journal*, 17, 60–68.

Fusco, C. (1998). Lesbians and locker rooms: The subjective experiences of lesbians in sport. In G. Rail (Ed.), *Sport and postmodern times* (pp. 87–116). Albany: State University of New York Press.

Gill, D. (2001). Feminist sport psychology: A guide for our journey. *The Sport Psychologist*, 15, 363–372.

Granskog, J. (2003). Just "tri" and "du" it: The variable impact of female involvement in the triathlon/duathlon sport culture. In A. Bolin & J. Granskog (Eds.), *Athletic intruders: Ethnographic research on women, culture, and exercise* (pp. 27–52). Albany: State University of New York Press.

Guthrie, S. R., & Castelnuovo, S. (2001). Disability management among women with physical impairments: The contribution of physical activity. *Sociology of Sport Journal*, 18, 5–20.

Hall, M. (1988). The discourse of gender and sport: From femininity to feminism. *Sociology of Sport Journal*, 5, 330–340.

Hall, M. A. (1996). *Feminism and sporting bodies*. Champaign, IL: Human Kinetics.

Harding, S. (1990). Feminism, science, and the anti-enlightenment critiques. In L. J. Nicholson (Ed.), *Feminism/postmodernism* (pp. 83–106). New York: Routledge.

Harding, S. (1998). *Is science multicultural? Postcolonialism, feminism, and epistemologies*. Bloomington, IN: Indiana University Press.

Hargreaves, J. A. (1993). Gender on the sports agenda. In A. G. Ingham & J. W. Lay (Eds.), *Sport in social development* (pp. 167–186). Champaign, IL: Human Kinetics.

Hargreaves, J. A. (2000). *Heroines of sport: Politics of difference and identity*. London: Routledge.

Hartsock, N. (1990). Foucault on power: A theory for women? In L. J. Nicholson (Ed.), *Feminism/postmodernism* (pp. 157–175). New York: Routledge.

Kaskisaari, M. (1994). The rhythmbody. *International Review for the Sociology of Sport*, 29(1), 15–24.

Kosonen, U. (1993). A running girl: Fragments of my body history. In L. Laine (Ed.), *On the fringes of sport* (pp. 16–25). Sankt Augustin, Germany: Academia Verlag.

Kosonen, U. (1993). Personal is scientific! In L. Laine (Ed.), *On the fringes of sport* (pp. 48–57). Sankt Augustin, Germany: Academia Verlag.

Krane, V. (1997). Homogeneity experienced by lesbian college athletes. *Women in Sport and Physical Activity Journal*, 6, 141–163.

Krane, V. (2001). One lesbian feminist epistemology: Integrating feminist standpoint, queer theory, and feminist cultural studies. *The Sport Psychologist*, 15, 401–411.

Laslett B. & Thorne, B. (1997). Life histories of a movement: An introduction. In B. Laslett & B. Thorne (Eds.), *Feminist sociology: Life histories of a movement* (pp. 1–27). New Brunswick, NJ: Rutgers University Press.

Laslett B., & Thorne, B. (1997). *Feminist sociology: Life histories of a movement.* New Brunswick, NJ: Rutgers University Press.

Lenskyj, H. (1994). Sexuality and femininity in sport contexts: issues and alternatives. *Journal of Sport and Social Issues,* 18(4), 356–376.

Markula, P. (2003a). Postmodern aerobics: Contradiction and resistance. In A. Bolin & J. Granskog (Eds.), *Athletic intruders: Ethnographic research on women, culture, and exercise* (pp. 53–78). Albany: State University of New York Press.

Markula, P. (2003). The technologies of the self: Sport, feminism and Foucault. *Sociology of Sport Journal,* 20, 87–107.

McDermott, L. (2000). A qualitative assessment of the significance of body perception to women's physical activity experiences: Revisiting discussions of physicalities. *Sociology of Sport Journal,* 17, 331–363.

McDonald, M. G., & Birrell, S. (1999). Reading sport critically: A methodology for interrogating power. *Sociology of Sport Journal,* 16, 283.

Miller, E. M. (2000). Dis. *Sociology of Sport Journal,* 17, 75–80.

Miller, L., & Penz, O. (1991). Taking bodies: Female bodybuilders colonize a male preserve. *Quest,* 43, 148–163.

Oglesby, C. (2001). To unearth the legacy. *The Sport Psychologist,* 15, 373–385.

Orlans Meadow, K. P., & Wallace, R. A. (1994). *Gender and the academic experience: Berkeley women sociologists.* Lincoln: Nebraska University Press.

Rail, G. (2002). Postmodernism and sport studies. In J. Maguire & K. Young (Eds.), *Theory, sport & society* (pp. 179–207). London: Elsevier.

Richardson, L. (1997). *Fields of play: Constructing an academic life.* New Brunswick, NJ: Rutgers University Press.

Sandoz, J., & Winans, J. (1999). *Whatever it takes: Women on women's sport.* New York: Farrar, Straus and Giroux.

Scott, J. W. (1992). "Experience" In J. Butler & J. W. Scott (Eds.), *Feminist theorize the political* (pp. 22–40). New York: Routledge.

Scraton, S. (1992). *Shaping up to womanhood: Gender and girls' physical education.* Buckingham, England: Open University Press.

Scraton, S., & Flintoff, A. (2002). Sport feminism: The contribution of feminist thought to our understandings of gender and sport. In S. Scraton & A. Flintoff (Eds.), *Gender and sport: A reader* (pp. 30–46). London: Routledge.

Stanley, L. (1992). *The auto/biographical I: The theory and practice of feminist auto/biography.* Manchester, UK: Manchester University Press.

Stratta, T. M. P. (2003). Cultural expressions of African American female athletes in intercollegiate sport. In A. Bolin & J. Granskog (Eds.), *Athletic intruders: Ethnographic research on women, culture, and exercise* (pp. 79–106). Albany: State University of New York Press.

Struna, N. (2000). Social history of sport. In J. Coakley & E. Dunning (Eds.), *Handbook of sport studies* (pp. 187–203). London: Sage.

Sykes, H. (1998). Turning the closets inside/out: Towards a queer-feminist theory in women's physical education. *Sociology of Sport Journal,* 15, 154–173.

Theberge, N. (1985). Toward a feminist alternative to sport as a male preserve. *Quest*, 37, 193–202.

Theberge, N. (1987). Sport and women's empowerment. *Women's Studies International Forum*, 10, 387–393.

Theberge, N. (1997). "It's part of the game": Physicality and the production of gender in women's hockey. *Gender and Society*, 11, 69–87.

Theberge, N. (2000). *Higher goals; Women's ice hockey and the politics of gender*. Albany, NY: State University of New York Press.

Theberge, N. (2000). Gender and sport. In J. Coakley & E. Dunning (Eds.), *Handbook of sport studies* (pp. 322–333). London: Sage.

Thompson, S. (1988). Challenging the hegemony: New Zealand women's opposition to rugby and the reproduction of a capitalist patriarchy. *International Review for the Sociology of Sport*, 23(3), 205–212.

Thompson, S. (1999). *Mother's taxi: Sport and women's labor*. Albany: State University of New York Press.

Veijola, S. (1994). Metaphors of mixed team play. *International Review for Sociology of Sport*, 29(1), 31–50.

Vertinsky, P. (1994). Gender relations, women's history and sport history: A decade of changing inquiry, 1983–1993. *Journal of Sport History*, 21(1), 1–58.

Wachs, L. F. (2003). "I was there . . .": Gendered limitations, expectations, and strategic assumptions in the world of co-ed softball. In A. Bolin & J.Granskog (Eds.), *Athletic intruders: Ethnographic research on women, culture, and exercise* (pp.177–200). Albany: State University of New York Press.

Wheaton, B., & Tomlinson, A. (1998). The changing gender order in sport? The case of windsurfing subcultures. *Journal of Sport and Social Issues*, 22, 252–274.

Wray, S. (2002). Connecting ethnicity, gender and physicality: Muslim Pakistani women, physical activity and health. In S. Scraton & A. Flintoff (Eds.), *Gender and sport: A reader* (pp. 127–140). London: Routledge.

Wright, J., & Dewar, A. (1997). Women speak out about physical activity. In G. Clarke & B. Humberstone (Eds.), *Researching women and sport* (pp. 80–95). London: MacMillan.

PART I

Feminist Sport Studies:
Stories of Discovery
and Dismissal

Chapter 1

"To Not Just Live My Life, But To Create It": A Life of Feminist Researcher Arja Laitinen

Ulla Kosonen

In her writing, Arja Laitinen often cited aphorisms. In the title I have rephrased her favorite one from Goethe, to describe Arja's life that came to a premature end: In 1999 she, at the age of 50, died of breast cancer. While this was a great loss for Arja's two young sons, her partner, and her family and friends, it was also a loss for the budding feminist sport sociology community in Finland that Arja had helped to initiate and develop. In this chapter, I hope to highlight Arja's versatile life as a researcher, teacher, a feminist academic, and an activist to map her role as a pioneer of Finnish feminist research in the sport sciences. I begin by describing Arja as a feminist university teacher to locate her work within the development of Finnish sport research. I then focus on Arja's research path that evolved from feminist sport research to consultancy within a women's institute. I hope to further illuminate this path by including quotations from Arja's personal notes, and from memories and interviews with former students, colleagues, and friends.*

---

*I would like to thank Leena Laine for her substantial contribution and Riitta Pirinen for her useful comments in the process of writing this chapter.

STARTING AS A FEMINIST TEACHER AND SOCIOLOGIST IN SPORT SCIENCES

Arja Laitinen arrived at the Department of Social Sciences of Sport in Jyväskylä in 1976. The Faculty of Sports Sciences was founded in Jyväskylä University in 1968 as the first and only higher education institution to offer education and research in sport science in Finland. Kalevi Heinilä was appointed as a first professor in sport sociology in 1971. In 1975 which the UN proclaimed as the year of women, the department established a research project in women's participation in the Finnish sports culture. The final report, which contained basic statistical information on women's participation at different levels in sports, was published in 1977 (Heinilä, 1977). Therefore, Arja entered the department by the time it was taking its first steps toward research on *equality* and sport.

Arja had completed her master's in social sciences at the same university in the Department of Sociology. The Finnish mainstream sociology at the time was survey research following the quantitative tradition of American sociological research. However, during the 1970s and 1980s this tradition was challenged by critical Marxist research (and later in the late '80s followed by the postmodern wave). Arja, educated in the mainstream sociology and without a sport background, admitted that she often felt as an outsider in her new working place where most of her colleagues had an active sporting interest. The research in sociology of sport at Arja's arrival followed the development of the mainstream sociology in Finland: its methodology was quantitative and its focus on organizational sociology. While there was an evolving Marxist sport research it was dismissed at the department; the same fate, as I will later demonstrate, was waiting for feminist sport research. It wasn't until feminist research during the '80s that qualitative research was introduced to the social sciences of sport.

Arja's position as assistant professor included teaching courses in sociology, sport sociology, leisure sociology, women and sport[1], and supervising master's students. The students remember Arja as a warm and supportive teacher who, instead of assuming the position of an authoritarian scientist, wanted to foster relationships based on mutual interaction and respect. Her teaching philosophy was to bring social theory and methodology as close to students' everyday experiences as possible.

I have fond memories of Arja Laitinen's research seminars. The small lecture rooms were usually packed with students from different levels and different pathways. The dense physical atmosphere brought us close to each other and encouraged a lively exchange of thoughts. Arja's style of handling things in a humane and understanding way also made it easier

Arja Laitinen in 1990s (Photo: Arinna Oy)

*to create an open conversation. Arja was open to students'
opinions, thoughts, and questions. She urged us to question
arguments rather than accepting them as facts of life. She
brought the central theories of sociology close to us students,
and these theories became meaningful rather than abstract jar-
gon open only to few experts. Arja didn't use the theories to
shield her expertise. In terms of these qualities Arja differed
from her colleagues in many ways.* (Tarja Tapper, a student in
sport administration in the late 1980s)

Arja's research seminars often inspired students to engage in new, innovative projects including research in women's physical culture. These seminars also supported Arja's own interest in feminist research on sport.

In one research seminar, male students predicted that female students
would find it difficult to get jobs in the field of sport administration. These
comments prompted Arja to wonder about the actual employment rates of
the female sport science graduates. As a result the students started to engage in small projects regarding the post graduate employment rates. This
situation revealed the further need (lack) of research concerning women
and sport in Finland. Arja began to accumulate close connections with the
growing feminist movement inside and outside of the university.

"MOVEMENT CULTURE AND WOMEN"—A FEMINIST RESEARCH PROJECT

In the late 1970s, there was an evolving movement of "New Feminism" by small radical groups within different sectors in the Finnish society. This feminist movement also initiated an establishment of women's studies and feminist research groups at several Finnish universities in late 1970s. The first national, interdisciplinary meeting for women researchers was organized by the Finnish Academy and Ministry of Education in 1980. This was a starting point for further local and nationwide activity (Alanen, Rantalaiho, & Saarinen, 1985). In 1986 it was possible to write:

> There is a strong feeling among feminist researchers that the work they are doing represents a significant paradigm challenge within the social sciences. This scientific revolution will mean a thorough revision of the normative, theoretical, conceptual and methodological rules of social research. (Saarinen, 1992, p. 116)

As feminism in Finnish academia evolved in the late '80s, a network for women's research and a journal specializing in research on women was established. Institutes for women's research, professorships, and regular women's studies courses in different universities followed. The development of the feminist studies in the sports sciences and the impact of Arja's research can be understood against this development of feminist research in Finland. It is also noteworthy that Arja's research area, the sports sciences, was not popular within the Finnish "mainstream feminist research."

In the early '80s, based on her discussions with other Finnish researchers interested in women and sport, Arja set to further investigate the invisibility and marginalization of women in Finnish sport culture. When Arja's work as a feminist sport researcher began to take shape, she also attended international conferences on women and sport. She writes about how one conference, particularly, played a significant part in the birth of feminist sport research in Finland.

> During the time I was developing the student project [on the employment of female sport science graduates] I met my first [Finnish] colleague interested in women's sport at the Sport and International Understanding Congress (Helsinki, 1982). Our conversation at the congress initiated an idea about some form of co-operation. We decided to apply for a grant for sociological and historical research on women's sport. The Ministry of Education rejected our research [application] on women's discrimi-

nation [in sport], but we continued to develop the idea in spite of our disappointment. (Arja's notes)

In the following year, together with Leena Laine, Marjo Raivio, Riitta Pirinen, and Ulla Kosonen, a research project, later titled "Movement Culture and Women" (MCW) was founded. The first seminar on "Women and Sports Culture" was organized in 1983. It was a smallscale conference that was to facilitate reciprocity and discussion between the researchers and women from the field of sport administration and sport organizations who had vastly different experiences, it was noted, from each other (Laitinen, 1983; 1985).

In the beginning the MCW project was based at two consecutive levels of research. The first focused on *women in sport culture*: the sport participation within women's life course, sport as a profession, and women's sport in the mass media. At the second level the MCW investigated women's *movement culture*. The aim was to view women's movement culture holistically by connecting individual women's life courses with the historical and societal structure (microsociological research within a macrosociological frame) (Laitinen, 1983). The MCW project further aimed to examine women's sport and physical activity from a multidisciplinary perspective. In addition, the project explicitly assumed a feminist research perspective that emphasized women's experience. Finally, the goal was to create a feminist research project for women, a project that provided information from women (researchers) to (physically active) women. In its time, the MCW project differed quite sharply from the mainstream, quantitative Finnish research in sport sociology: the research approach was largely qualitative, new research methods such as life story interviews and memory work were introduced, and interdisciplinarity was encouraged. For example, Arja writes:

> I had learned to collect data about the life course through structured questionnaires…Two months of fieldwork and observations increased my criticism of this research methodology that resulted in turning people into numbers and tables. People's experiences and the context for their social interaction vanished from such research data and research reports. My interest in life history as a method, growing out of my fieldwork, arose again. (Arja's notes)

While the late 1980's life histories and autobiographical writing had become more visible within the Finnish social sciences, in the sport sciences such subjective methodologies were often considered "unscientific." The work of MCW, therefore, served as a pioneering attempt to introduce new ways of studying sport.

Not only did the MCW project engage in nontraditional forms of research, it also aimed to challenge the hierarchical manner such projects were often conducted. Every member of the MCW project, including the research assistants and transcribers, were invited to join the meetings. The meetings always began with a "How are you?" round or "an opening of the circle": everyone had a chance to tell her news and feelings. The idea was also to meet each other at the individual, personal level, not only as a researcher. The meaning of the starting and finishing rounds was also methodological.[2] Arja describes the principles of the group:

> Everybody always attended the meetings regardless of how far they were in their studies. Later, when the group had a person who specialized in transcribing the interview tapes, she also came to all the research meetings and parties. The pervading philosophy of the project was to provide a supportive and caring research environment. The support was directed to the person's entire life. The goal was to create a good atmosphere and a steady foundation for research. (Arja's notes)

Arja further characterized the MCW project as dynamic and flexible. All formalities and hierarchy were avoided: the members of the project were working as a collective. As the only member of the group to have a position at the university Arja took the responsibility for the administrative tasks. Other tasks from presentations in different meetings to interviews by media—which in those days had a great interest in women and sport research—were circulated. To my experience the holistic working methods of MCW were unique compared with other feminist groups in the Finnish universities. MCW was an innovative and creative community, and at the same time a warm and supportive "home" for feminist researchers living in margin.

A FEMINIST CONFERENCE ON WOMEN AND SPORT: A DREAM COME TRUE?

Right from the beginning of her time in the department of social sciences of sport, Arja was inspired by the international developments in sport feminism and she managed to invite feminist researchers to visit her department:

> I became involved with issues about women and sport when Joan Duda visited the department in 1981. After this start, I invited, among others, such feminist sport researchers as Kari Fasting and Gertrud Pfister in 1983 and Nancy Theberge in

1985. In 1987 an international conference brought the researchers mentioned above to Jyväskylä and expanded the discussion to Canada (Ann Hall), Germany (Sabine Kröner), and Poland (Teresa Wolanska), as well as elsewhere. (Arja's notes)

An international conference in 1987, titled The International Congress of Movement and Sport in Women's Life was an important event for Arja and others in the MCW project. It proved an interesting learning experience in more than one way.

The original vision was to organize a feminist conference with an emphasis on informal meetings and conversations rather than formal talks and keynote addresses. However, another proposal from the faculty of sport sciences suggesting a similar conference theme emerged and eventually resulted in a jointly organized conference. It followed formal traditional conference arrangements, but included experts, sessions, and new working forms from the MCW project's original proposal. For example, the international contacts that the project had created now paid off and several feminist sport scholars were invited as keynote speakers to the conference. In addition, there were physical activity workshops such as oriental dance and performances where women from different countries introduced the audience to physical activities of their homeland. The actual conference was followed by a free seminar, where participants had a chance for a further discussion on the future of feminist sport research. This follow-up seminar that took place in an informal natural setting of a Finnish lakeside and forest was a warm and inspiring meeting and formed an important starting point for building international networks among feminist sport researchers around the world.

Arja also presented a keynote speech in the conference. Her speech sketched the state of women in the Finnish academic world in general, and in the sport sciences in particular. Arja concluded: " Sport science is research by men on men and is one expression of the masculinity of our culture" (Laitinen, 1989a, p. 211). At the Finnish universities, the highest academic positions, teaching positions, and research committees were dominated by men. Arja emphasized, however, that "micro-inequities become visible in different kinds of situations in the everyday culture of science" (Laitinen, 1989a, p. 216). Such micro-inequities were related to administration, interaction with other universities (e.g., funding for visiting professors), research practices (scholarships, research funding, research design), and everyday work practices. In Finland it was difficult to find women researchers who focused on studying women in sport and Arja introduced the work of the MCW project as an example of such research. Her presentation, particularly her comments on the treatment of women researchers within the sport sciences, caused a strong reaction among the audience. Some thanked Arja for her brave comments, but others were baffled and even offended. Some male colleagues accused her of falsely pointing the finger at her own department. Some of them even stopped greeting her for several years. Why did her presentation cause such a storm of emotions?

In her talk, Arja analyzed the state of sport science and the research community in Finland from a feminist perspective and her analysis hit too close to home. The reaction also demonstrated that the school of sport sciences did not embrace feminist research. What was the everyday experience for the members of the MCW project came as a shock to the male researchers in the audience, particularly when presented in an international venue and as a part of a keynote speech.

Later, Arja confessed to her MCW colleagues how hurtful she found the reactions to her presentation despite the plentiful positive feedback. After the presentation, her life at work became increasingly painful. In addition, Arja's qualitative research was viewed with suspicion in the sport science community that cherished objective research.[3] Subsequently, the research by the entire MCW project was characterized as unscientific by official evaluators and grant applications by the project researchers were turned down time after time. As a research project, MCW received funding from the Ministry of Education (the main funding body for sport science research in Finland) only in 1984–1985. Due to the treatment she met at the university, Arja began to think of leaving the sport sciences.

AN AVANT-GARDE SPORT RESEARCHER IN FINLAND

"Standing-up-and-fighting-like-a-man is a good deal easier than sitting down and writing like a woman" (Stephanie Markman)

This line from the poem that I hung on the wall in the front of my desk in the early 1980s seems accurate now when I reflect upon myself and my work as a researcher in the sport science research project "Movement Culture and Women." As a member of the MCW project I, as an active female researcher, now recognize the meaning of the title of the above poem: "Male Tradition." My work in MCW has consisted of answering questions and challenges from "the outside." I have spoken in seminars, attended meetings and committees, and written articles on the women's movement culture, but the conditions of my research have been dictated by the demands of others, not my own needs. What I have done has not stemmed from my own interest: the life stories of women. I have not planned my research activities rationally in advance; rather, my research process had grown from intuition. During these years there was seldom time to "sit down and write like a woman;" the commissioned articles always had "death lines" (as I started to call them to stick to my schedule—in vain, I now realize). (Arja's notes)

In this note from early 1990s Arja refers to the tremendous need for expertise in women and sport and how she was often invited to speak to women's sport organizations and other organizations about the topic. Despite her numerous engagements inside and outside of academia, Arja managed to write quite extensively on the issues of women and sport. To illustrate Arja's influence on Finnish sport sociology, I will now briefly review the main themes of her published research.

FEMINIST UTOPIAS IN SPORTS

Arja was very interested in exploring future visions for women's sport that would operate independent from the mainstream sport culture. According to her, the Finnish sport culture was structured around "visibility." Arja analyzed the impact of this situation:

When in other countries, women's sport participation has increased explosively . . . in Finland, on the contrary, we cannot talk about a women's revolution of sport. The male values of sport have been accepted by women . . . Sport participation, however, can liberate women's bodies from social control. But often, women's fitness movement, dance, and even Finnish women's gymnastics are founded on the male image of women as they attempt to mould the female body to the currently desirable slender, slightly muscular, and youthful shape. This image is not created for women, but mainly for men. (Laitinen, 1986, p. 147)

To counter the problems of the present sports culture, Arja developed an idea of alternative movement culture, which liberates, instead of controls, women (Laitinen, 1989a; 1989b). Before this culture could actualize, women (and men) needed to become aware of the profound impact of sexual politics present in sports. Therefore, for Arja, awareness was a precondition for the development of an alternative physical culture. This awareness must take place at two levels: first, a social awareness of discrimination in sporting contexts, and second an awareness of one's own body, bodily memories, and their connection to larger social practices. Arja's vision took a clear shape when she participated in a research project called "The Future of

Physical Culture in the Changing City," which contemplated the future of physical culture to develop models for alternative future scenarios. Arja's task in this project was to develop alternative future models of physical culture from women's perspectives (Laitinen, 1987b).

In her part of the project, Arja presented four models as a point of departure: 1) A programmed competition society: "Sport that feels like work;" 2) A society of healthy competition: "Sport as recreation and preparation for work;" 3) A cultural society of self-education: "Pleasure of bodily experiences—pleasure and experience stemming from self-expression and one's own movement;" 4) A society of well-being and community: "Life is not just work—time for movement" (Laitinen, 1987b). The first and second scenarios reflected the realities of (women's) sport in Finland and while far from ideal, Arja saw these as the most likely future of sport and physical activity. In "a society for healthy competition" women participated in male-dominated sports, but competed in their own sports. Arja believed that the first scenario of programmed competition society was the most ominous future. Humans in this environment, as it is based on technology, have to learn to act like machines: efficiently, rationally, and systematically without ethical values or emotions. Arja's ideal future scenario centered on the last two options. In the third option, "a cultural society of self-education," art occupied a central role in movement culture. This type of aesthetic physical culture concentrated on the individual and was pursued in small gyms. The fourth scenario was based on well-being, taking care of one's health and communality: people play, hike in nature, or organize communal physical activities together. In this scenario, people exercise in close connection with the rhythm of life and nature. Deriving from these two visions, Arja was interested in the development of sport facilities that would complement her ideal future scenarios. This was her utopia of facilities for women:

> The center would have a rather small gymnastics hall for little girls that is painted with sensitive colours and feels safe: adults of different ages would have their own facilities for exercise. Further, there would be special facilities with video and music equipment with a possibility for live music accompaniment for apparatus gymnastics, elite level artistic gymnasts and rhythmic gymnasts to fine tune their movement routines. A studio with barres and mirrors would also be reserved for dancers. Near the center would be room to sit and a café, as well as a children's play area. There would also be a place for theatre movement. There would also have to be some facilities for education such as seminar rooms. Eastern forms of physical activity emphasizing spirituality would balance the area of physical culture, as the center would have a quiet and warm room for yoga and other activities. Women

could also take care of their health through physical exercise in the center. There would be a health education unit where also the so-called healthy people would be educated to take care of their health through exercise. Various groups of "ill" people would also get a chance for suitable exercise. Aesthetic and artistic values would be emphasized in the architecture and the surroundings. The present angular sport architecture of straight lines would be replaced with versatility and round shapes. The facilities would have many plants and flowers. (Laitinen, 1987b, pp. 149–150)

Considering that Arja wrote her vision for feminist sport almost 20 years ago, she appears well ahead of her time. It is no wonder that her work was considered "radical" as most feminist sport researchers still attempt to come to grips with women's contradictory positions in today's male dominated sport world. Arja, being a visionary, was also interested in autonomous forms of women's physical activities. The peace movement provided one such alternative.

The ideal of peace was central to Arja's life philosophy. After the Congress on Sport and International Understanding (Helsinki 1982) Arja became interested in the role of physical activity in the peace movement. In addition, she wanted to find ways to include the work for peace in her teaching. Physical activity was used to promote peace and protest against nuclear weapons the first time when three Norwegian women planned a "marathon" march for peace from Copenhagen to Paris in 1981. In 1982 another march for peace took place from Moscow to Minsk in the Soviet Union, and a third march was organized from New York to Washington in 1983 in the United States. Other physical activity events, such as bicycling marches, skiing, rowing, and swimming events were later organized to promote peace. With her students Arja interviewed Finnish peace marchers who participated in the events in 1981, 1982, and 1983. For these participants, physical activity—walking—was a visible and practical way of promoting peace. It didn't require any equipment and enabled the peace activists to create a close connection with people in three different social and political contexts (Laitinen, 1988). Arja also considered the peace marches as an example of women's physical activity that differs from the strictly formulated and competition-oriented definitions of male sport.

SPORT IN WOMEN'S LIFE: METHODOLOGICAL APPROACHES

Arja was the first sport sociologist in Finland to study the meaning of sport in individual women's lives. Her point of departure was a life scheme model, presented between 1953 and 1971 by anthroposophists M. Noers and B. Lievegood (Laitinen, 1987a). They argued that human life history consists of biological and psychological lives that are shaped by the social life. Based on this model, Arja emphasized that social science should not exclude the biological human being (Laitinen, 1987a, pp. 89–91). In addition, Arja noted, the notion of time shaped an individual's perspective into his/her life experiences. Therefore, it was important to analyze how different forms of social time, working time, family time, and sporting time intertwined in women's life courses. Finally, instead of a quantitative analysis Arja wanted to follow Bertraux's idea of the life history research that focuses on individual women's lived experiences (Laitinen, 1987a; see also Laine, 2004).

> I wanted to study social reality holistically through people's everyday lives rather than through researcher's abstract jungle of concepts and methodology. At the same time this also reflects my desire to dissociate myself from a macro-sociological, abstract analysis of society that does not touch the individual. My research derives from the experiences of the individual and then attempts to understand how their life stories "evolve," and then aims to find a connection between the individual's life and the social reality. The central sociological theme is to find the invisible ties between a person's reality and social reality. (Arja's notes)

This philosophy guided Arja's research project on the life courses of 43 influential Finnish sport women. She interviewed elite athletes, women involved in sport organizations, and women involved in sport administration. Arja's preferred interview technique was "active listening," during which the researcher and the interviewee both are involved in a process of creating knowledge.

> A researcher is expected to start the conversation, to set certain limits and at least to some extent conduct the situation. She is also assumed to ask the questions. A feminist, conversational interview tracing a life story, unlike the mainstream interview methods that recommend collecting "material from research objects," creates space for the interviewee to ask questions, because both participants in the discussion are subjects. (Arja's notes)

Here Arja engaged in ongoing feminist discussion of how to reduce the hierarchical power relations between the researcher and the researched. Her interest in power relations translated into further investigations in the lives of marginalized groups.

Arja's interest in ethnic, marginalized (grassroots) cultures was obvious when she, in the beginning of the 1980s, participated in fieldwork study in a Mexican country side village. In addition, she had earlier collected stories told by Karelian immigrant families within a larger research project on Karelian immigrants. More than 400,000 Karelians were removed from the Eastern part (Karelia) of Finland, when this area was connected to Soviet Union as a consequence of World War II. These immigrants were resettled all around Finland, and as "foreigners," speaking with a distinct dialect and mostly of Greek Orthodox faith (the majority of Finns are Lutherans) they formed a minority culture within the dominant culture. When developing the research plan for her dissertation, Arja planned to analyze women athletes' life courses and Karelians' stories side by side looking for parallels between the experiences of these two groups. She was interested in subjugation and power; alienation within the dominant culture; the invisibility of one's culture; and the living in both one's own and the dominant cultures. Her research questions focused on the formation of individuals' aims in life, the cultural awareness of women athletes and Karelians, and the linking of individuals' life histories with its societal context. Her exciting plan to combine these two different materials challenged the limited scope of quantitative Finnish sport sociology. Arja had designed and organized her doctoral dissertation based on this data, but her plans never materialized to the final point. The isolation she had experienced as a feminist researcher in the sport sciences and the tendency of the Finnish sport science community to underrate qualitative research made it more difficult to complete the project. Even after 15 years' intensive work for the department, Arja's work received no support while male colleagues' research was pushed forward. In 1996, having left the university and after recovering from the first period of cancer, Arja applied for a grant to finish her dissertation. The application was rejected.

OPENING UP NEW DOORS

Since the beginning of the 1980s Arja had become increasingly critical of the power games played at the university. She had also conducted "a minor revolution" in her private life as she describes it in her notes. Here she refers to her own background as growing up in a family of a Lutheran priest and with traditional family values. She started to challenge these values and to desire a life on the basis of her own set of values. Arja's choice of divorce and later opting for a de facto relationship instead of marriage reflect this desire. In addition, these external changes were linked to an internal growth: she took a major step to find a spiritual home within anthroposophy.

Arja had worked with different women groups to find a community that would embrace the principles that guided her research: equality, attention to women's culture by increasing the awareness of women's condition, the holistic self, and the ideals of peace movements. Such a community began to evolve through her involvement with the local Steiner Society. She worked actively in the society that maintained a day-care center and a school, both attended by her two sons. She also deepened her knowledge on Steinerian philosophy by studying such practical aspects of it as organic farming and eurhythmics. Here Arja finally met other women who shared her dream of combining their theoretical knowledge with practical work.

This group of women founded a private institute titled "Arinna" (Institute for Human Encounter) in 1992. Arja decided to leave the university and later stated that the decision was one of the most important steps in her life. Arinna is a small group of 4–6 women who are colleagues and friends. They work as consultants to give psychologically and educationally grounded workshops and courses for individual women and women's groups at the working places and organizations. Their working methods, which aimed to connect different areas of the self in everyday life, are often unconventional and versatile including artistic and bodily expression. All

Arja Laitinen lecturing on a course. When working in Arinna Institute in the 1990s one of Arja's special interests was the problems women faced at their workplaces. Her courses that addressed these problems were attended by women from various positions from cleaning ladies, housewives, unemployed to women executives. (Photo: Arinna Institute)

Arinna's projects are set out as humanitarian: the idea is to engage in projects that directly benefit women and their communities.

Arinna colleagues remember Arja as a supportive person who always encouraged others. They further mention that truthfulness characterized Arja's approach to life. She accepted challenges to fulfill her tasks, even when being nervous and afraid of the responsibilities that followed. The colleagues consider it was love, love for people and love for work, which inspired Arja to overcome fear and take action toward what she considered important. She also enjoyed her work immensely: it was an inspiration, not a tedious responsibility. Within Arinna, Arja had found her "own mission" and she knew now "what the world asked from her" although it meant living in constant insecurity and uncertainty. An important part of Arja's work continues to live with Arinna.

SAYING GOOD-BYE

> Being a feminist is difficult; we spend a lot of time talking about survival. Other women at the faculty contact me wanting to discuss their feelings of being a woman researcher in a male dominated field. (Arja's notes)

Many aspects of Arja's pioneering work have now become an accepted part of the social sciences of sport. However, her thoughts still challenge us to think about sport, physical activity, and women in a different light and call for societal change. Her research philosophy, her activism, and her involvement in the MCW research project created a path for feminist sport research in Finland, research that was much ahead of its time. In many ways, Arja's legacy also lives within Finnish sport science research.

The following note demonstrates how Arja's research interest is parallel with today's feminists' interests in sport:

> I was fascinated by the idea to study the "secret" of those rare women working actively within sport culture instead of conforming to or leaving the masculine world of sport. In addition, due to my own feminist interest I wanted also to study whether the women were active and emancipatory in terms of their thoughts, choices, and operation modes from a feminist perspective. Had they consciously developed a so-called women's sport culture? (Arja's notes)

Arja's retirement and later her death left a huge hole in this field of study. It could be argued that women's sport research in Finland rested on the shoulders of few activists (Arja and the other members of the MCW project) and after her, there was no one to continue the work at the Department of Social Sciences of Sport. At the same time, feminist research increased, specialized and institutionalized into women's studies programs at the University of Jyväskylä and other universities in Finland. Perhaps the discontinuity of feminist sport research tells us something about the difficulty of being a feminist researcher in the area of sport sciences, a difficulty that takes an unnecessary heavy toll on loving, modest, and enthusiastic individuals like Arja.

Arja, however, left behind a large material heritage of publications, lectures, and research data and her work has emerged in a new way in the process of writing this chapter. For example, although the initial MCW project is now finished, the current research of the former MCW researchers is still invigorated by the fire of enthusiasm that Arja fed with her curiosity, openness, and faith. Arja's work shows that research knowledge can be created in connection to lived experiences for the benefit of people. While this book and this chapter have highlighted Arja's contributions, it has also been a part of the mourning process of her colleagues. The conversation with Arja continues.

ACKNOWLEDGMENTS

The Department of Social Sciences of Sport at Jyväskylä University has financially supported the writing and translating of this article. Hannu Tervaharju translated the first version of article from Finnish to English.

ARJA LAITINEN'S LIFE COURSE AND WORK

1949   Arja is born in Seinäjoki as the fifth child of seven. Her father was a dean in the Lutheran Church; her mother stayed at home. Arja spent her childhood in various parts of Ostrobothnia. Graduation from high school 1968.

1968   Arja pursues studies in sociology at the University of Jyväskylä. Master's in Social Sciences 1972.

1972–1975   Research assistant at the Department of Sociology. Participates in research project on the adaptation of Karelian immigrants in Finland.

1970s   Marriage and divorce. De facto relationship and birth of the first son in 1979. One of the founders of Jyväskylä Anthroposophical Society.

1976–1991   Research Fellow at the Department of Social Sciences of Sport, University of Jyväskylä.
1978   In Mexico pursuing studies in rural sociology.
1980   Licentiate thesis in sociology on the Karelian immigrants.
1980s   Arja becomes interested in feminism and joins a feminist awareness group. Arja supervises postgraduate work on women's positioning in sport-related employment.
1984   The Movement Culture and Women (MCW) project receive funding from the Ministry of Education. More researchers join in the project and funding is arranged to employ a project secretary. Arja begins to study the life course of women in sport.
1987   The International Congress of Movement and Sport in Women's Life. Several positions at the university and the sport science community. Presentations and articles about research on women and sport. Educates herself toward the end of the 1980s at the anthroposophical Snellman Academy. Starts making plans to found an educational center in cooperation with others.
1992   Participates in the founding of Arinna – Institute for Human Encounter. Arja educates herself at home and abroad while simultaneously working as an educator and researcher (1991–1999).
1992   Birth of the second son.
1995   Arja is diagnosed for the time first with breast cancer. The cancer recurs in 1998.
1999   Arja dies.

SELECTED PUBLICATIONS BY ARJA LAITINEN

Laitinen, A. (1983). *Liikunta ja nainen [Women and sport]*. Planning of Physical Culture. Teaching Report Number 10. Department of Sociology. University of Jyväskylä, Finland.

Laitinen, A. (1983). Naistutkimus ja naisnäkökulma tutkimukseen liikuntatieteissä – tarvitaanko sitä? [Women's studies and the feminist point of view in sports research - are they needed?]. *Liikunta ja tiede*, 6, 293–294.

Laitinen, A. (1984). Women's sport - overview of Finnish women's physical culture and physical activeness. In K. Olin (Ed.), *Contribution of sociology to the study of sport*. Festschrift book in honour of Professor Kalevi Heinilä. University of Jyväskylä. Studies in Sport, Physical Education and Health, 18, 167–191.

Laitinen, A. (1984). Katsaus liikuntasosiologiseen naisurheilututkimukseen [A survey on the women's research in sports sociology]. *Liikunta ja tiede*, 6, 272–278.

Laitinen, A. (1985). Nainen ja urheilu Pohjois-Amerikassa. [Women and sport in North America]. *Liikunta ja tiede*, 4, 186–187.

Laitinen, A. (1985). Liikuntakulttuuri ja nainen - LIINA -projekti. [The movement culture and women - the MCW-project]. *Liikunta ja tiede*, 4, 177.

Laitinen, A. (1986). Liikuntakulttuurin muutos - naisopiskelijatko haasteryhmä? [The change in the sports culture – Female students challenging the culture? *Liikunta ja tiede*, 3, 144–149.

Laitinen, A. (1987). Naisliikuntakulttuuri tulevaisuuden kaupungissa [Women's movement culture in the future city]. In P. Kettunen & K. Sajavaara (Eds.), *Yliopiston mielijuohteita Jyväskylästä* (pp. 131–150). Jyväskylä: Jyväskylän yliopisto.

Laitinen, A. (1987). Seuran päämäärä – elävää todellisuutta. [The goal of a sport club – living reality?]. *Kisakenttä*, 5, 197–199.

Laitinen, A. (1987). Liikunta, naiset ja elämänkulku [Movement, women and the life course]. In T. Pyykkönen (Ed.), *Liikkuva nainen. Tieteen näkemyksiä naistenliikuntaharrastuksesta* (pp. 84–97). Lappeenranta: Liikuntatieteellisen Seuran julkaisu 109.

Laitinen, A. (1988). Naistutkimusprojekti liikuntatieteissä [A feminist research project in sports sciences]. In Simonen L. (Ed.), *Naistutkimuksen ajankohtaisia ongelmia* (pp. 103–133). Yhteiskuntatieteiden tutkimuslaitos, sarja C 30. Tampere: Tampereen yliopisto.

Laitinen, A. (1988). Kaksikasvoinen liikunta [The double faced movement]. In H. Jalkanen, L. Lestinen, K. Ollila, A. Palmroth, T. Timonen, R. Wahlström, & M. Vaittinen M. (Eds.), *Rauha kasvaa meistä - Peace grows in people's minds* (pp. 88–10). Mänttä.

Laitinen, A. (1989). On movement by and for women: A process – oriented approach to research. In M. Raivio (Ed.), *Proceedings of the Jyväskylä Congress on Movement and Sport in Women's Life* (pp. 208-228). Volume I Reports of Physical Culture and Health 66. Jyväskylä, Finland: Jyvaskylan yliopisto.

Laitinen, A. (1989). Future perspective of women's movement culture. In J. Hovden & K. Pedersen (Eds.), *Women in sport - sport for women?* Constructing scenarios and utopias from a women centred perspective (pp. 62–78). Report from a Nordic Research seminar arranged in Alta 29th and 30th of May 1989. Finnmarksforskning. Rapport 1/1989. Alta, Norway.

Laitinen, A. (1989). Frigjort kroppsbevegelse - bevisst bevegelse i kroppen. En feministisk utopi. *Nytt om kvinneforskning*, 4, 52–58.

Laitinen, A. (1989). Finnisher Frauensport in der Gegenwart. In C.Peyton & G. Pfister (Eds.), *Frauensport in Europa. Informationen – Materialen* (pp. 132–142). Hamburg: Czwalina.

Laitinen, A. & Paananen, I. (1989). Tanssi elää - tilaa tanssille. [The dance lives – space for dance]. *Liikunta ja tiede*, 2, 104–105.

Laitinen, A., & Tiihonen, A. (1990). Narratives of men's experiences in sport. *International Review for the Sociology of Sport.* 3, 185–202.

Laitinen, A. (1990). Matka liikkeen ytimeen.[A journey into the core of the movement] *Liikunta ja tiede*, 2, 60–62.

Laitinen, A. (1992). "Äitee" ladun aukaisija ['Mummy' - opener of the ski track] *Liikunta ja tiede*, 6, 4–9.

Laitinen, A. (1992). Naiset ja urheilumuutokset nykyhetkestä tulevaisuuteen [Women and the changes in sport from now to future]. In K. Olin, H. Itkonen, & H. Ranto (Eds.), *Liikunnan muutos, murros vai kaaos?* (pp. 30–32). Helsinki, Finland: Suomen Työväen Urheiluliitto.

Tikka, M. & Rantamaa, P., & Laitinen, A. (1994). *Matkalla ajassa. Tekstejä iästä, elämänkulusta ja vanhenemisesta [On a journey in time. Writings on age, life course and aging].* Jyväskylän ikääntyvien yliopiston raportit ja seminaarityöt. Jyväskylä, Finland: Jyväskylän yliopisto.

Harvey, C D H., Bond, J.B. Jr., Laitinen, A., & Sommer, R. (1995). *Intergenerational interaction in Finland. Family matters.* Autumn 1995, Issue No. 40. Australian Institute of Family Studies.

NOTES

1. A course titled "Movement Culture and Women" (MCW) was first taught in 1983. Later, other researchers from the Movement Culture and Women research project also participated in the planning and lectures in this course. Arja taught the course for the last time in 1993. In 1995, women were omitted from the content of the course and it was renamed as "Sport Culture and Difference."

2. The "Opening Circle" method advocates that the start of the meeting significantly affects the working of the group. The goal of the opening round is to get rid of the topmost feelings to enable the participants to move to the actual work freed from any burdening thoughts. The goal of the finishing round is to assess what the members of the group have gained from the meeting to ensure that all participants were genuinely present in the meeting. The method is still used in all kinds of women's groups.

3. One example is the Ministry of Education's Evaluation of Finnish Research in Sport (1991). Riitta Pirinen recalls that this evaluation was a severe shock to Arja.

REFERENCES

Alanen, L., Rantalaiho, L., & Saarinen, A. (1985). *Naisen historiallisuus: yhteiskunta, yksilö, sukupuoli.* Seminaariraportti [The historicity of the woman: Society – individual – gender. Seminar Report], Tampereen yliopisto: Yhteiskuntatieteiden tutkimuslaitos. Second Edition.

Heinilä, K. (1977) (Ed.). *Nainen suomalaisessa liikuntakulttuurissa* [Women in the Finnish sport culture]. Jyväskylän yliopisto: Liikuntasuunnittelun laitos. Tutkimuksia n:o 15.

Laine, L. (2004). Unfortunately she was the winner. In J. Bale, M. K. Christensen, & G. Pfister (Eds.), *Writing lives in sport. Biographies, life-histories and methods* (pp. 115–129). Aarhus University Press.

Laitinen, A. (1983). *Liikunta ja nainen* [Sport and women]. Jyväskylän yliopisto: Liikuntasuunnittelun laitos. Opetusmonisteita n:o 10 [Seminar Report].

Laitinen, A. (1985). Liikuntakulttuuri ja nainen – LIINA-projekti [The movement culture and women – MCW-project]. *Liikunta ja Tiede*, 4, 177.

Laitinen, A. (1986). Liikuntakulttuurin muutos – naisopiskelijatko haasteryhmä? [The change in sports culture – Female students as challengers?] *Liikunta ja Tiede*, 3, 144–149.

Laitinen, Arja (1987a). Liikunta, naiset ja elämänkulku [Movement, women and the life course]. In T. Pyykkönen (Ed.), *Liikkuva nainen. Tieteen näkemyksiä naisten liikuntaharrastuksesta.* (pp. 84–97). Lappeenranta: Liikuntatieteellisen Seuran julkaisu n:o 109.

Laitinen, A. (1987b). Naisliikuntakulttuuri tulevaisuuden kaupungissa [Women's movement culture in the future city]. In P. Kettunen & K. Sajavaara (Eds.), *Yliopiston mielijuohteita Jyväskylästä* (pp. 131–150). Jyväskylä, Finland: University of Jyväskylä Press, 131–150.

Laitinen, A. (1988). Kaksikasvoinen liikunta [The double faced movement]. In H. Jalkanen, L. Lestinen, K. Ollila, A. Palmroth, T. Timonen, R. Wahlström, & M. Vaittinen (Eds.), *Rauha kasvaa meistä – Peace grows in people's minds.* (pp. 88–110). Mänttä.

Laitinen, A. (1989a). On movement by and for women: A process-oriented approach to research. In M. Raivio (Ed.), *Proceedings of the Jyvaskylä Congress on Movement and Sport in Women's Life* (pp. 208–228). Reports of Physical Culture and Health, 66. Jyväskylä, Finland.

Laitinen, A. (1989b). Future perspective of women's movement culture. In J. Hovden & K. Pederson (Eds.), *Women in sport – sport for women? Constructing scenarios and utopias from a women centred perspective* (pp. 62–78). Finnmark Distrikthogskole: Finnmarks Forskning Rapport, 1989:1.

Saarinen, A. (1992). Feminist research – An intellectual adventure?. Research Institute for Social Sciences, The University of Tampere: Centre for Women's Studies and Gender Relations 4.

Chapter 2

From Pre- to Postfeminism: A Four-Decade Journey

M. Ann Hall

Feminism and Sporting Bodies: Essays on Theory and Practice (Human Kinetics, 1996) traces my 30-year journey across the feminist terrain from the mid-1960s to the mid-1990s. It tells of my struggle to understand what various feminisms could contribute to our understanding of women in sport, and to our efforts to make the sports world a better place for women. The book was one of the most difficult writing projects I have ever attempted. Limited by the publisher to a small paperback, it was agony deciding what to include and what to leave out, then condensing it all into something clear and accessible. The book has sold more than 2,000 copies to date (despite being overpriced) and is listed in the catalogue of nearly 500 libraries worldwide. It has also been translated into Japanese.

The first chapter, "Research Odyssey of a Feminist," is the story of how I came to feminism both intellectually and as an activist. It is included here in much the same version appearing in the book although I have edited it for clarity and context. I also bring my story up to date and comment upon current developments in feminist sport studies.

RESEARCH ODYSSEY OF A FEMINIST

The term *feminism* was not part of my vocabulary until I read Betty Friedan's *The Feminine Mystique* in the mid-1960s while completing my after-degree teacher training. I grew up in Canada in the 1940s and 1950s, when "feminist" (like "career woman") had become a dirty word. According to Friedan, early feminists had fought for and eventually won the right to vote. They had "destroyed the old image of women, but they could not erase the hostility, the prejudice, the discrimination that still remained" (Friedan, 1963, p. 100). Although her book interested me, I found it difficult to identify with her central thesis that white, middle-class, American housewives were lost, incomplete, disappointed, and almost despairing because of "the problem that had no name." At the time, I was in my early twenties, freshly trained, wildly enthusiastic, and about to embark on a career as a high school physical education teacher. It was full speed ahead into the world of work—not marriage and a family—smugly confident I would escape the boredom and despair Friedan described.

After less than a year in my new career, I was shocked at the blatant discrimination and impossible conditions in which I was expected to teach and encourage young girls to acquire an interest in physical activity. The only female physical education teacher at my school, I was working around the clock preparing lessons (in three subject areas), administering an intramural program, coaching all the girls' teams, and teaching my lessons in a small, dingy gym while my three male counterparts took the best facilities and equipment, and lounged about just waiting for me to crack up. My solution at the end of the school year was to leave and return to university. No one ever asked why I was leaving, and I carried those awful memories with me for a long time; they fueled much of what I did and thought from then on. It has now been 40 years since I landed at the University of Alberta to begin graduate work.

At an international conference held a few years after I returned to graduate school I was giving one of my first academic papers: "The Role of the Safety Bicycle in the Emancipation of Women" (the "safety" bicycle was the first bicycle with rubber tires rather than bone-jarring metal ones). I concluded, rather grandly, that not only did women use the bicycle as a means of defying tradition, but it was plausible that many reforms in women's rights would not have come about so quickly without the safety bicycle.[1] The paper was a product of my master's thesis, a history of women's sport in Canada prior to World War I. After my presentation, an American fellow approached me and stated accusingly: "You must be a women's libber." My quizzical expression prompted him to tell me about the women's liberation movement in the United States, and I listened in amazement. It was the late 1960s, and I knew of no such movement in Canada; even if there was one, I was too busy establishing my new career as a university physical education instructor to take notice. At the time, establishing my career meant teaching a variety sport activities, coaching the women's swim team, administering women's athletics, establishing a new subfield called the "sociology of sport," and trying to figure out how and in what area I would conduct research.

Becoming a Positivist

In 1971 I went to the University of Birmingham in England to do doctoral work, which allowed me space and time to think about feminism again. I read a number of influential books, all published in the early 1970s—specifically Kate Millett's *Sexual Politics*, Germaine Greer's *The Female Eunuch*, Shulamith Firestone's *The Dialectic of Sex*, Eva Figes' *Patriarchal Attitudes*, Robin Morgan's anthology *Sisterhood Is Powerful*, Juliet Mitchell's *Woman's Estate*, and Sheila Rowbotham's *Women, Resistance and Revolution* and *Women's Consciousness, Man's World*. These books are now considered among the classics of second-wave feminism in the English-speaking world.[2] I also read Simone de Beauvoir's *The Second Sex*, which had been published in French in 1949 and in English in 1953. I simply could not get enough of these books, but paradoxically, although I knew beyond question I was a feminist, I could not relate this extracurricular reading to my doctoral research. How would the researcher and the feminist become one?

To my knowledge, I was the first Canadian to undertake a doctorate in physical education in England. This made me an oddity because the area was not fully recognized in Britain as a legitimate university subject. My degree was earned entirely through research, and I had taken to England a straightforward question: Why do some women make sport and physical activity an important part of their lives and others do not? When I began my doctorate, I had no formal background in either sociology or sport sociology. Along with physical education, my undergraduate training had been in mathematics and statistics; consequently, the natural science model seemed the most appropriate to answer my question. I was interested in the "whys" of women's involvement in sport, or lack of it, and building a causal mathematical model to explain these whys seemed eminently worthwhile and challenging. Moreover our exemplars in the sociology of sport at the time were proponents of the quest for empirically verifiable, formal theory. In the end, I produced a substantial multivariate statistical analysis that "proved," among other things, that the more you liked physical activity and sport when you were younger, the more likely you were to keep doing it when you were older. My dissertation, *Women and Physical Recreation: A Causal Analysis*, certainly lived up to a quote I had placed at the beginning: "Don't be afraid to oversimplify reality. It will always be possible to introduce complexities a few at a time" (Blalock, 1971, p. 196).

I had become, to put it simply, a positivist, or someone who believes that (a) reality consists of what is available to the senses, (b) the natural and social sciences share a common logical and methodological foundation, (c) the goal of social research is to create universal laws of human behavior, and (d) there is a fundamental distinction between fact and value creating the grounds for an "objective" social science (Hughes, 1980).

Unfortunately I had then no clear understanding of the epistemological and methodological foundations of social research and little knowledge of the variety of research methods, including qualitative ones, available to us now. I learned all this on my own, an experience that later prompted me to introduce a course for incoming physical education graduate students on social research applications to leisure and sport, which I taught for more than 20 years.

My supervisor at the University of Birmingham was Charles Jenkins, a wonderfully sensitive man. His intellectual interests were amazingly eclectic, and although he supported the positivist turn in my work, he did try to interest me in the work of those at the Centre for Contemporary Cultural Studies: people like Stuart Hall, Paul Willis, and Charles Critcher. The Birmingham school, as it became known, was at the forefront of cultural studies, a form of critical cultural analysis initially developed among Left-leaning, post-war British intellectuals.[3] However, there was little work on leisure or sport being conducted at the Birmingham Centre in the early 1970s; there were no women and certainly no feminists, although by the end of the decade, feminism had forced a major rethink of every substantive area of work within cultural studies.

In 1973 Charles Jenkins and I organized a conference at Birmingham on Women and Sport. Our purpose was to explore the relationship between biological and cultural influences on women's sport participation through a series of invited papers. Among others, we invited Paul Willis from the Birmingham Centre, who at the time was working on his dissertation, the often cited *Learning to Labour: How Working Class Kids Get Working Class Jobs*, to give a paper. He and I presented papers during the same session. His was a brilliant and insightful discussion of the role of sport in the reinforcement of common-sense ideologies that assert the superiority of men and of how women collude in these ideological definitions.[4] Mine was a complex multiple regression analysis in which I tried to explain the relationships among all the variables in my dissertation. At one point, I remember displaying a slide with the title: "How to Regress in One Easy Lesson." The irony of all this escaped me at the time.

Researching "Women in Sport"

I returned to teaching with my newly earned PhD. I wanted to continue doing research in the area of "women in sport" but the disciplinary perspective was unclear. Having narrowed down the options to the social sciences, I was uncertain whether it would be history, sociology, psychology, or social psychology, not that I had much training in any of these disciplines. American sport sociologist Susan Birrell (1988) was absolutely correct when she stated: "The decade of the 1970s is marked by unevenness in focus and quality as the field struggled first for identity and then for legitimacy" (p. 463). She went on to point out that women in sport as an area of study must be seen against a backdrop of other social forces. Certainly significant were changes in physical education, which at the time was transforming itself from a profession into an academic discipline, or more accurately a series of subdisciplines now readily identified as the history of sport, sociology of sport, psychology of sport, and so forth. It was, therefore, logical to develop a multidisciplinary women in sport area. Also of importance was second-wave feminism, which produced the women's movement and a steady growth in women's sport.

The context of Birrell's observations was the United States, and although Canada has followed the American experience in some areas, it has not in others. Legislative and institutional changes in women's sport in the United States, such as the passage of Title IX in 1972,[5] the formation of the Women's Sports Foundation in 1974, and the expansion of opportunities in sport for girls and women, were only marginally felt in Canada during the 1970s, although 1974 did mark the beginning of federal government involvement in the issues with the organizing of the first National Conference on Women and Sport. On the academic front, since most Canadian physical educators teaching in universities went to the United States for doctoral-level training (I was an exception), they brought back the need to compartmentalize the field into its various subdisciplines, and we all felt the same pressure to create our own research specialties. Mine was to be the vaguely defined area of women in sport.

By the mid-1970s I had become immersed in the Canadian women's movement. My tales from that period are too long to narrate here, but through helping to found, or volunteer in, several feminist organizations like the Alberta Status of Women Action Committee, the Canadian Research Institute for the Advancement of Women, and the Canadian Association for the Advancement of Women and Sport, I gained an invaluable network of feminist colleagues across the country. I interacted with them through committee meetings, board meetings, funding crises, hiring committees, marches, lobbying, and celebrating women's culture with feminist sisters both within and outside academe. My involvement taught me an extremely valuable lesson: As feminists, our theory, politics, and practices are inextricably linked. Those working in the academy, whose focus is research and scholarship, must work with those on the front line—be they activists, "femocrats," shelter workers, or volunteers—so that together we are doing critical political work. Through the years, I have continued to help document our progress in challenging gender inequality within sport and physical education in Canada and to speak out when necessary.

Moving Beyond the Psychological

Feminist theory, a more sophisticated understanding of sociology, and feminist political work were the major influences on my academic research and scholarship as I undertook the task of helping to shape the sociological study of women in sport. The work in that area during the early 1970s, as Susan Birrell (1988) rightly pointed out, was dominated by psychological rather than sociological analyses of women's place in sport. In fact, my first research article, published in England, was entitled, "A 'Feminine Woman' and an 'Athletic Woman' as Viewed by Female Participants and Non-Participants in sport" (Hall, 1972). Using a semantic differential as an attitude measurement tool, I found that nonparticipants showed considerably more "dissonance" between the two concepts than did participants and that this difference was statistically significant.[6] What was I trying to do? Mindful of the popular and often pejorative image of the female athlete as "unfeminine," I wanted to see if this stereotype prevented some women from taking an active interest in sport and to show that for women who did participate, there was a greater congruence between the two images. My conclusion was naive and demonstrated a minimal understanding of the cultural forces and ideological practices at work:

> The present study does seem to suggest that perhaps participation in sport among women could be increased if the image associated with athletic women were somehow changed, so that it became more congruent with the stereotype associated with feminine women. This would also involve the concomitant change in the feminine image toward a direction more consonant with athleticism. (p. 46)

Again Susan Birrell (1988) hit the proverbial nail on the head with her critique that this early research, mine included, "relied on methodologically primitive attempts to measure complex psychosocial constructs; conceived of women as not fitting into sport; and by subtly assuming that the problem behind women's low involvement lay within, tended to blame women for their own lack of participation" (p. 467). The topics in Psychosocial Aspects of Women in Sport, a course I introduced to my department in the early 1970s, reflected this psychological and individualistic bias. These included sex differences, sexual role behavior, tomboyism, attitudes toward women athletes, the personality traits of women athletes, fear of success, role conflict, psychological androgyny, the apologetic, and socialization. An understanding that sporting practices are historically produced, socially constructed, and culturally defined to serve the interests and needs of powerful groups in society still was missing.

Recognizing the Relevance of Feminism

Despite the growth of the sociology of sport in the 1970s, it was clear that girls and women were not represented in the studies and literature. By 1976 there were 13 texts and anthologies (all from the United States) that had the sociology of sport as their focus. Only three of these had a separate chapter or section devoted to females; of some 200 separate articles in the anthologies, fewer than one tenth were written or co-written by women. The material on females in these texts and anthologies represented less than 3% of the total content. This made me angry. I knew there was more research and scholarship about women than was being acknowledged, and I was becoming acutely aware of the male bias in sociology. Feminist sociologists were addressing this androcentric perspective, as were feminist scholars in the humanities and other social sciences.

Though there was little feminist scholarship to read in the late 1970s, I searched out and consumed everything I could find with one objective: applying it to the study of girls and women in sport. My published writing from this period, aside from attempting to expand the sociological knowledge base about females in sport, represents a plea to my colleagues in physical education and the sociology of sport to recognize the relevance of feminism.

Early in my academic career, wanting to learn more about sociology, I embarked on a self-directed reading course in the history of social thought, contemporary social theory, and the epistemological debates within social research methodology. Several colleagues helped me, most of them males who were engaged in producing radical critiques of sport in Western societies. They were reading social theorists like Anthony Giddens, Pierre Bourdieu, Paul Willis, Antonio Gramsci, and Raymond Williams and were attempting to apply theories of power, social reproduction and practice, and cultural struggle and production to an analysis of the historical and cultural construction of modern sport. I read their work as well as the theorists from whom they drew their inspiration. I also read with great fervor emerging feminist theory, which, for the most part, my colleagues and the social theorists ignored.

Slowly I came to two major insights. The first was that social psychological research, with its emphasis on sex roles and sex identity, not only demanded a substantive critique but was potentially harmful because it continued to perpetuate the very stereotypes researchers in the field wished to eradicate. Within the context of women and sport research, social psychological research needed to be replaced by a gender and sport discourse that treated gender as a relational category just like class or race (see Chapter 2 in *Feminism and Sporting Bodies*). This led me to my second insight: For most radical theorists class was *the* primary form of domination, and it was going to be a long, hard battle to get them to recognize the gender blindness of their critiques (see Chapter 3 in *Feminism and Sporting Bodies*).

By the mid-1980s I was no longer alone in recognizing the potential of feminist theory and analysis for gender relations and sport. Susan Birrell, herself one of those who has contributed significantly to the women in sport discourse, documented this work, although primarily in North America (Birrell, 1988). Certainly we all owe a debt to the earlier efforts of Eleanor Metheny, Marie Hart, Ellen Gerber, Jan Felshin, Pearl Berlin, Dorothy Harris, and Carole Oglesby. As Birrell suggested, the work of Hart and Felshin in particular should be singled out because it was "grounded in a feminist sensibility, yet little theoretical work was available to help them frame their arguments" (p. 468). Twenty years ago I was unduly critical of this work because in my view it lacked the necessary theoretical sophistication. In hindsight, now that I am in my sixties with several generations of scholars coming up behind, my own work also lacked the sophistication they bring. We are products of our times in ways we do not realize until we look back.

In the early days, my colleagues in sport and physical education—both male and female—were almost entirely resistant to feminism. Now, despite pockets of intransigence, there is a small but critical mass of feminist and pro-feminist scholars around the world whose focus is the sociological study of gender and sport. Their work appears regularly in the books, journals, and conference programs of our field.

My nonsporting feminist colleagues are mostly bemused by my continuing fascination with sport. For them, the highly competitive, sometimes violent, overly commercialized sports world represents distinctly nonfeminist values and is a world they generally ignore. Few are active in sports, although some certainly exercise for health and well-being; for many, negative childhood experiences in school physical education turned them off long ago. In my women's studies classes, I sometimes had to overcome the initial negative reaction of a student who found it difficult not to associate me with a much disliked PE teacher.

Despite this often schizophrenic existence, I saw my task as advocating the inclusion of sport on the feminist agenda and ensuring that feminism was very much a part of the sport agenda. One way I tried to do this was through my university's women's studies program, which I helped to establish. Over the years, I taught and held a variety of administrative positions in the program. However, I found it a continual struggle to get discussions about women's sport included in the women's studies curricula.

REMAINING CONTENT OF *FEMINISM AND SPORTING BODIES*

There are five remaining chapters in *Feminism and Sporting Bodies*. Chapter 2 examines how the discourse of gender and sport had changed since its earlier, psychological beginnings by outlining the differences between categorical and distributive research and thirdly, relational analyses. The primary focus of *categorical research* is quantifying and empirically studying sex or race differences in athletic participation, performance, and abilities, while attempting to explain their existence in terms of biological factors and socialization. *Distributive research* examines the distribution of resources (e.g., competitive opportunities, coaching positions, administrators, income levels, sponsorship) and focuses on inequality in opportunities, access, and financial resources. *Relational analyses* begin with the assumption that sporting practices are historically produced, socially constructed, and culturally defined to serve the interests and needs of powerful groups in society. Sport, therefore, is seen as a cultural representation of social relations and here includes gender, class, and race relations. Clearly, I am in favor of the latter, and I develop this further in the next two chapters by examining the meaning, implications, and potential of feminist cultural studies applied to sport. Where Chapter 3 focuses on theory, history, sexual difference, and masculinity, Chapter 4 examines the relatively new (at least then) cultural criticism surrounding the *body*. In the remaining two chapters, I examine the notion of *feminist research*, especially as praxis, and how that research can be applied to the sociocultural study of sport. I also argue that sport is a political site, and specifically a location for the resistance and transformation of gender relations.

BRINGING MY STORY UP-TO-DATE

After more than 30 years at the University of Alberta, I retired in 1997. Retirement, however, has not meant the end of my research and writing. My master's thesis, completed in 1968, was a history of women's sport in Canada prior to World War I. Twenty-five years later, I decided to continue researching the history of women's sport in Canada. Why? First, there was still no comprehensive history, which in some ways I found disappointing, but given the enormity of the task, I now understand why. Second, I wanted to write a much different history than was the case 30 years ago. Along with many exemplary studies in women's sport history, there were several decades worth of feminist historiography, none of which was available to me in the 1960s. Finally, I was fortunate to receive a substantial research grant, which provided the necessary funds to hire research assistants, travel to archives, conduct interviews, and much else. The project was no where near completion when I retired, and it kept me occupied until the publication of *The Girl and the Game: A History of Women's Sport in Canada* (Broadview Press) in the spring of 2002. I have also published another (short) book, several articles, and book chapters, all concerned with women and sport, and have kept up a steady practice of encouraging and reviewing the work of others. At the time of writing, I am completing the revisions to *Sport in Canadian Society*, a textbook published with several colleagues more than 10 years ago. Historical research, especially cultural history, continues to attract my attention. Future projects may include a history (1917–1940) of the Edmonton Grads women's basketball team, one of Canada's most successful teams. As well, I am thinking about a cultural history of women's athletic bodies. No doubt other projects will come to the fore. The best thing about "retirement" is being able to focus on one project at a time, to work at one's own pace, or indeed not work at all. This brings me to reflect upon developments in feminist sport studies since the mid-1990s, at least as I see them.

FEMINIST SPORT STUDIES IN THE POSTFEMINIST ERA

The 1990s saw the rise and popularization of the term "postfeminism." In *Feminism and Sporting Bodies* I mentioned a postcard kept above my desk: "Post Feminism – keep your bra and burn your brain," never imagining the extent to which "postfeminism" would come to dominate not only media insistence on feminism's demise but also the theoretical debates within the academy. I am referring to the North American context here, and more specifically the United States, although in Canada we have also been affected by these developments.

Within the media and popular consciousness, postfeminism is most identified with the hostile backlash against second-wave feminism, and some of the most powerful cornerstones of the modern women's movement (equality for example). Within academic and intellectual circles, postfeminism represents a methodological or theoretical shift, not unlike postmodernism, poststructuralism, or postcolonialism. The term is highly contentious and invested with many meanings, summarized here by Misha Kavka (2002):

> The media have claimed it for the "backlash" girls of conservative feminism, the Third Wave claims it for a younger generation of culturally savvy feminists who seek "to use desire and pleasure as well as anger to fuel struggles for justice"; poststructuralist academic feminists claim it for a pluralistic theoretical feminism that repudiates the supposed essentialism of the second wave; and "I'm not a feminist but . . ." latecomers often claim it for a performatively wry and even lighthearted attitude to the self-serving proclamations of the masculine order. . . . The most worrying definition of "postfeminism," however, belongs to that group of mostly younger women, now headed towards or in the early stages of a career, who believe that feminism has already done its work by achieving as much social equality for women in the home and workplace as one could hope or even wish for. (p. 32)

To what extent have these multiple meanings of "postfeminist" intersected with feminist sport studies? Given the limitations of space, I can only sketch this intersection and point to several issues and problems, which in my opinion need our immediate attention.[7] I cannot agree with Susan Birrell (2000) when she states that "references to a postfeminist era are both wrong-headed and politically dangerous" (p. 71). We (of the second wave) cannot simply dismiss the "post" in postfeminism, especially from the perspective of feminist activism in sport. We need to understand and engage its multiple meanings because like it or not in some sense we are in a postfeminist era.

Let me start with one of the more positive aspects of postfeminism—the notion of a "third wave"—and its relationship to feminist sport studies. Feminist activists and women's movement historians use the "wave" model to describe the women's movement in North America (especially the United States). The first wave encompasses the early 20th century fight for suffrage; the second characterizes women's liberation and women's rights activism beginning in the late 1960s; and the third wave signals a new generation of feminism representing younger women who came of age in the late 1970s through to the late 1980s.[8] Third-wave feminists clearly wish to distinguish themselves from "postfeminists"— young, conservative anti-feminists who explicitly define themselves against and criticize feminists of the second wave. In *Turbo Chicks: Talking Young Feminisms*, a recent collection of young Canadian feminist voices, the third wave is defined as:

> . . . a diverse group of primarily young women, born into a world changed by feminism and other social justice movements and trying to put their diverse feminisms into practice in this world, acknowledged to be complex, contextual and ever shifting. For this generation, feminism should prioritize not just gender but all of the intertwining axes of identity and experience including race, class, ability and sexuality. The third-wave movement and aesthetic is associated with cultural activism (zines, riot grrrrl bands, guerilla subvertising), the challenging of identity boundaries and a revelling in female power whether through our bodies, sexuality, work, art or activism. (p. 352–353)

One of the most articulate and prolific spokeswomen for third-wave feminism, and for its relationship to women's sport, is Leslie Heywood, who teaches in the English department at the State University of New York, Binghamton. From her earlier work on women's bodybuilding (*Bodymakers: A Cultural Anatomy of Women's Bodybuilding*) and a disturbing memoir of her experiences as a young athlete (*Pretty Good for a Girl*), to her latest book coauthored with Shari Dworkin (*Built to Win: The Rise of the Female Athlete as Cultural Icon*), Heywood has consistently argued for a third-wave feminist analytic. What this is, however, is not so easy to define.

Aligned with cultural studies, a third-wave feminist analysis of sport focuses on the cultural work done by female (and male) athletes in late capitalism. It claims a break from aspects of second-wave feminism, specifically the essentialism of cultural (sometimes called "radical") feminism, which argues for a female sporting counterculture where male values are exorcized and female values nurtured. From a third-wave perspective, binaries like male/female, active/passive, violent/peaceful, competitive/cooperative and so forth belong to long contested essentialist constructions of masculine and feminine "nature." In this sense, it has much in common with postmodern and poststructural versions of feminism. Third-wave feminists are at ease with contradiction and accept pluralism as a given: strong female athlete images perform negative and affirmative cultural work simultaneously; competitive and participatory models of sport *both* offer a range of possibilities for women (and men); market conditions can be oppressive to some, empowering to others, and offer the potential to do progressive *and* regressive cultural work, sometimes at the same time. Third-wave feminist methodology bridges the linguistic and the empirical, mixes the theoretical and the textual with the empirical and structural, and makes use of multiple rhetorical strategies that mingle narrative, critical, creative, and expository writing.[9]

I am not suggesting that we all jump on the third-wave feminism bandwagon. For one, this sort of academic work is difficult to do, and requires creative writing skills we do not all necessarily possess. Michael Messner (2002) suggests that although third-wave feminism is promising and potentially important, it is not a major break from second-wave feminism. Rather, he argues, "I read it as a newer, youthful continuation of individualist, middle-class liberal feminism that has found fertile ground in the political spaces opened by NOW, Title IX, and affirmative action and in the expansive cultural spaces created by the successful corporate-media co-optation of feminist slogans and symbols" (note 30, p. 204). Although I agree that third-wave feminism is not necessarily discontinuous with second-wave feminism, it is unfair to characterize it as middle-class and liberal for the reasons discussed earlier.

Third-wave feminist analyses of sport, especially those arguing that sport is an unlikely form of what Leslie Heywood calls "stealth feminism," are a useful antidote to the increasing number of anti-feminist tomes appearing in press. At the top of my anti-feminist list would be Jessica Gavora's *Tilting the Playing Field: Schools, Sports, Sex and Title IX*. Her book has received extensive coverage in the media, almost all highly positive, because it confirms the ideological message being sent out by the Bush administration that Title IX has been killing male high school and college sports programs throughout the United States. Gavora (according to the book jacket) is the chief speechwriter for the U.S. Attorney General and a senior policy advisor at the Department of Justice. Again space does not permit a thorough analysis and critique of *Tilting the Playing Field*, but anyone wishing to understand the mindset of young "postfeminists" should read this book. Second-wave feminism, according to their analysis, has made women the unnecessary "victims" of male power, and the modern feminist movement has become irrelevant to the vast majority of women. Gavora argues (with substantial statistics) that because of the proportionality requirement of Title IX, mandating equal athletic participation opportunities for females in proportion to their numbers at a given school or college, males are losing opportunities to play and compete. Opposing groups, like the Women's Sports Foundation, present their own set of counter statistics, claiming Gavora's book is "full of misinformation and inaccuracies, and is largely extremist rhetoric."[10] The rancor of the debate is not surprising, but what is startling is the extent to which anti-feminists like Gavora have been influenced by biological determinist arguments claiming girls and women have *naturally* less interest in playing sports than do boys and men. Boys and girls, she argues, are hardwired to pursue different interests (like sport) and since sex differences are not socially constructed, there is no point deconstructing them through enlightened public policy. So much for decades of feminist research to the contrary.

A couple of other books to put on your anti-feminist reading list are Rene Denfeld's *Kill the Body, the Head Will Fall: A Closer Look at Women, Violence, and Aggression* and Precilla Y. L. Choi's *Femininity and the Physically Active Woman*. Denfeld's book is both fascinating and disturbing. As an amateur boxer, she takes us inside the world of women's boxing—what it's like to go one on one with a sparring partner or actual opponent, what it's like to get punched in the face—no question, she is a good writer. She also re-examines assumptions and stereotypes about women, aggression, and violence, claiming they have been misrepresented, even falsified, by second-wave feminists. Her main point is that women have the potential to be, and in some cases are, just as physically aggressive and violent as are men. They are not, indeed need not be "victims"; they should learn to look after themselves, become more aggressive. At the other end of the spectrum is Precilla Choi's argument that the masculine "sporty" type is the main reason why many girls and women do not participate in sport. Although her book examines (but does not critique) some of the latest (indeed feminist) research, it harks back to an earlier period of social psychological research on women and sport long since abandoned.

I want to conclude by making two additional observations, which at first glance may not seem intertwined. The first is the noticeable absence of sport studies within feminist academic literature and scholarship. Every three months I receive my copy of *Feminist Periodicals: A Current Listing of Contents* listing the table of contents of approximately 180 feminist magazines and academic periodicals (in English). Rarely do I find articles related to women's sport, physical activity, or even leisure. Somewhat better is the yearly *New Books on Women and Feminism*, which has a separate section on "Sports and Recreation," although it lists everything from how-to manuals and personal memoirs to more academic books. The point is that feminist sport studies, whether second wave or third wave, is making little or no impact on feminist scholarship and women's studies programs, at least in North America.

My second observation is the ever-widening gap between those who "do" theory and research and those who are the practitioners and activists in women's sport. I discussed this in *Feminism and Sporting Bodies*, but would argue the problem is far more serious now than it was in the mid-1990s. To put it simply, our critical academic work is being ignored by the new policy makers and "femocrats" of women's sport, who are reluctant to engage with those who criticize the status quo.[11] National and international women sports movements have become overly governmental, while grassroots organizers (and critics) are increasingly ignored, sidelined, or displaced by glossy new committees. In her recent book, *Heroines of Sport: The Politics of Difference and Identity*, longtime women's sports activist Jennifer Hargreaves argues that if the international women's sports movement is to grow in effectiveness, "it needs to find ways of reaching those women who are marginalized in their own countries, to transform the existing sets of power relations and to 'reach out' and 'pull in' women from underprivileged backgrounds and involve them in a process of reconstruction" (p. 231). I could not agree more.

At the risk of ending on a cynical note, I suggest that unless feminist sport scholars (of both the second and third waves) find better ways to contribute to feminist scholarship in general and women's studies in particular, and at the same time influence the practitioners and policy makers of women's sport, we and our work are in danger of becoming irrelevant.

ACKNOWLEDGMENTS

This chapter is adapted, by permission, from M. A. Hall, 1996, *Feminism and sporting bodies*, Champaign, IL: Human Kinetics, 1–9.

NOTES

1. I have more recently revisited the role of the bicycle in the physical emancipation of women. See *The Girl and the Game: A History of Women's Sport in Canada* (pp. 15–20).

2. It is called second-wave feminism to distinguish it from the earlier women's rights movement, which came to a halt in many Western countries after World War I when women were granted the right to vote. Dale Spender (1985), in *For the Record: The Making and Meaning of Feminist Knowledge*, reviews and interprets many of these classics, as well as others. It is well worth a read.

3. For useful and concise discussions concerning the theoretical origins of cultural studies and their application to sport studies, see Hargreaves and McDonald (2000) as well as Andrews (2002).

4. A version of Paul Willis' paper, with the title 'Women in Sport in Ideology,' was published in J. Hargreaves (Ed.), *Sport, Culture and Ideology* (pp. 117–135); it was also reprinted in S. Birrell & C L Cole (Eds.), *Women, Sport, and Culture* (pp. 31–45). For a version of my own contribution to this conference, see Hall (1976).

5. Now in its 30th year, Title IX is a federal act that states: "No person in the United States shall, on the basis of sex, be excluded from participation in, be denied the benefits of, or be subjected to discrimination under any education program or activity receiving federal financial assistance." This legislation and its implementation has significantly affected the growth of girls' high school and women's collegiate athletics in the United States, but it is under increasing attack by those who wish to see its effect diminished.

6. A semantic deferential is an instrument that measures meaning as a relational concept. A semantic scale is composed of a series of polar (opposite-in-meaning) adjectives: for example, happy-sad, fast-slow, aggressive-passive, hot-cold. Respondents are asked to rate or evaluate a particular concept, for example an "athletic woman," in relation to these polar adjectives. It is then possible to draw a profile, and obtain an overall score, of how respondents "rate" this particular concept.

7. Nor is this section intended as a review essay of where we are at with regard to feminist theories of sport, gender studies in sport, or feminist cultural studies of sport. For current summaries and analyses of these areas, see Birrell (2000), Theberge (2000), and Hargreaves and McDonald (2000).

8. The term "third wave feminism" came into public consciousness with the founding of the Third Wave Foundation in the United States in 1992. For a useful introduction to third wave feminism, see Heywood and Drake (1997), pp. 1–20. The wave model is not, however, without its problems and dissenters; see in particular Springer (2002) who argues that the wave model excludes feminists of color.

9. My interpretation of the third-wave feminist analytic has been summarized from Heywood and Dworkin (2003), pp. 8–24.

10. Donna A. Lopiano (Executive Director) Women's Sports Foundation responds to Title IX attack. Online at http://www.wfnet.org/news/story.php?story_id=94 accessed 24 March 2004.

11. I am indebted to Margaret Talbot for applying the term "femocrats" to this group of women managers, policy specialists, and bureaucrats now working in governmental and nongovernmental sport organizations from the local to the international level—see Talbot (2000).

REFERENCES

Andrews, D. L. (2002). Coming to terms with cultural studies. *Journal of Sport and Social Issues*, 26, 110–117.

Birrell, S. J. (1988). Discourses on the gender/sport relationship: From women in sport to gender relations. *Exercise and Sport Science Reviews*, 16, 459–502.

Birrell, S. J. (2000). Feminist theories for sport. In J. Coakley & E. Dunning (Eds.), *Handbook of Sports Studies* (pp. 61–76). London: Sage.

Birrell, S. J. & Cole, C L (Eds.) (1994). *Women, sport, and culture*. Champaign, IL: Human Kinetics.

Blalock, H. M. (1971). Theory building and causal inferences. In H. M. Blalock & A. B. Blalock (Eds.), *Methodology in social research* (pp. 155–198). London: McGraw-Hill.

Friedan, B. (1963). *The feminine mystique*. New York: Norton.

Gavora, J. (2002). *Tilting the playing field: Schools, sports, sex and Title IX*. San Francisco: Encounter Books.

Hall, M. A. (1971). The role of the safety bicycle in the emancipation of women. *Proceedings of the Second World Symposium on the History of Sport and Physical Education* (pp. 245–249), Banff, Alberta, May 31–June 3, 1971. Edmonton: University of Alberta.

Hall, M. A. (1972). A "feminine woman" and an "athletic woman" as viewed by female participants and non-participants in sport. *British Journal of Physical Education*, 3, 43–46.

Hall, M. A. (1974). *Women and physical recreation: A causal analysis*. Unpublished PhD thesis, University of Birmingham, Birmingham, England.

Hall, M. A. (1976). Sport and physical activity in the lives of Canadian women. In R. S. Gruneau & J. G. Albinson (Eds.), *Canadian sport: Sociological perspectives* (pp. 179–199). Toronto, ON: Addison-Wesley.

Hall, M. A. (1996). *Feminism and sporting bodies: Essays on theory and practice*. Champaign, IL: Human Kinetics.

Hall, M. A. (2002). *The girl and the game: A history of women's sport in Canada*. Peterborough: Broadview Press.

Hargreaves, J. (Ed.) (1982). *Sport, culture and ideology*. London: Routledge & Kegan Paul.

Hargreaves, J. (2000). *Heroines of sport: The politics of difference and identity*. London and New York: Routledge

Hargreaves, J. & McDonald, I. (2000). Cultural studies and the sociology of sport. In J. Coakley & E. Dunning (Eds.), *Handbook of Sports Studies* (pp. 48–60). London: Sage.

Heywood, L. (1998). *Bodymakers: A cultural anatomy of women's bodybuilding*. New Brunswick, NJ: Rutgers University Press.

Heywood, L. (2000). *Pretty good for a girl: An athlete's story*. Minneapolis: University of Minnesota Press.

Heywood, L., & Drake, J. (Eds.) (1997). *Third wave agenda: Being feminist, doing feminism*. Minneapolis: University of Minnesota Press.

Heywood, L., & Dworkin, S. L. (2003). *Built to win: The female athlete as cultural icon.* Minneapolis: University of Minnesota Press.

Hughes, J. A. (1980). *The philosophy of social research.* London: Longman.

Kavka, M. (2002). Feminism, ethics, and history, or what is the "post" in postfeminism? *Tulsa Studies in Women's Literature,* 21, 29–44.

Messner, M. A. (2002). *Taking the field: Women, men, and sports.* Minneapolis: University of Minnesota Press.

Mitchell, A., Rundle, L. B., & Karain, L. (Eds.) (2001). *Turbo chicks: Talking young feminisms.* Toronto: Sumach Press.

Spender, D. (1985). *For the record: The making and meaning of feminist knowledge.* London: Women's Press.

Springer, K. (2002). Third wave black feminism? *Signs: Journal of Women in Culture and Society,* 27, 1059–1082.

Talbot, M. (2000). Femocrats, technocrats and bureaucrats – women's contested place in the Olympic movement. Paper presented at the *Symposium to Celebrate 100 Years of Women in the Olympics,* Pre-Olympic Scientific Congress, Brisbane, Australia, 11 September.

Theberge, N. (2000). Gender and sport. In J. Coakley & E. Dunning (Eds.), *Handbook of Sports Studies* (pp. 322–333). London: Sage.

Chapter 3

Verifying the Values and Sparking the Spirit: Research and Practice on Motivation in Sport Psychology

Joan L. Duda

> *And when the moon*
> *is a light on the surface of the water*
> *we can hear the common longing.*
> *And we are asking*
> *why we are here?*
> *Only for this moment*
> *like a burst of flame.*
> *the answer is then as a declaration. It is for love.*
>
> —Poem found on Arja Laitinen's desk,
> October 1999

Love and all its manifestations, such as caring, connection, comfort, commitment, and confirmation of the precious worth and capacity of (an)other(s) and the self, truly marked the life of my dear and long-time friend, Arja Laitinen. Drawing from our many dialogues over the years, I have no doubt that she felt such love in her own encounters with the important people who made up her day-to-day world. As epitomized in the affection for and admiration of Arja revealed by the authors contributing to this volume, she was the kind of person who also radiated love to those acquaintances and family members around her.

In this contribution, however, I would like to focus on a different type of love, namely an ardor for and the injection of personal passion in one's work. It was clear that Arja was ardent about her professional activities, such as her earlier scholarship on feminism, sport, and physical culture at the University of Jyväskylä or later efforts with Arinna centered on telling the life stories of Finnish women. She approached such endeavors with intrinsic zeal and dedication. What was also evident from my conversations with Arja was that she was keenly aware of and energized by how her own values, experiences, and concerns infused and informed her professional contributions.

The aim of this paper is to share a bit about my own professional journey as a teacher, scholar, and practitioner in the field of sport psychology. It will be a story of love that is told with love, for I truly feel blessed to be able to study what I study and I am truly touched to have the opportunity to contribute to this text. It also will be a narrative on the discovery and rediscovery of fervency and the role of values in my work. Moreover, this saga will touch upon my understanding of how such personal enthusiasm and ideals juxtapose with how I view and approach my major area(s) of academic interest.

As a young girl, I thought (perhaps also because my teachers suggested this) that I would grow up to be a writer. In each case appreciating the power, symbolism, sound, and elegance of words, I enjoyed reading and time flew by in my literature classes. Mixing and mincing metaphors, there was much glee and satisfaction as I forged on with my latest poem, essay, or song. In essence, writing was a vehicle for expressing what I was feeling, how I saw events and situations in my world, how I would like things to be, and what I thought were feasible alternatives in terms of how we/I could fix or modify what was happening. Writing was a way of making sense of life circumstances and trying to find myself in the midst of it all.

This mode of expression continued through my days as an undergraduate student in psychology and women's studies at Rutgers University. However, as I moved toward graduation and then continued on with my education as a graduate student in sport psychology, my relationship with writing and, to some degree, my way of looking at the world started to alter. Particularly as I commenced my doctoral degree study, I was learning the tools and outlook of a scientist and was introduced to the order and security of logical positivism and empirical reductionism. This paradigmatic perspective presumes that

> there is an objective causal order that is ontologically independent of human inquiry, perception, and action, an order whose character does not vary with the theoretical commitments, interests, or values of the people investigating it. Second, [it]

presupposes that underlying this objective causal order are laws that are independent, both ontologically and causally, of human inquiry, perception and action. (Schwartz, 1990, p. 7)

As I tried to develop my capabilities as a researcher in sport psychology, I strove to employ valid and reliable assessments of the constructs of interest and utilize methods marked by as much internal and external validity as possible. Surrounded by data (actually keypunch cards and large, cumbersome outputs in those days), it was conveyed to me that the ultimate ambition was to be a "neutral, value-free truth seeker who tries to understand the world [of sport] in a totally objective manner" (Howard, 1985, p. 255). My writing now was supposed to become a way of impartially posing questions, dryly stating "facts," and dispassionately interpreting findings with the previous scientific literature and the epistemic rules of "sound" research as my pillars and guideposts. I liked what I was investigating but was unsure of how much of Joan was in the mix. In any regard, I tried to avoid this confusion and did my best to keep "her" at bay.

I met Arja soon after I completed my PhD at the University of Illinois, namely in September 1981. The job market in higher education in the early 1980s was at an ebb in the United States and an opportunity to pursue a visiting professorship overseas caught my imagination. When I told people that I was going to Europe for a semester to teach and do research, they immediately thought London, Paris, Rome, Madrid . . . No, that's not where life's course took me. I found myself in Jyväskylä, Finland (needed to look it up on a map, the city and the country!), with the hours of sunlight starting to diminish and the snow and cold temperatures coming to camp in—and Arja Laitinen as my office mate. My months in Jyväskylä were a most rewarding adventure. I discovered that I could live abroad and, even though I missed "home," found such international experiences personally comfortable and stimulating at the same time. Moreover, I was captivated by what I gleaned about other people and myself by being part of a foreign culture. And yes, I forged a special friendship with my office mate, Arja, that never diminished as a function of ensuing distance and passing years.

Following my semester in Finland and a brief postdoctorate experience back at my doctoral alma mater, the next step was my first bona fide position as a faculty member (albeit still designated "Visiting") in the Department of Kinesiology at UCLA. One day early in my stint at this university, I went to hear a lecture by Professor Evelyn Fox Keller. Her talk covered a number of areas, touching on issues relating to the philosophy of science and the impact of gender on scientific paradigms and assumptions. She also spoke of her work analyzing the career of the biologist/ geneticist Barbara McClintock, and gave examples of Dr. McClintock's personal connection with the phenomenon she investigated (in this case, the chromosomal characteristics of corn!). If someone in the "hard sciences" whose daily research activities involved a nonhuman study participant (notice the sense of control implied regarding the scientist over the study participants when we use the word "subjects" to describe those who are cooperating with us with respect to forging new knowledge!) perceived herself to be linked to what she studied, what was I doing trying to separate myself from what and whom I investigated (or should I say allowed me to investigate)? Alas, in terms of my personal research agenda in sport psychology, I became attuned to the realization that "I" was there all along. The place of values was verified and the new challenge was to come to grips with how such values were manifested in my research and applied work, my outlook on the research and practice of my colleagues, and their reactions to my contributions to the field.

Values can be defined in relation to the principles or criteria evoked to ascertain the relative worth, merit, or importance we place on objects, actions, states of being, ways of life, institutions, etc. (Schwartz, 1990). With respect to research and application in sport psychology specifically, values can be translated as the "guiding principles that [we assume] can promote human welfare" (Prilleltensky, 1997, p. 520). I came to realize after further explorations into the pitfalls of positivism and premises of a postmodern psychology (Gergen, 1994, 2001), that acknowledging a degree of relativism in and bringing a value-laden approach to scientific inquiries does not constitute a drawback. Rather, it is the failure to recognize the impact of our subjectivity and humanism in the research enterprise that can cause bias and blind us in terms of the moral implications of our work. Indeed, an unswerving devotion to a value-free research process becomes the capricious culprit and one has to wonder how we, as scientists, can be enlivened and enriched by an exercise from which we make ourselves divorced. Such a standpoint also seems to distrust the "self-correcting" approach to knowledge that science represents. That is, "through strong empirical research, good theories gain support and bad theories sow the seeds of their own destruction" and "science, as a way of knowing, ultimately transcends the imperfections [and perhaps personal values] of its individual practitioners" (Sternberg & Grigorenko, 2002, p. 1129, 1130). Science can handle, and perhaps even welcomes, the influx of nonepistemic and epistemic values into the fray.

In the remaining parts of this chapter, I would like to discuss the ways I see values permeating my major research focus in sport psychology, i.e., the investigation of the nature, antecedents, and consequences of motivational processes in sport. My proposition here is fourfold: (1) Why we study a phenomenon is influenced by personal values; (2) How we study a phenomenon is impacted by personal values; (3) How we interpret the results of our research is predisposed by personal values; and

(4) Personal values come into play in our approach to applied work and when we consider the practical implications of existing research findings.

MY MOTIVATION TO STUDY MOTIVATION IN SPORT

I always knew Arja as an active woman. Walking, running, dancing, skiing—or sailing and swimming at one of the many serene Finnish lakes—movement was a fundamental part of who she was. As her professional work exemplified, she saw the importance of physicality in the lives of women; as a median of empowerment, as an expression of personal meaning, as a way to commune with one's self, others, and nature.

This was definitely something I shared with Arja, for as long as I could remember, I recall myself jumping, biking, throwing, kicking, batting, and sprinting around from place to place. Indeed, even nowadays, I keep trying to move with frequency and intensity in accordance with (and sometimes in opposition to) the constraints now put upon me by hectic life schedules, nagging and new-found injuries, and the fact that the activation level and reserves are not quite what they used to be. For me, perhaps because I was born in a suburban and inhabitant dense community in New Jersey, USA, rather than in a less populated Scandinavian country with an abundance of green and beautiful free space, my fervor for moving translated into a longterm engagement in organized sport in contrast to a primary involvement in unstructured, outdoor activities—as was the case for Arja.

According to Howard (1985, p. 255) "values can legitimately and fruitfully affect the choice or selection of questions for study." As it always has been an endemic aspect of who I am and what I do, I value sport in my life. What a "kick," then, when one can enter into a career investigating a phenomenon deemed personally enjoyable. With respect to my personal interest in *studying sport*, it is also appealing to me that sport is a cultural artifact; it mirrors society and this relationship is reciprocal as sport also has an impact on the social order. So, I have also been captivated to study sport as a social construction and as a vehicle by which we can shape the larger community(ies) surrounding us.

Why the fascination with *motivation* in contrast to other topics within the broader realm of sport psychology? Difficult to say, but from a conceptual and practical perspective, I have continuously been absorbed with why some individuals begin participation in sport and other physical activities, why some maintain their engagement, and why some become disenfranchised and discontinue involvement.

As a student of the topic of motivation, I appreciated that the sport setting is an excellent forum in which to explore motivational processes. It is said that the study of motivation begins and ends with a consideration of behavior (Roberts, 1992). Behaviors indicative of motivation, such as performance and exerted effort, are more readily observed and assessed in sport than in other settings, such as the academic environment. Moreover, sport tends to be a voluntary activity and, therefore, a most telling setting in which to study persistence (a hallmark indicator of motivation).

Finally, why *study motivation in sport?* Besides being an inherently intrinsically rewarding activity, there are the implications of sport participation for public health to be considered. The contribution of regular physical activity to the quality of life has been well-documented (e.g., Sallis, Patterson, Bueno, & Nader, 1988). Sport *can and should* reflect a popular and rather social alternative for engagement in physical activity for young and old and among the proficient as well as the less able. We only need to figure out how we can foster motivation so that people would want to and are more able to pursue such an alternative.

THE MANNER IN WHICH TO STUDY SPORT MOTIVATION: A PERSONAL CHOICE

The vehicle through which we try to study and make sense of a phenomenon, such as sport motivation, is a theoretical position. As psychological theories contain suppositions about how something works and are designed to predict outcomes of differential value to different scientists, it is apparent that value judgments come into play when selecting a theoretical framework. As one of my mentors, John Nicholls, proposed

> . . . differences among scientific theories involve differences in the purposes of those who construct [and choose] the theories. People with different priorities ask different questions and tell different stories about the world. Scientific theory is, in this view, very much a personal, social, human affair. (Nicholls, 1992, p. 101)

As a PhD student, I was exposed to a number of contemporary theories of achievement motivation that were having their mark on contemporary psychology and sport psychology circles based on traditional, epistemic, scientific "rules." What "caught my fancy" were the achievement goal frameworks (Ames, 1992; Dweck, 1986, 1999; Nicholls, 1984, 1989), as particularly formulated and proffered by John Nicholls.

In general, achievement goal frameworks hold that achievement goals, reflecting ways in which individuals define their competence and subjectively define success, are the guiding principles for ensuing cognitions, emotions, and behaviors. The framework advocates the relevance of two major goal states, namely task and ego involvement. When in a state of task involvement, people tend to focus on the task at hand and construe their ability in a self-referenced manner. In this case, learning, personal improvement, and the exhibiting of effort occasion feelings of success. When ego-involved, improvement and insight are not enough. In a state of ego involvement, the concern is with demonstrating superior competence relative to others. If high normative ability is evident, the person in question experiences personal success.

Nicholls (1989) holds that individuals differ in their dispositional pronenesses for task and ego involvement. That is, we vary in the degree we are characterized by two orthogonal goal orientations (i.e., a task and ego orientation). Achievement goal frameworks also assume that the psychological environment impacts the goal states realized in achievement settings. These perceived "motivational climates" (Ames, 1992), which are created by significant others such as parents (White, Duda, & Hart, 1992), teachers/coaches (Newton, Duda, & Yin, 2000), and peers (Vazou, Ntoumanis, & Duda, in press), are distinguished by the degree to which they set the stage for a differential emphasis on task or ego criteria for success.

Because perceived competence and resulting feelings of success are more within a person's control, it is theoretically expected that situational and/or dispositional task goals should correspond to positive motivational outcomes (Nicholls, 1989). It is also presumed that an emphasis on ego goals should be coupled with positive outcomes (at least in the short term) as long as the individual is confident she/he possesses high ability. Motivational problems are proposed to result when a person doubts her/his competence and is directed toward securing ego goals (Dweck, 1999; Nicholls, 1984, 1989).

In our earlier work, we tested the hypothesized relationships regarding achievement goals and achievement-related beliefs, cognitive responses, and behavioral patterns in sport (see Duda, 1992, 1993, 2001, for reviews). In general, the findings were consonant with theoretical predictions. Among a constellation of variables, we found that an examination of the achievement goals of athletes and/or their views regarding the prevailing motivational climate on their team, provided insight into their beliefs about the determinants of sport success, views about the purposes of sport participation, enjoyment of and satisfaction with their sport, experienced stress and coping responses, and behaviors such as performance/skill development, exerted effort, and task choice.

What captured my attention in the achievement goal frameworks? First, it made sense to me that more insight into motivational patterns would be provided if we consider individuals' personal meanings of achievement events and subjective notions of success (and failure) rather than viewing positive and negative achievement outcomes (such as winning and losing) as objective entities. Second, I believe that a critical period for enhancing motivation for sport engagement is childhood and the achievement goal frameworks have a developmental component (e.g., Fry & Duda, 1997; Nicholls, 1989). Third, as mentioned above, the frameworks place importance on individual differences between people but do not then "blame the victim" and assume some in-bred personality flaw is responsible for motivational deficits. Rather, the nature of the social environment fashioned by significant others is considered critical to motivational striving and the individual differences in question (namely, people's goal orientations) are considered to be tendencies that can be modified.

Lastly, it became apparent to me that I not only wanted (from a theory) insight into the *quantity* of motivation evident in the physical domain but also the *quality* of that motivation. With respect to someone participating in sport, she/he exhibits high (quantitatively speaking) motivation if she/he is acting invested at a particular point of time and is performing well. In contrast, the quality of motivation is revealed by a consideration of such factors as: (a) how does this athlete feel about her/his investment?, (b) does this athlete's investment in sport enhance her/his physical, psychological, moral, civic constitution?, (c) given a choice, would this athlete want to invest in sport over time?, and (d) has this athlete maximized her/his capabilities in sport and do we witness a pattern of long-term accomplishment? Achievement goal frameworks provide strategies for investigating such issues and propose mechanisms regarding why variation in the quantity *and* quality of sport motivation may exist.

Programmatic lines of work are, hopefully, dynamic and do go through different phases and permutations. Specifically, I have found myself in more recent work trying to push achievement goal frameworks to not only explicate differences in achievement-related responses (e.g., views about what it requires to be successful, perceived competence, performance-related anxiety) but also allow some comprehension of when and why sport involvement might be health conducive or health compromising (Duda, 1996, 2001). Indicative of this line of inquiry, research has found goal orientations and/or perceptions of the task- and ego-involving features of the climate to be predictive (in theoretically consonant ways) to correlates of and reported eating disorder symptoms among high-level competitive female gymnasts (e.g., Duda, Benardot, & Kim, 2004). Among competitive body builders, other studies have found those that took performance-enhancing drugs to be higher in ego orientation and perceived a more ego-involving training environment than their counterparts who were lower in ego orientation and viewed the climate as less ego-involving (Duda & Law, 2004).

This concern with explaining variability in the welfare of individuals has led to efforts to integrate achievement goal frameworks with (an)other conceptualizations of motivation. Searching for amalgamation and complementarities between theoretical perspectives, I believe, can only deep en our knowledge and widen our interpretive window. In essence, I concur with Lau (2002, p. 1126) who argued that

> if scientific theories and methodologies provide only a partial and always incomplete picture of reality, then the adoption of multiple theoretical perspectives and methodologies will serve only to enrich the understanding of psychological phenomena.

In the more recent work (e.g., McArdle, Duda, & Hall, 2004; Reinboth, Duda, & Ntoumanis, 2004; Standage, Duda, & Ntoumanis, 2003a), we have attempted to join together principles and constructs embedded in achievement goal frameworks and Self Determination Theory (SDT) (Deci & Ryan, 2000; Ryan & Deci, 2000). The latter theory reflects an approach to the study of human motivation in its broadest sense (i.e., not specific to achievement activities). SDT points to the relevance of human beings' "evolved inner resources for personality development and behavioral self-regulation" (p. 68) and assumes behavior is goal-directed. Like the achievement goal approach, SDT focuses on the *content* of goals. However, attention is also placed on the regulatory processes associated with different goal contents (Deci & Ryan, 2000). Also in contrast (or addition to, which is how I see the picture) achievement goal frameworks, SDT proposes that the concept of innate psychological needs is fundamental to variability in motivational processes and outcomes. The fulfillment of these basic needs (in particular, the need for competence, autonomy, and relatedness) is held to correspond with more self-determined motivational regulations (e.g., intrinsic motivation to engage in the activity at hand). Thwarting of these needs is predicted to be aligned with less self-determined regulations, such as extrinsic motivations for activity engagement.

For me, an appealing feature of SDT is that the concepts of self-determination and need satisfaction are held to be pertinent to the exhibiting of enhanced *hedonic* and *eudaimonic* well-being. Hedonic well-being is usually defined with respect to indicators of pleasure attainment and/or the avoidance of psychological, emotional, or physical discomfort (e.g., happiness, positive mood, lower incidence/intensity of negative mood states) (Deci & Ryan, 2002; Ryan & Deci, 2000). Eudaimonic well-being is reflected in the degree to which individuals are functioning fully and optimally (Deci & Ryan, 2002). This latter type of well-being is typically operationalized in SDT research in regard to indices of vitality and mental health. Most relevant if one is concerned with discrepancies in the quality of the sport experience, Ryan and Deci (2000) have argued that SDT also has predictive utility when it comes to the "darker side of human existence."

In terms of trying to pull together some of these pieces of a larger conceptual puzzle, we have found task orientation to correspond to more intrinsic motivational regulations in the physical domain. Ego orientation is typically unrelated to intrinsic motivation but positively associated with more extrinsic regulations (Standage, Duda, & Ntoumanis, 2003b). Further, perceptions of a task-involving climate are positively linked to greater need satisfaction (Reinboth et al., 2004; Standage et al., 2003a). Most exciting in my view, some of our most recent studies have indicated a positive interdependence between task goal focus and hedonic well-being (e.g., reported positive mood states) as well as eudaimonic well-being (e.g,. subjective vitality, self-esteem). An emphasis on ego goals, whether reflected by personal orientations or the perceived climate operating, has been aligned with diminished psychological (e.g., the stability and contingency of self-esteem appraisals) and physical (e.g., the reporting of physical symptoms) well-being among athletes (McArdle & Duda, 2003; Reinboth & Duda, 2004).

VALUES AND THE INTERPRETATION OF FINDINGS

According to Sheldon, Schmuck, and Kasser (2000, p. 1152), "empirical 'facts' can support many incompatible theoretical positions and are always theory dependent and thus value dependent." Their position doesn't imply that the epistemic rules and values of science do not point us toward some consensus and provide standards for choosing among competing theoretical explanations (Howard, 1985). It does suggest, however, that everything is not "clear cut" and there are often "shades of gray" in research findings that are viewed through our own value-colored lens.

Let me try to flesh out this point a little more clearly in terms of recent professional experiences. Currently in the achievement goal literature, there is some controversy (e.g., Duda, 1997; Hardy, 1997). I have no doubt that a degree of controversy is inevitable when a line of work becomes popular and has so many practical implications for the sport domain. To begin with, other researchers have questioned whether task goals are always so adaptive and appealing in sport (Hardy, 1997). The existing sport achievement goal literature, of which my work within this body of work has been particularly targeted, has also been interpreted as suggesting that ego orientation "is the bad guy" and then criticized for this suggestion (Hardy, 1997). In essence, there have been defensive responses to any potential attacks on the worthiness of ego goals and counter proposals generated, which argue that such an achievement goal is needed and can be beneficial in sport (e.g., Harwood, Hardy, & Swain, 2000). Along the same lines, the advocacy for an ego orientation has been particularly fervent regarding its necessity at the elite level and questions have been posed regarding whether it is possible for task involvement to exist among elite performers (Harwood et al., 2000). Indeed, some colleagues have questioned the applicability of key goal concepts and basic tenets of achievement goal frameworks to the highest levels of sport competition (Harwood et al., 2000).

For the record, I do see how (and indeed have written about how) an ego goal focus, if coupled with high perceived ability and/or a strong task orientation, could result in positive *achievement* outcomes, such as good performance (Duda, 2001). It should be noted as well that the founding father of this approach to motivation, namely John Nicholls, much earlier recognized these possibilities (Nicholls, 1984, 1989). With respect to the debate summarized above though, perhaps one reason for such variability in positions about the pluses and minuses and relevance of task and ego goals revolves around how (as researchers and/or practitioners in sport psychology) we define a positive (achievement) motivational pattern. To some degree, this goes back to the point raised previously about motivation quantity *and* quality. In my view, a motivation response (or pattern of motivational responses) is deemed adaptive and desirable if it/they reflect the quantity and quality facets of motivation and achievement. To me, the former without the latter could never be considered truly positive or adaptive. My position does not alter on this issue as a function of whether the athletes in question are true beginners, recreational, or representative of the highest echelons of sport (Duda, 1997; Pensgaard & Duda, 2004).

More specifically, in the prevailing prism that researchers and practitioners in sport psychology use to examine and interpret "achievement" and motivational patterns, do we primarily consider short-term competitive outcomes such as who won a particular race or what team secured the championship? Do we reflect on sustained excellence among the talented? Regardless of skill level, is a desirable achievement/motivational pattern signified when people work to maintain their capacities and skills and investment in the sporting realm throughout the lifespan? Is it relevant whether people overcome physical, mental, and/or emotional challenges and give their best effort? When deciding on whether someone is optimally motivated, do we bear in mind when they are faced with "failure" and/or doubting themselves in the sport arena (e.g., because of an injury or performance slump) or just look at their cognitive, affective, and behavioral responses when "things are going good"? Finally, when characterizing indices of high-achievement motivation, do we take into account the *means* to achievement and the *cost* of achievement for the individuals in question?

In my perspective, the elements of the sport experience embedded in these queries are not independent but rather significantly interrelated in the daily, real-life operation of sport. However, I think it is important to recognize that sometimes, in certain value systems or perspectives on sport, these elements can be at odds. I, on the other hand, wish they were not deemed incompatible and do not believe they *have to be* or *should be* in conflict, in any particular sport *or* at any competitive level.

The central point here however is that, in terms of *my* interpretation of research findings regarding the implications of task and ego goal orientations *and* perceptions of a task-involving and ego-involving climates (Duda, 2001), one needs to consider *all the aspects of the quantity and quality of motivation* reflected above when judging whether observed results are indicative of a positive or negative (achievement) motivational pattern. Just showing that a particular achievement goal at times and among certain sport participants corresponds to winning, high confidence, superior performance doesn't do the trick. This is a limited, and arguably a value-fueled, way of judging a motivational perspective adaptive or less desirable. Wearing my value-coated glasses when reading through the plethora of studies on dispositional and situational achievement goals in sport, I say let's fan the flames of task involvement and do what we can to keep ego involvement in check! This is the way to go if we want to lay the foundation for quality and sustained engagement and maximal accomplishment in sport.

THE VALUE OF ONE'S WORK: WHERE DO WE GO FROM HERE—IN PRACTICE?

In my own professional pursuits and perspective on the field, I have never accepted a presumed inevitable division between research and application. In contrast, I have always felt that sport psychology theory and research *can* and *should* inform practice. After all, why do we do research? Is it solely to fill journals, impress colleagues in the discipline, and ensure our survival and promotion within the academic milieu? Or, is the driving force and passion behind our scholarship to enlighten and perhaps empower change regarding the failings within sport and/or reinforce and provide better insight into all the good "things"?

Also contrary to any assumed dichotomy between research and practice, I have always thought too that what coaches, athletes, spectators, and those not involved think and do *can* and *should* impact theoretical understanding and future research efforts in sport psychology. Over the years, a number of research questions that my colleagues and I pursued have germinated from what was actually happening in the "real world" of sport.

With respect to the potential implications of research for practice, I find it most unsatisfying and perhaps somewhat unpalatable when it is suggested that we shouldn't question or try to modify the status quo (especially at the elite level) because "that's the way sport is." Injustices, costly consequences for participants, breakdowns in moral functioning, punitive and dehumanizing features of the environment, there are professionals in sport psychology who say "take it or leave it" (the latter meaning either reconsider doing research or practice because your outlook is not in touch with the way it is—and must be?—or redirect your research efforts and gear your proposals for change to nonelite sport populations and systems). I feel that such a position reflects narrow and static thinking and can be considered indicative of circumventing our personal and professional responsibilities. With respect to trying to evoke change, "our obligations as citizens . . . are considerably broader than our obligations as scientists" (Miller, 1970, p. 1063). As professionals in sport psychology, we are indeed in the position to ask "why?" in terms of what is happening in sport, and to suggest some alternatives and then ask "why not"? In turning a critical eye to sport and contemplating a new order, I concur with Miller (1970, p. 1063) who argued that

> the most urgent problems of our world today are the problems we have made for ourselves. They have not been caused by some heedless or malicious inanimate Nature, nor have they been imposed on us as punishment by the will of God. They are human problems whose solutions will require us to change our behaviour and our social institutions. (Miller, 1970, p. 1063)

At the very least, we should consider our personal values and assumptions and ask ourselves what ideals and standards do we wish for people and for society at large in terms of sport engagement and consumption? Let's lay it on the line and further the debate in a constructive manner. With respect to such an exchange,

> the objective is not to reach consensus among all [sport] psychologists nor to foist on the public a particular conception of the good life and the good society [and a "good" world of sport] . . . The objective is to generate dialogue about the different conceptions of the good society [and a better sport] and how to get there. (Prilleltensky, 1997, p. 518)

CLOSING CONSIDERATIONS REGARDING VALUES AND THEIR VALUE TO PRACTICE

Without questioning Baconian logic, which assumes that the predictive accuracy, internal coherence, and practical significance of a theory are elementary to its validity (Howard, 1985; Ryan & Deci, 2000), I continue to be more mindful of and at ease with the infiltration of values in my personal scholarship and applied endeavors. In attempting to further elucidate the moral implications of my work, I have found the framework proposed by Prilleltensky (1997, p. 518) to be useful. He suggests that it is paramount that researchers and/or practitioners in psychology gain awareness of and articulate the *values, assumptions, and practices* marking our discourse and actions. Prilleltensky holds that these three are highly interdependent with values influencing our working assumptions about people and problems, and such assumptions having a logical concordance with our practice strategies and approaches.

Values. Employing Prilleltensky's (1997) diagnostic framework, it is clear to me that I value (i.e., I am concerned about and empathetic toward) the physical *and* psychological welfare of individuals involved in sport. This is considered to reflect the values of caring and compassion (Prilleltensky, 1997). I am also focused on the principle of self-determination; i.e., within sport, people have the right to pursue their own selected, personally meaningful goals and feel some control over their sport involvement. Other values that are endemic to my sport psychology work are human diversity, democratic participation, and distributive justice. With respect to the former, I believe the world of sport should be accessible and attractive to both genders and all people of all ages, social classes, races, ethnicities, and sexual orientations. I also am committed to the amenable and dignified expression of different social and cultural norms and viewpoints in the realm of sport. Indeed, there is not one but many sport participations and experiences. In terms of democratic participation, I concur that sport engagement should ultimately allow and encourage individuals "to feel part of the world around them" and uphold "personal rights and social responsibilities." That is, sport can and should be a vehicle for promoting citizenship and involvement in the democratic process (Bredemeier & Shields, in press). Finally, in my value system, the resources to engage in and possibility for the obtaining of "goods" (whether extrinsic and/or intrinsic, collective and/or individually oriented) through sport should be fair and equitable.

Assumptions. According to Prilleltensky (1997), implicit or explicit *assumptions* in our research, theoretical formulations, and applied activities expose our "moral standpoint." For example, in terms of the suppositions deemed to be operating in my applied work, we would need to consider how I plan to use the information stemming from my own and others' research on sport motivation. With respect to this issue, I do assume it is important to take this work and translate it for practitioners, via workshops, practical articles, one-on-one consulting with athletes or coaches, and I am committed to doing so.

It is also important to ascertain my conception of the "good life" among those in and outside of the sport system. (Hopefully) consonant with my values, I see the "perfect" sport domain as one in which all participants (athletes, coaches, officials, administrators) feel self-determined and have the opportunity to maximize their physical, mental, emotional, and spiritual potentials. In truth, I wish this for all individuals in all facets of their lives.

To further elucidate the moral fabric of applied work, Prilleltensky (1997) would also suggest that it is relevant to examine my vision of an "ideal" sport system and outlook on what I would consider a more desirable reciprocity between sport and society. The "ideal" sport system, in my view, is one that encourages a healthful sport involvement throughout the lifespan and continuously contributes to personal growth. With such aims accomplished, sport would indeed be a vehicle for contributing to a better society on the whole rather than echoing or exacerbating societal ills.

Practice. Finally, Prilleltensky's (1997) framework proposes that there are five distinguishable aspects of psychological *practice* that are colored by our values and assumptions, namely (a) problem definition, (b) views on the role of the people we are working with, (c) views on our role as sport psychology researchers and/or practitioners, (d) preferences regarding intervention strategies, and (e) perspectives on the timing of interventions. For example, in my consulting activities, I am not primarily oriented toward "treating" sport-related problems encountered by athletes or coaches. Rather, the emphasis is to direct efforts toward the prevention of such problems and identify and try to further enhance athletes' and coaches' strengths in contrast to a heavy focus on countering weaknesses. When and where possible, I try to work with significant others in the sport system (e.g., coaches, parents) to facilitate a task-involving climate *and* work with athletes (and coaches) to foster their task-involving/self-determining self-regulation skills. All in all, I see myself as a facilitator who is in partnership with those with whom I am working. Everyone has expertise and experience to share, and my knowledge (which, in a large part, draws from research and theory!) is one piece of the puzzle. If the consultation goes well, my services as a sport psychology consultant should be needed less and less and eventually, perhaps not at all!

A FINAL THOUGHT

The last time I saw my friend Arja Laitinen was in June 1999. Arja came to visit me for a week while I was on research leave in Spain. We spent a lot of time during those days discussing many of the issues raised above in terms of her and my recent professional (pre)occupations. As was the case for as long as I knew her, Arja was very much in a personal growth mode—planning, contemplating, integrating, engaging—even though physically she was very far from being well. We also talked about much larger considerations such as what our lives might be about, where are they going, and the underestimated value of whole, disease-free bodies. Although such exchanges are sorely missed, their form, content and *Arja's spirit* continue to inspire and challenge me.

REFERENCES

Ames, C. (1992). Classrooms, goal structures, and student motivation. *Journal of Educational Psychology*, 84, 261–274.

Deci, E. L. & Ryan, R. M. (2000). The "what" and "why" of goal pursuits: Human needs and the self-determination of behavior. *Psychological Inquiry*, 11 (4), 227–268.

Deci, E. L., & Ryan, R. M. (2002). On happiness and human potentials: A review of research on hedonic and eudaimonic well-being. *Annual Review of Psychology*, 52, 141–166.

Duda, J. L. (1992). Sport and exercise motivation: A goal perspective analysis. In G. Roberts (Ed.), *Motivation in sport and exercise* (pp. 57–91). Champaign, IL: Human Kinetics.

Duda, J. L. (1993). Goals: A social cognitive approach to the study of motivation in sport. In R. N. Singer, M. Murphey, & L. K. Tennant (Eds.), *Handbook on research in sport psychology* (pp. 421–436). NY: Macmillan.

Duda, J. L. (1996). Maximizing motivation in sport and physical education among children and adolescents: The case for greater task involvement. *Quest*, 48, 290–302.

Duda, J. L. (1997). Perpetuating myths: A response to Hardy's 1996 Coleman Griffith Address. *Journal of Applied Sport Psychology*, 9, 303–309.

Duda, J. L. (2001). Goal perspectives research in sport: Pushing the boundaries and clarifying some misunderstandings. In G. C. Roberts (Ed.), *Advances in motivation in sport and exercise* (pp.129–182). Champaign, IL: Human Kinetics.

Duda, J. L., Benardot, D., & Kim, M-S. (2004). *The relationship of the motivational climate to psychological and energy balance correlates of eating disorders in female gymnasts*. Manuscript under review.

Duda, J. L., & Law, J. (2003). *Reported and intended use of steroids and human growth hormone in competitive body building: An achievement goal theory approach*. Manuscript under review.

Dweck, C. (1986). Motivational processes affecting learning. *American Psychologist*, 41, 1040–1048.

Dweck, C. (1999). *Self theories: Their role in motivation, personality, and social development*. Psychology Press: UK.

Fry, M. D., & Duda, J. L. (1997). Children's understanding of effort and ability in the physical and academic domains. *Research Quarterly for Exercise and Sport*, 68, 1–14.

Gergen, K. J. (1994). Exploring the postmodern: Perils or potentials? *American Psychologist*, 49, 412–416.

Hardy, L. (1997). Three myths about applied consultancy work. *Journal of Applied Sport Psychology*, 9, 277-294.

Harwood, C., Hardy, L., & Swain, A. (2000). Achievement goals in sport: A critique of conceptual and measurement issues. *Journal of Sport and Exercise Psychology*, 22, 235–255.

Hoshman, L. T., & Polkinghorne, D. E. (1992). Redefining the science-practice relationship and professional training. *American Psychologist*, 47, 55–66.

Howard, G. S. (1985). The role of values in the science of psychology. *American Psychologist*, 40, 255–265.

Kendler, H. H. (1999). The role of value in the world of psychology. *American Psychologist*, 54, 828–835.

Lau, M. Y. (2002). Postmodernism and the values of science. *American Psychologist*, 57, 1126–1127.

McArdle, S., & Duda, J. L. (2003). Understanding variability in the achievement experiences and well-being of perfectionists: A motivational processes/social contextual approach. In R. Stelter (Ed.), *New approaches to exercise and sport psychology: Theories, methods and applications* (p. 110). Copenhagen, Denmark: Institute of Exercise and Sport Sciences Press.

McArdle, S., Duda, J. L., & Hall, H. K. (2004). *Young athletes striving for perfection: Examining variability in achievement experiences from a motivational perspective*. Manuscript under review.

Miller, G. A. (1970). Psychology as a means of promoting human welfare. *American Psychologist*, 25, 1063–1075.

Newton, M., Duda, J. L. & Yin, Z. (2000). Examination of the psychometric properties of the Perceived Motivational Climate in Sport Questionnaire - 2 in a sample of female athletes. *Journal of Sport Sciences*, 18 (4), 275–290.

Nicholls, J. G. (1984). Achievement motivation: Conceptions of ability, subjective experience, task choice, and performance. *Psychological Review*, 91, 328–346.

Nicholls, J. G. (1989). *The competitive ethos and democratic education*. Cambridge, MA: Harvard University Press.

Nicholls, J. G. (1992). The general and the specific in the development and expression of achievement motivation. In G. Roberts (Ed.), *Motivation in sport and exercise* (pp. 31–56). Champaign, IL: Human Kinetics.

Pensgaard, A. M., & Duda, J. L. (2004). *Relationship of situational and dispositional achievement goals to coach ratings, perceived stressors, and performance among Olympic athletes*. Manuscript under review.

Prilleltensky, I. (1997). Values, assumptions, and practices: Assessing the moral implications of psychological discourse and action. *American Psychologist*, 52, 517–35.

Reinboth, M., & Duda, J. L. (2004). Relationship of the perceived motivational climate and perceptions of ability to psychological and physical well-being in team sports. *The Sport Psychologist*, 18, 237–251.

Reinboth, M., Duda, J. L., & Ntoumanis, N. (2004). Coaching factors, need satisfaction, and the psychological and physical welfare of young athletes. *Motivation and Emotion*, 28, 297–313.

Roberts, G. C. (1992). Motivation in sport and exercise: Conceptual constraints and convergence. In G. Roberts (Ed.), *Motivation in sport and exercise* (pp. 3–30). Champaign, IL: Human Kinetics.

Ryan, R. M., & Deci, E. L . (2000). Self-determination theory and the facilitation of intrinsic motivation, social development, and well being. *American Psychologist*, 55, 68–78.

Sallis, J. F., Patterson, T. L., Buono, M. J., & Nader, P. R. (1988). Relation of cardiovascular fitness and physical activity cardiovascular risk factors in children and adults. *American Journal of Epidemiology*, 127, 933–941.

Schwartz, B. (1990). The creation and destruction of value. *American Psychologist*, 45, 7–15.

Standage, M., Duda, J. L. & Ntoumanis, N. (2003a). A model of contextual motivation in physical education: An integration of self-determination and goal perspective theories in predicting leisure-time exercise intentions. *Journal of Educational Psychology*, 95, 97–110.

Standage, M., Duda, J. L., & Ntoumanis, N. (2003b). Predicting motivational regulationsin physical education: the interplay between dispositional goal orientations, motivational climate and perceived competence. *Journal of Sports Sciences*, 21 (8), 631–647.

Vazou, S., Ntoumanis, N., & Duda, J. L. (in press). Peer motivational climate in sport: A qualitative inquiry. *Psychology of Sport and Exercise*.

White, S. A., Duda, J. L., & Hart, S. (1992). An exploratory examination of the Parent-Initiated Motivational Climate Questionnaire. *Perceptual and Motor Skills*, 75, 875–880.

PART II

Personal Experiences as a Source for Feminist Inquiry in Sport

Chapter 4

Doing Feminist Ethnography:
A Report from the Rink

Nancy Theberge

During the 1990s I spent a great deal of time at hockey rinks. My time at these arenas was the basis of the most extensive and engaging research project of my academic career, which began in the mid-1970s. Beginning with a doctoral dissertation on the Ladies Professional Golf Association (LPGA), followed by various projects including studies of women in volunteer positions in amateur sport, women in coaching, and media constructions of gender and sport, I have devoted much of my scholarly life to the study of gender and sport. My work in women's hockey, however, brought me into a world that was entirely new to me, that of the change room, practices and games that are the stuff of athletes' daily lives. This work is reported in my book, *Higher Goals: Women's Ice Hockey and the Politics of Gender*, and a number of journal articles and book chapters.[1] In this chapter I want to explore how the project that became *Higher Goals* evolved, as a case study in how a feminist sport sociologist does her work. Specifically, I will discuss some background factors that led me to this project, details of how I did the research, and issues that arose as I became an insider in the world of women's hockey. A concluding section reflects briefly on my relationship to women's hockey since completing the research. My interest to study this sport evolved from the interaction of some features of my personal and intellectual biography. So, I will begin this discussion with some background.

FROM CHILDHOOD SPORTING ATTACHMENTS
TO A CAREER AS A SPORT SOCIOLOGIST

My path to a career as a sport sociologist was different from that of many who work in the field, in that I have no background in either organized sport or physical education, save two years of required physical education in university in the late 1960s that at the time I saw as a nuisance. As a young girl growing up outside Boston in the 1950s and early 1960s, there were few opportunities for sport participation available to me. Despite this, my childhood was marked by a powerful attachment to sport. As the youngest child in a family with two older brothers, I grew up in a family where sport was a passion. Much of this energy was directed to baseball and following the fortunes of the local professional team, the Boston Red Sox. One of the ways I like to describe my path to an adult career of studying sport is that I do not remember a time in my childhood when I was not going to Fenway Park, the storied stadium where the Red Sox play. These trips were not frequent and when they did occur they were major outings. Three or four times a year my family would go into Boston to see a baseball game. During the rest of the season I watched games on television or fell asleep at night listening to broadcasts on a radio next to my bed. A nighttime ritual of falling asleep to baseball broadcasts is an image frequently associated with children of my era, though that image typically is one of a young boy. At the time, I had little sense that following sport had anything to do with gender.

During my first year as an undergraduate at the University of Massachusetts I took Introductory Sociology and quickly decided I had found an intellectual home. Although I did not know it at the time, during the years that I was completing an undergraduate sociology degree at Massachusetts, a graduate program in the sociology of sport was being assembled at this institution. Following graduation, in 1970 I began studies for a master's degree in sociology at Boston College. It was here that I discovered the sociology of sport. While taking a course in race relations, I decided to write a paper on the black athlete. In researching this paper, I found my way to literature in the then emerging field of the sociology of sport. And in seeking out this material, I learned that the University of Massachusetts had become perhaps the leading institution at the time to pursue graduate work in this area. Graduate studies seemed a perfect way to combine my twin passions for sport and social thought and in 1973 I returned to Amherst to begin doctoral work in sociology. While completing the general requirements for a PhD in sociology, I began my concentration in the sociology of sport with a dissertation on the LPGA (Theberge, 1977).

My choice of dissertation topics was my first conscious decision to focus on women in sport. As mentioned above, as a child I had given little thought to the gendered nature of sport, which I took largely for granted. By the mid-1970s, however, the women's movement had started to influence many women of my generation. I decided that for my dissertation I wanted to focus on women's sport, which had received very little attention in the growing literature in the sociology of sport. I chose golf because I wanted to study elite athletes, which at the time pretty much meant either Olympic sport or professional tennis or golf. I was able to make some contacts in golf, which led to the opportunity to conduct my dissertation research.

In 1976 I moved to my first postgraduate position at the University of Waterloo, where I have remained. Since then I have pursued a research agenda focused largely on women's sport. A key event in my career was a sabbatical in 1985, in which I was based in Norway and traveled extensively in Europe and particularly in the Nordic countries. Two features of that sabbatical leave are especially notable in regard to the present chapter. First, it was during this time that I met Arja Laitinen. On learning that I was in Norway, Arja invited me to Finland. I spent 10 memorable days in Jyväskylä in April 1985, where I stayed with Arja and her family and lectured at the university. Because of Arja's kindness and gracious hospitality in connection with this visit, I immediately said yes when asked to contribute to the present volume.

A TURN TO THE SOCIOLOGY OF THE BODY, PHYSICALITY, AND WOMEN'S HOCKEY

My sabbatical stay in 1985 in Europe was also notable because it played a major role in my growing interest in the sociology of the body, which became the basis for my research in women's hockey. During my time in Europe, I met a number of scholars who spoke of work in "body culture," the term used by many people I met in my travels. While I was then naively skeptical of what seemed to me a neologism, in subsequent years as the sociology of the body developed and gained visibility, and its relevance for the study of gender and sport became obvious, I turned increasingly to literature in this field as a basis for my own work.

In the early 1990s I was completing work on a research project on women in coaching. This project was originally conceived as a study of career mobility, concerned with trying to understand the mechanisms and processes that led to women's underrepresentation in coaching, especially at the higher levels of sport. The data collection for this project involved interviews with women coaching at the elite levels of Canadian sport. In speaking with the study participants, I learned that one of the main barriers to their career mobility concerned the physical practice of sport. Coaching is a technical activity, concerned with training athletes in skills and techniques, that is the *practice* of sport. Women coaches repeatedly faced assumptions that men are better athletes, with more experience and expertise in the physical practice of sport, and for this reason (and others), also are better coaches. These assumptions in turn became the basis of unequal professional opportunities and mobility (Theberge, 1993).

In part to follow up on this aspect of my research in coaching, and more generally in response to theoretical developments at the time that stressed the importance of the body in social life and gender relations specifically, I determined that I wanted to study women's experience of skilled physical practice. That is, I wanted to come to understand what it is like for women to be *really good* at some kind of bodily practice and the factors that condition that experience. With this broadly conceptualized interest, and given that I am a sport sociologist working in Canada, it might seem to have been foreordained that I would turn to hockey to pursue this topic. This was not the case. Although I grew up not far from Boston, the location of one of the original six National Hockey League (NHL) franchises, for some reason hockey was not part of my childhood sporting consciousness. On moving to Canada in 1976, I was struck by the heavy, at times it seemed excessive, focus of the sporting culture on hockey, which of course was a focus on men's hockey. In this context, while I became more aware of hockey, my interest remained limited. The turn to women's hockey was greatly facilitated by an epiphany that occurred on a Sunday afternoon in April of 1990. On that day I was "grazing" television stations and came across a broadcast of the championship game between Canada and the United States at the 1990 Women's World Ice Hockey Championships, being held in Ottawa. Despite my extensive involvement and interest in women's sport over the previous decade, I knew little about women's hockey and had never seen a women's hockey game. Watching that televised broadcast, I was fascinated by the action, and especially by the speed and physicality of the play.

In 1992, when I was ready to embark on a project on women's physicality, I retrieved the image of that hockey game and started to explore the possibility of doing some research in women's hockey. This began with a phone call to the offices of the Canadian Amateur Hockey Association (now Hockey Canada), where the official in charge of women's programs suggested I attend the upcoming annual general meeting of the Ontario Women's Hockey Association, scheduled a few weeks later in Toronto. I did so and with this began to lay the foundation for my research in women's hockey. This meeting turned out to be significant not because of its substance, which was devoted to administrative concerns and of little interest to me or my work, but because of a contact I made. One of the persons in attendance was a woman, Margot, who rose to speak about the girls' hockey program in her community, where I also live and work. I later introduced myself to her and as we chatted, I learned that she was an active player—in fact was a member of the Canadian national team that had won the 1992 World Championships in Finland the previous month—and the owner/operator of a girls' hockey camp on the campus of the university where I teach. I asked her if I could spend some time at the camp and she readily agreed.

In July, I renewed this acquaintance and went to the camp on the first day. I was warmly welcomed by the rest of the staff and subsequently spent much of the week at the camp, talking to coaches, players, and their parents. The most important contact I made at this camp was with John. He coaches the Blades, then (and now) one of the best teams in women's hockey, and the team that Margot played on at the time.[2] The Blades played in the Provincial Women's Hockey League, which was based in the Metropolitan Toronto area. As earlier with Margot, I asked John if I could learn more about the team and he readily agreed.

In November, shortly after the Blades' season started, I went in to a game in Toronto, met John and made arrangements to come in to meet the team at a practice the following week. Following the practice, John brought me into the change room, introduced me to the players, and left the room. I recall that meeting, now more than ten years ago, almost as clearly as if it happened yesterday. When John and I entered the room, the players were lively, and some noisy, as they joked and jostled with one another. They then settled down as I gained their attention. I circulated a letter I had written describing myself as a sociologist interested in doing research in women's hockey, outlining my interests and containing my request to spend some time with the team. The letter also indicated the terms of my proposed association with the team, including that I would keep players' individual identities anonymous. Most players read the letter but only a few had much to say. One commented on the formality of the university letterhead on which the letter was printed. Another, reacting to the promise of anonymity, called out that she wanted her name included in any publications. At a personal level, I had some distinct impressions. One was consciousness of being in a space—the change room of a women's team—that was foreign to me and regret that I had missed out on the experience of being an athlete and a member of a team such as this one. In contrast to this sense of missed opportunity, another sensation that occurred at the same time was excitement over the recognition that I had gained access to a setting that would allow me to investigate some key issues in the study of gender and sport.[3]

At this point, it may be useful to remark on the state of the study of women in sport when I began this project in 1992. In the 1980s there was a well-developed literature on women in sport that was heavily, though not exclusively, focused on distributive issues of opportunity, participation, and resource allocation.[4] As a result, it was by then well established that women were vastly underrepresented in sport and when they did participate, they received unequal funding and other forms of support. There was less information on the experiences of women athletes, of the sort that an ethnographic study such as I was embarking on could provide. Additionally, there was particularly little information on the experiences of women in team sports. In this context, I knew that I wanted to come to understand women's experiences of skilled physical practice, and do so in a sport setting.[5] I also felt it important to focus on the under-examined context of team sport.[6]

My research agenda had another specific goal. As part of my intention to examine gender and sport I wanted to explore the dynamics of heterosexism and homophobia. Along with the emphasis on distributive aspects of gender, by the early 1990s it had become well established that sport is homophobic. In women's sport, this was manifest in the paradoxical conditions of both denying the lesbian presence in sport and placing pressure on women in sport to counteract lesbian stereotypes of women athletes through overt displays of femininity. In my work with the Blades, I was committed to exploring how heterosexism and homophobia worked, by examining the experiences of lesbian players and their relations with their heterosexual teammates, as well as coaches and others in positions of power. I did not know what I would find but I was certain that this would be a key aspect of the social world I had set out to explore, and to do this adequately and honestly it was critical to examine the dynamics of homophobia and heterosexism.[7]

My initial meeting with the team in early December, 1992, marked my entry into the research setting.[8] The fieldwork continued through the remainder of the 1992–93 season, ending in April, and the entire 1993–94 season, from September until April. I had access to all team activities and, most crucially, to the change room before and after games and practices. Generally, in each week there was one practice, a home game and an away game. Other team gatherings included occasional social events such as the annual Christmas party, fund-raising activities, including a dance and boat cruise, and tournaments, including the provincial and national championships. The latter were especially important to team dynamics and by extension my own work as they were the few occasions when the team was gathered for an extended period of several days.

From the moment I gained access, I assigned a high priority to the fieldwork, that is to being with the team for whatever it was doing. There were two reasons for attaching such importance to spending time with the team in the variety of circumstances that occurred in the course of a season. The first was to secure my status as a member of the Blades, albeit one with a special role. I reasoned that if the players were expected to come to all team activities, and I wanted access to the players' lives, it was important that I be as committed as they were. Second, I knew that for the purposes of my efforts to understand the Blades, it was essential that I be with the team on both the routine and exceptional occasions. By understanding the routine experiences, such as the mid-season practice where seemingly nothing new happened, I was better positioned to comprehend the extra-ordinary events, such as winning the national championship, or the one fight I observed in the course of my two years with the Blades.[9]

While time with the team was the focal point of my work, my data gathering extended beyond the Blades. In the summer of 1993, I attended two girls' hockey camps operated by members of the team (in addition to that held by the player from my home town, Margot) and in the fall of 1993 and winter of 1994 I attended tryouts for the national team, where a number of the Blades and players on other teams in their league were competing for positions. In the spring of 1994 I attended the World Championships in Lake Placid, New York. In the summer of 1994 I trav-eled to Western Canada where I interviewed players and coaches from a team that historically has been a main rival of the Blades at national championships, and attended another girls' hockey camp where I inter-viewed a number of players and coaches. On all these occasions, in addi-tion to observing the activities and conducting formal interviews, I met and chatted with people involved in women's hockey in various capaci-ties. Through all these experiences I developed something of a presence in the women's hockey community, which was extremely helpful when I subsequently approached an individual, say a coach or administrator, to request an interview or some information. All this was done with the in-tention to better understand the world of women's hockey and specifi-cally, the experiences of the Blades and Blades' players.

BEING IN THE FIELD WITH THE BLADES

My approach to the fieldwork with the Blades was to be with the team but not of it. This involved a continuing process of negotiating the boundaries and content of my relationships with individual players and the team. (This point is discussed in more detail later in the chapter.) When I was with the team (as opposed to with individuals), I rarely initi-ated conversations or interactions. When a remark was directed to me, I answered or picked up on the point in a manner that was courteous. At the same time, I tried to be helpful in ways that did not compromise my role as independent observer. For example, during the pregame prepara-tion period in the change room, players would on occasion ask me to per-form a task such as delivering a message or a hockey stick in need of taping to someone in the arena. In the second season of my fieldwork, I also became the guardian of the key to the team change room during games. In performing these tasks, I attempted to maintain a balance be-tween being helpful while not assuming the role of team assistant or "gofer." In doing so, I also tried to operate on the basis of both common sense—this player needs to have her stick delivered to someone for taping and I can easily step outside the change room while she and the others carry on with getting dressed for the game—and a realization that another side of my gaining access to the team for my own purposes of doing research was to give back in whatever ways were possible and appropriate. In the long term, I intended to reciprocate through the contribution my work made to advancing understanding and dispelling myths about women athletes and women's sport. In the short term, giving back took the form of providing assistance that would on occasion make the players' lives a little easier.

Throughout the course of the project I remained conscious of my special status, which required both that I have an easy and trusted access to the group but that I not lose the distance that would enable me to apply critical insights in my analysis. Within this framework, I recall an occasion early on in the field work when, while standing in the change room (which was so crowded with players and their equipment that there were no empty seats) as the players carried on their pre-game preparation and chattering among themselves, I wondered: What can these women be thinking about this other woman in their midst, whose purpose for being here seemingly is to wait for something to happen? Most often, I directed my awareness of my own status toward maintaining a keen eye for events and dynamics related to my research and to making sure that I kept in confidence everything I took in.

RELATIONSHIPS WITH PLAYERS AND THE TEAM

My associations with individual players varied. I became friends with only one player, Margot. This relationship evolved from special circumstances. The travel demands of this project posed a major challenge for me. Because of the distance between my home and the team's base and other playing venues in the Toronto area, each team event required a trip of more than four hours, including two-plus hours for traveling and another two hours with the team. Compounding these demands was the fact that most of these trips took place on winter evenings, when driving conditions were always potentially threatening. The travel demands for the project were greatly eased when, early on, I began to ride to games and practices with Margot and her husband Don, who drove with her to games and practices. Over the course of time, we became good friends. I made sure to monitor my discussions with Margot, taking special care that in the frequency of our contact and the privacy of our car trips, I did not slip out of my commitment to maintain confidences. These rides were particularly useful in enhancing my knowledge about the game of hockey. Margot, Don, and I would talk about that afternoon or evening's game, plays that occurred and other aspects such as the actions of officials. I filed the insights from these conversations along with everything else I observed and followed up on points and issues that were of interest for my work.

At the other end of the spectrum, there were a few players with whom my association was distant, though still cordial. With these women, I typically exchanged greetings and they responded to my questions but they were otherwise not as forthcoming as most of their teammates. On reflecting on this, I took the position that so long as I was operating within the ethical guidelines established for the project and there was no evidence of unhappiness with my involvement with the team, the arrangement was satisfactory. As it turned out, in the case of the two players who were most distant, in both cases I came to have reassuring and even gratifying feedback. With one, my concerns about her feelings about my association with the team were dispelled when we met for an interview following the first season of my research. She was honest, forthcoming, and interested in my work to a degree I had not appreciated.

The second instance of a player whose feelings about my work I questioned involved the player who had been the most reserved in her interactions with me. Unlike all other players on the team, she remained distant throughout the course of my work. I should note here that this player was not demonstrably unfriendly, she was simply not forthcoming. This changed following the completion of the project. When *Higher Goals* was published, I sent messages to players offering to provide them with copies if they wished. This player asked for a copy and after reading the book, sent me a message in which she described the book as "wonderful."

She went on to indicate she wished she had been friendlier but in truth, had been hesitant about my work with the Blades. Her greatest concern was how I would see and write about the "lesbian presence." We then had an exchange of messages, in which I shared my own reflections at the time on our relationship. During the course of my work I came to see this woman as a dedicated and skilled hockey player, committed to the team and to being the best player she could be. I was confident that I took the same approach to my work with the Blades and in the belief that she would respect this. This confidence enabled me at least in some measure to resolve my own ambivalence arising from her possible concerns about my presence on the team. Our exchange on this issue, following the completion of the project and my withdrawal from the team, was extremely gratifying.

With most of the players, I developed warm and friendly relations. We exchanged greetings regularly and in time I came to know them as individuals. On the occasion of a boat cruise in Toronto that was a fundraising effort for the Blades, I stayed at the home of a player and her partner so that I would not have to make the late evening drive home. (My regular driving companions missed this event.) On the team bus ride to Ottawa for the 1993 national championships, I sat with a player who was known for her quiet manner in the change room and learned that her shy demeanor in this group setting belied a talkative nature in more individualized contexts. This player's father came to most games and practices and I also got to know him well. Early on in my work, he thanked me for the interest I was showing in women's hockey. In these and other ways, I negotiated the boundaries of personal relationships in a professional context.

In addition to these associations with individual players, I also developed a relationship with the team. This too required reflection on my part, to be as clear as possible on how I was managing the boundaries of this relationship. One aspect of this is that I became a fan of the team, rooting for them in games and tournaments. In this context, I clearly and admittedly lost some of my dispassion toward the Blades. I recognized, however, that this was quite likely inevitable, given my extensive and intimate association with the team. I trusted that when I completed the field research and separated from the team I would regain the distance I needed to write an account that was fair and honest.

My evolving association went beyond being a fan, as over time I came to be included in team activities. In the second year of my work, the team captain and another player approached me to ask if I wished to be involved in the secret Santa gift exchange at the team Christmas party. I initially demurred, indicating I wasn't sure I "fit" here. They reassured me that the team would like me to take part and I agreed to do so.[10]

Another instance of inclusion in team affairs had broader ramifications, or so I thought. In the winter of 1993 Blades players and coaches received new, very attractive lambskin team jackets. Henceforth they wore them to all team functions, and in doing so gained some notoriety in women's hockey for the striking (and at times intimidating) image they presented in arenas. At a fund-raising dance in the winter of 1994, a year after the players received the jackets and nearly a year and a half after I had begun my association with the team, Stephen, the general manager, presented me with one of these jackets. My reaction was a mixture of emotions. I was stunned, as I had no idea this was coming. I was also pleased and flattered. At the same time, however, I was concerned that this visible manifestation of my association with the team—wherein I would literally wear the Blades' colors on my sleeve—would appear to blur the independence I remained committed to maintaining, despite my intimate association with the team. Intensifying my ambivalence was the fact that it was clear that Stephen and the players expected me to wear the jacket when I was with the team, including to the national championships in Winnipeg a few weeks later.

Notwithstanding my mixed feelings, I wore the jacket henceforth at team gatherings, including in Winnipeg, and was happy to do so. My feeling was that the team had welcomed me into its life and by including me in the Christmas gift exchange and presenting me with the jacket, had conveyed some genuine sentiments. I accepted those sentiments and had little doubt I should reciprocate. To the extent I had a concern, it was not that I would be compromised by these gifts or the relationship they represented. My reservation was with the *appearance* of compromise and specifically, the message that might be conveyed by my walking around arenas, including at the national championships, in a Blades jacket. What would officials in the sport and players and coaches from other teams (some of whom I had or planned to interview) think? (And why did I care? This concern is discussed in more detail below.) Upon reflection, it seemed clear to me that I would just have to accept whatever implications arose from my now very visible connection to the team. As well, I realized that whatever ideas some observers had about my association with the Blades, they were probably in large measure already in place and only confirmed by my newly acquired jacket.[11]

WORKING THROUGH AMBIVALENCE

In all contexts when I was with the Blades, and indeed whenever I was in the field at a women's hockey event, I made a concerted effort to identify myself as an academic researcher gathering material for later publication. Nonetheless, and not surprisingly given that I became a regular presence at all Blades events, I came to be seen within the women's hockey community as a member of the Blades, albeit one whose status was unclear and/or odd. This association also required considerable reflection on my part, because of the Blades' position in women's hockey. This point requires some explanation.

During the course of my research, the Blades were the dominant team in women's hockey. For several years they had been the champions of their league, which saw the highest level of play in women's hockey anywhere in the world, and in that time had won the national championship twice. Their position in women's hockey derived not only from their dominance but also from their approach, which was aggressively and unremittingly in pursuit of excellence, defined not only by winning—although that was important—but by becoming the best players and team that they could be. In this pursuit, the Blades had become known for stacking players, that is bringing on to the team as many of the best players in women's hockey as possible. Critics argued that the resulting competitive imbalance was bad for the league and by extension, women's hockey. A related basis of concern was the team's "style," which emphasized professionalism and was manifest in an attention to detail. At a time when many women's hockey teams had to scrounge for funds to pay for ice time and equipment, the Blades were famous in the sport for having ample ice time, new equipment and uniforms that, in seeming contrast to those of their opponents, were never in need of repair. (The aforementioned jackets were the most striking example of the team's attention to style.) The team was able to provide these benefits because alone among organizations in women's hockey at the time, it aggressively sought sponsors and engaged in fundraising activities.

My response to being associated with the Blades had several dimensions. Although I understood it was not surprising I would be identified with the team, I was nonetheless concerned about this in regard to criticism from some observers that in some respects the Blades did not operate in the best interests of women's hockey. I had spent nearly twenty years engaged in feminist activism and scholarship concerning sport. Being in the field, however, brought me more deeply into the complexities of gender politics in sport than I had previously experienced. As I came to know the world of women's hockey and the Blades' position within this world, many of the elements of the critique of the Blades were revealed to me in their complexity. It was true, as the critics claimed, that in their aggressive approach to fund raising and securing the best players and providing for them, the Blades took care of their own. As I came to see it, however, the primary problem in this regard was a lack of support for women's hockey generally, which then made the Blades' determined efforts to obtain sponsorship and funding a distinguishing feature, against which other teams suffered in comparison. The fact that the positions of power on the team—the owner/general manager, the head coach, and his staff—were held by men ran counter to the feminist effort to change the gender structure of sport, a part of the feminist agenda for sport about which I felt particularly strongly. At the same time, the men associated with the Blades were highly committed to the team and their efforts benefited the players in numerous ways. I also came to see the Blades' emphasis on winning as one side of a commitment to enabling the players, individually and collectively, to become the best possible hockey players. At a time when few took women hockey players seriously as athletes, everyone on the Blades did so, without reservation or apology. I had great respect for this.

While not related to my identification with the team, there was another aspect of my work with the Blades that prompted ambivalence and considerable reflection. As explained at the outset, my initial motivation for this project was to explore women's experience of physicality. As it turned out—and again there is no surprise here—women's hockey and the Blades specifically provided a wonderful setting in which to pursue this interest. At the highest level of the sport, where the Blades are located, women's hockey is intensely physical. Play at this level is tough, aggressive, and often fearless. In 1987 I had published a theoretical discussion on "Sport and

Women's Empowerment," in which I argued that the physical nature of sport offers particular potential to empower women. Some five years later, I observed the realization, indeed the embodiment, of those ideas with the Blades. On a number of counts—as a feminist, as a woman who had grown up in an era when intense physical activity was not only denied but often not even considered for women, and in other respects I have not yet figured out—I loved watching and being close to the game action.

Part of that action is body contact, including the officially prohibited body checking. While the rules of women's hockey prohibit body checking, that is, checking a player for the purpose of taking her out of a play (as opposed to incidental contact that occurs in the course of making a play), players nonetheless check in different circumstances. Sometimes they do so without conscious intention; they react on instinct or play gets away from them. Sometimes they do so with intention; in these instances they hope they will not be caught but are prepared to be caught and penalized. Games between highly skilled teams, such as the U.S. and Canadian national teams, often see numerous examples of body checking, as officials decide to "let the players play."

The issue of body checking in women's hockey has several dimensions. As I became more involved in my work, and known for it, I frequently was asked to discuss this. Often the discussion was framed in a simplistic fashion: Why don't women body check?; Should women body check? There are several considerations to this issue, and at the risk of reproducing this oversimplification they include the following. Women are not taught to check, and when not enacted properly, body checking can be dangerous. This explanation, of course, does not explain why players are not taught to body check. Another point is that without body checking the game is different, in that there is a greater emphasis on speed and play making; each version of the game has merits. As well, the non-body-checking version of the game is more attractive to many players and their parents; this observation points to continuing cultural unease with aggressive physicality in women's sport. Finally, in many communities where programs are not extensively developed, girls' teams include players of a wide range of ages and sizes, making body checking impractical and even dangerous. Overlaying all these considerations is the issue of the difference or similarity of men's and women's sport. To the question "Why don't women body check?," with the implication that perhaps they should, is the response, "Women don't have to play like men" and in the absence of body checking, "the women's game is a better game." The latter point has considerable validity when women's hockey is compared to the aggressive physicality of play in the NHL, which is often characterized by gratuitous violence.[12]

As I learned about women's hockey, and spent a great deal of time at the highest levels where players are very skilled, I came to love the physicality of the sport, wherein I saw power, creativity, and physical mastery. In the end, the greatest ambivalence I experienced in conjunction with my research in women's hockey was not in regard to my association with the Blades but over the issue of checking. I saw more than a few instances of body checking in which a player took an opponent out of a play cleanly, followed by the player who had been hit getting up and moving on. And in interviews with players who competed when body checking was allowed in women's hockey, I heard testimony of the satisfaction players experience in enacting this skill, as well as their respect on observing and even on occasion receiving a good, clean body check. At the same time, I recognize the potential for injury, and both the validity and importance of the observation that women need not play like men. My purpose here is not to resolve the debate and my own ambivalence but to note it. And more, to note that I came to learn that when I spoke of this issue, if I betrayed my attraction for the physical element of the game my remarks sometimes became a target of concern and on occasion criticism for, as one observer put it, endorsing the adoption of one of the worst features of men's sport, excessive violence. It was in this context that I most often reflected on the possible challenge to my credentials as a feminist that were prompted by my attraction to and observations on physicality in women's hockey.

NEGOTIATING BOUNDARIES

As the above account makes clear, an ongoing issue in my research was the negotiation of boundaries with individual players on the team and with the Blades organization. I began the fieldwork with an expectation that I would be an observer, whose role was to take in, reflect upon, and make sense of all that I saw. Before long, of course, my involvement with the team became more complicated. This was an outcome of several features of the setting and my work, which have been noted in the course of the above discussion. One of these features was the sheer amount of time I spent with the team, in contexts that were marked by highs and lows— games poorly played and championships won; internal frictions and overcoming these to "gel" as a team—along with the more mundane elements of the team's life such as mid-season practices and routine chatter. In this context, it was important that my manner be cordial while not intrusive. Another factor that influenced my relationship with the team was my clear attraction to and appreciation of what the Blades represented in women's sport: commitment to enabling women to become skilled athletes (though as noted there were additional elements of the Blades' model that promoted ambivalence on my part). Yet another factor was my acute awareness that in letting me into their lives the players and coaches had provided access to an experience that was not only a wonderful research opportunity but enormously enjoyable. To be on the inside of a championship women's sports team was new and exciting for me. I felt a deep sense of gratitude to all associated with the team for providing a wonderful opportunity, both personally and professionally.

In the midst of the above conditions and even as my own involvement took on the routine character of the team members, I never lost sight of the fact that as a researcher, I needed to be conscious of how I negotiated the boundaries of my status. In particular, I was mindful that when I went to analyze and write up the materials, I would need to be clear on my vantage point as a scholar trying to make sense of the lived experiences of women athletes. As a strategy for negotiating the boundaries of my involvement, during the period when I was conducting my fieldwork I endeavored to be aware of my identification with the team and vigilant in my observations and recording of those observations, so that when I withdrew from the field and set about to make sense of my materials, I would have a complete account. I also trusted that when I withdrew, I would regain the sense of dispassion I needed to complete the analysis and, with the extensive documentation of my fieldwork and interviews and my own critical feminist perspective, I would be well prepared to write a full and fair account of the Blades and the world of women's hockey.

CONNECTIONS WITH HOCKEY FOLLOWING COMPLETION OF THE FIELD RESEARCH

I concluded the fieldwork portion of my research at the end of the 1993–1994 season. By then, I had been with the team for nearly two full seasons and it was time to begin the process of writing up the analysis. I then moved to a new place in my relationship with women's hockey. My time with the Blades, and especially the hours I had spent rinkside during games, convinced me that playing hockey is great fun and that I would like to try the game myself. In order to do this, I first had to learn to skate and to this end, I started taking skating classes. Skating did not come easily to me but I made some progress. My career on the ice came to an abrupt end in February, 1996, when while skating I fell and broke my right wrist. (I am right handed.) My assessment is that I finally improved to the point where I could fall hard enough to do some damage. With this, my hopes to play hockey were terminated as I put away my skates for good.

Since completing the research for *Higher Goals*, I have retained an association with women's hockey, although from some distance. During the course of writing the initial drafts of the book, I sent copies to players and solicited their comments. The feedback I received was positive, mostly on the order of observations that in telling the Blades' story, I got it "right." Some of the most interesting and meaningful feedback came from lesbian players on the team. A couple indicated their agreement with my analysis of the dynamics of homophobia, which I characterize as one of inclusiveness on the team but lesbian invisibility in more public contexts. One lesbian player, however, felt that in discussing the dynamics of homophobia, I had exaggerated its significance in the life of the team. I respect her position, which, on reflection, I think is a statement of the view, detailed in the book, that the Blades "are about what happens on the ice."[12] That is, the unifying interest and central dynamic of the Blades was playing hockey and in this regard, sexual orientation was beside the point. In my research, I explored the broader context in which this effort takes place and my observations and analysis indicate that one important dimension of this context is homophobia and heterosexism.

Apart from exchanges during the preparation of the manuscript and following the publication of *Higher Goals*, I have had little contact with players save Margot, who has moved to another community and whom I see on occasion. For the first few years following the completion of my work with the Blades, I was able to maintain a sense of close attachment with women's hockey because through my research I had met many of the coaches and players on the 1998 Canadian Olympic team, which received considerable publicity in the period leading up to and through the Olympic Games. It was with great interest that I followed the fortunes of the team throughout the Olympic tournament. Most of this generation of players has since retired and I now have only a few personal connections to women active in the sport.

I also attend few games, despite the fact that there is now a well-established semi-professional league, the National Women's Hockey League (NWHL), which was formed in 2000 with the amalgamation of the premiere leagues in Ontario (where the Blades play) and Quebec. Once attending events no longer was part of my work, it became more difficult to find the time to do this. There have, however, been exceptions, which I have greatly enjoyed. In the winter of 2001, one of the legendary players in women's hockey, Angela James, retired and during an NWHL game an event was held to mark the occasion. Through my research, I had come to know Angela and wanted to be present for this occasion. I went in to the game, which was the occasion for a kind of reunion of players I had known in the course of my work, and exchanged friendly greetings with many of these players.[14]

In the spring of 2002 I attended the championship game of the NWHL, which is now the premiere competition in Canadian women's hockey. This occasioned a bit of shock on my part. During the period of my research, 1992–1994, games in the Blades league—recall that this was the highest level of women's hockey and the precursor to the NWHL—

were played in small, out-of-the-way and often uncomfortable arenas, before crowds of perhaps 50 people, all of whom had a personal association with a player on the ice. In contrast, the 2002 NWHL championship game was played in a modern, comfortable arena seating in the vicinity of 5,000 people, filled nearly to capacity. On arriving just as the game was starting, I had trouble finding an empty seat. The atmosphere in the arena was greatly enlivened by the presence of entire sections of seats filled with young girls, many wearing the sweaters of their own hockey teams, screaming and cheering on the players. As well, the game was broadcast on cable television. In this setting, I could not help but marvel at the changes in women's hockey that had occurred over the previous decade. That game was won in overtime by the Blades, with only two players remaining from the years I spent with the team. On that occasion, I again set aside any pretense to dispassion and rooted enthusiastically for the team that had enabled me to venture deep inside the world of women's sport and in doing so, provided the opportunity to pursue the most interesting and rewarding research project of my career to date.

NOTES

1. For additional references, see Theberge (1995); (1997); (1998).

2. John and the Blades, as well as Stephen, mentioned below, are pseudonyms.

3. The central, and related, issues examined in *Higher Goals* are women's sport as a setting for the construction of community, and the gendering of physical practice.

4. In addition, there was an extensive social psychological literature on issues related to role conflict among women athletes.

5. This discussion appears in Theberge (2000), chapter 7. See also Theberge (1997).

6. This discussion appears in Theberge (2000), chapter 6. See also Theberge (1995).

7. This discussion appears in Theberge (2000), chapter 5. See also Theberge (1995).

8. In addition to the players and John, the other key individual on the team was Stephen, the owner/general manager. Despite his central role on the Blades, I never was formally introduced to Stephen but in the course of my first few weeks on the team I came to learn about his place in the Blades organization and then gave him a copy of the introductory letter I had written. Like John, Stephen was extremely helpful and supportive of my work.

9. The game in which the fight occurred is discussed in *Higher Goals*, pp. 127–128.

10. In the gift exchange, I received a copy of a recently published book on girls' hockey, the first book on the sport. This volume was an instructional manual

with profiles of well-known players, including several Blades. The player who gave it to me autographed the book and then arranged for the rest of the team to do the same. This gift is now a cherished memento of my time with the Blades.

11. I still have the jacket and wear it on occasion with particularly fond memories. It has become a collector's item as a few years after I completed my research the Blades took on a new major corporate sponsor and changed the team colors to conform to the corporate colors of their new sponsor.

12. A more fully developed discussion of issues surrounding body checking is found in *Higher Goals*, chapter 7.

13. See *Higher Goals*, chapter 3.

14. The reunion was also a visible indicator of changes in regard to homophobia and the "lesbian presence" in women's hockey. One of the former Blades with whom I exchanged greetings was at the game with her lesbian partner and their infant twins; another former player was with her lesbian partner and their son. During the period of my research, lesbian players were out to the team but in public settings their lesbian identities were largely invisible.

REFERENCES

Theberge, N. (1977). *An occupational analysis of women's professional golf.* Unpublished Doctoral Dissertation, University of Massachusetts.

Theberge, N. (1987). Sport and women's empowerment. *Women's Studies International Forum*, 10 (4): 387–393.

Theberge, N. (1993). The construction of gender and sport: Women, coaching and the naturalization of difference. *Social Problems*, 40 (3): 301–313.

Theberge, N. (1995). Gender, sport and the construction of community: A case study from women's ice hockey. *Sociology of Sport Journal*, 12 (4): 389–402.

Theberge, N. (1997). It's part of the game: Physicality and the production of gender in women's hockey. *Gender & Society*, 11(1): 69–87.

Theberge, N. (1998). Same sport, different gender: A consideration of binary gender logic and the sport continuum in the case of ice hockey. *Journal of Sport and Social Issues*, 22 (2): 183–198.

Theberge, N. (2000). *Higher goals: Women's ice hockey and the politics of gender.* Albany: State University of New York Press.

Chapter 5

Coping with Trauma:
Staying the Course

Carole A. Oglesby

Arja was born 11 years after me and thousands of miles separated us. I never was privileged to meet her but who could fail to notice how eyes lit up when colleagues spoke her name? How could one miss the change in voice tone, which communicated, without direct words, unspeakable loss of a soul taken from us too soon?

Never having met her, I felt uncomfortable and out of place, at a gathering of women focused on shaping a project that would memorialize her being, her life, and its impact. As the outlines of this book began to emerge, I felt a shift to growing comfort. I felt a sense of belonging, absolutely and perfectly, to a community of spirit of which Arja was an exemplar. She was a shining example yet one with all of us in terms of a set of shared experiences: feelings, set-backs, and satisfactions. In this chapter, I explore one daunting facet of our common set of experiences: that of trauma.

The word "traumatized," as a descriptor of a psychological state, was most familiar in the context of war. After WWI, it was particularly recognized that some veterans were "shell-shocked"; neither able to put certain memories and events behind them nor "explain" what had happened to them to those who had not experienced the war. The Veterans of Foreign Wars (VFW), founded in the early 1900s in the USA, grew from 5,000 members in 1915 to 200,000 in 1936 and was dedicated to the special medical and long-term care needs of men who were unable to adjust to post-war lives (http://www.wfw.org;aboutus/abo_ourhistory.htm).

I mention the VFW because in 1992, in the USA, an organization was formed for which Arja would have easily qualified. It was/is called "Veteran Feminists of America (VFA)" with goals: to document our history; honor our heroes; enjoy the sisterhood; help rekindle the spark of the feminist revolution and pass the torch to later generations (Ceballos, 2002). The VFA consciously self-describes within the context of revolution, "a (so-far) blood-less revolution," (Heide, 1978, p. 195) with casualties, set-backs, and victories, and memories appearing to bear the character of psychological trauma.

I do not wish to be understood as describing Arja, or any sport feminist, as helpless victims. Nor do I wish it to appear that I am reducing the whole of life history to pre-, actual, and post-trauma. Rather, I am utilizing this opportunity to apply my own scholarly training and personal experiences to offer alternative interpretations and shed light on the path of change-makers like Arja. My hope is that, in so doing, like-intentioned individuals will less often stumble and fall in the darkness of surprise and confusion.

Sport feminists commit to transform sport—its form, its conduct, and its research. Sport has often been intensely reviled and revered but, as with other human institutions, its forms and practices are highly resistant to change. Its most ardent devotees are primarily men, and often men of privilege, who view critical change discourse as unnecessary, outlandish, or even destructive.

Any individual, but particularly a woman, who dares to challenge the sporting order may be banished and vilified in diverse ways (many made manifest throughout this book). Arja was both a challenging advocate and ahead of her time, thus she faced extremes of resistance and disappointment, as dedicated feminists often have. I will raise disturbing questions about what effects these consequences may have had on her life.

In earlier work, I have made a distinction between cooperative and assertive advocacy. In cooperative advocacy with sport or sport science bodies, the mainstream organizations determine a need to make change, or add female leadership, in order to create more inclusive or "women-friendly" environments. After this determination, the organization turns to a woman's organization, or an individual woman, to aid in the achievement of the elusive goal. Cooperative advocacy of this nature is not always easy, but it is congenial.

Arja's life, like almost all sport feminists, was dominated by assertive advocacy in which the "mainstream or establishment" is taken on through the utilization of law, economic forces, concepts of justice and fairness, or personal charisma, in order to create change. Assertive advocacy can be dangerous and lonely. It is my contention that the involved individual often becomes vulnerable to high-level stress and, what psychologists call, trauma.

Being traumatized has long been understood as a state brought on by war, violence, and/or disaster. Some are now referring to this type of trauma as "Big T trauma." Recently, however, psychologists have begun to realize another type of trauma resulting from insidious, pervasive, lower threshold stressors, which can eventually engender similar effects to "Big T trauma." My contention is that many sport feminists, like Arja, experience "Little t trauma." Thus, we would benefit from proceeding through our lives with this awareness in order to better weather the storms and stay the course with contentment, satisfaction, and health. In sections that follow, I describe briefly (a) the nature and consequences of trauma; (b) the identification of experiences in my own career and work, which may have risen to levels of trauma, and (c) ways to cope and transcend traumatic circumstance, to some degree self-chosen in the conduct of our commitments to institutional change.

BIG T AND LITTLE T TRAUMA

Many believe that ordinary life in the waning of the twentieth and birth of the twenty-first centuries has become increasingly stressful. Newspapers, radio, television newscasts are filled with details of crime, cruelty, natural and human-created disaster, economic and cultural dislocation as reflected in such statistics as increasing drug and alcohol use, suicide and divorce (Williams & Sommer, 1994). Reports of occurrences of anxiety disorder and depression are at all time highs (Sue & Sue, 1990). Stress theory has been designated one of the central paradigms of the 20th century in psychology (VanderKolk, McFarlane, & Weisaeth, 1996) and posits that excessive demands on an organism produce a typical, pervasive, and repetitive sequence of neurophysiological response. This response yields a characteristic three-phase form: acute response, resistance; either recovery or exhaustion (VanderKolk et al., 1996). Notable scientific work on this phenomenon has been conducted from a variety of disciplines and orientations including medicine (Selye, 1974); psychology (Lazarus & Folkman, 1984); and animal models of inescapable shock (Seligman, 1992).

Traumatic stress, however, has been associated with events such as war, captivity, torture, disaster, and racial extermination. Shalev (1996) maintains that "historically the field of traumatic stress has evolved independently from the pre-existing domain of stress and coping. Despite attempts to articulate links . . . there has been little research between the two fields" (p. 92). Under the rubric of theoretical and applied work on Post Traumatic Stress Disorder (PTSD), advances have been noted in distinguishing among the variation of human response to life events. Shalev (1996) pointed out that events, ostensibly not involving extreme stress, are seen as threatening by some survivors while others report the event as only challenging. He stated further and that "no one has successfully distinguished traumatic from stressful events" (p. 92).

Williams and Sommer (1994) suggest that, to be classified as traumatic, an event must be perceived and processed as serious enough to challenge basic human assumptions of safety, predictability, justice, and fairness. The "psychologically traumatic event," as described in Williams and Sommer's work, was more broadly conceived than that typical of previous PTSD work and, thus, seemed designed to bridge the foci of both the daily life stressor's and the tragic. VanderKolk et al. (1996), claim that PTSD-like symptomology is probably more common than imagined. They cite survey data on 1,200 American adolescents in which 23% were victims of physical or sexual assaults and one in five developed PTSD. A similar survey showed "76% of adolescents reported being exposed to extreme stress" (p. 5).

Williams and Sommer (1994) identify four types of events that define possible "traumatic stressors"; (a) unanticipated single event beyond the range of normal, daily stress; (b) enduring repetitive occurrences tending to elicit numbing, dissociation, rage states, and/or unremitting sadness and denial; (c) compounding or additive effects of low-level, insidious stressful events; (d) an alteration in one's basic relationship to the biosphere through exposure to toxicity, which cannot be escaped. Meek (1990) adds that losses of loved ones and valued friends, positive aspects of one's self and developmental losses can also be considered traumatic.

In occurrences labeled as traumatic, there is an overwhelm of sensation in which the brain's interpretive capacities shift from "fight/flight" in the face of preventable danger to the catatanoid (freezing) reaction universal among animals. This reaction includes a paralysis of initiating behavior and a numbing by which affective and pain responses are blocked (VanderKolk, 1984). High levels of activation in the midbrain can facilitate the storing of emotional responses and other sensory impressions based on fragments of information (VanderKolk, 1996). An "uncoupling" seems to occur between the stimulus event and attendant emotion. The organism's capacity to properly categorize and evaluate the experience is impaired or incapacitated (VanderKolk, 1996).

To summarize, an intense or emotion-charged event may result in a dissociation of event characteristics and emotion; an incomplete or inadequate evaluation and integration of the meaning of the event may result or there may be no memory at all of the event (amnesia); a high-level retention of sensory fragments of the event (hypermnesia) may be subsequently and frequently remembered spontaneously (in full-blown post-traumatic stress disorder called a flashback).

When we read or hear reports of horrific, single occurrences of violence or natural disaster, it is well understood that there may be immediate, or delayed, and very long-lasting psychological symptomology for those involved. The "little t" trauma research and theory is pointing out that the pervasive, insidious stressors, which may be related to self-chosen paths of transformation and resistance, can also result in subclinical symptoms of trauma. In addition to the neurophysiological consequences already described, the experiencing of shame, self-blame, loss of capacity for self-care, denial, and unremitting sadness are common emotional byproducts of little t trauma (Nathanson, 1998). In reflecting on my own life, and on countless informal discussions with colleagues, I have identified many, many events that fit the hallmark descriptors of little t trauma. Likewise these reactions of self-blame, shame, denial, and sadness are familiar, if not welcome, companions. In the next section, I will make these assertions more concrete.

SPORT FEMINISTS' TRAUMA

In this analysis I focus on events and consequences that flow from the relatively self-chosen path of sport feminist visionary and groundbreaker. I ruled out life traumas shared eventually by most of us including divorce, ill health, and awareness of mortality. I have the aching fear that, for Arja, this last trauma was both a consequence and stimulus event with which she had to cope.

In Arja's life, she chose the area of movement activity and women because of her passionate honesty. She chose it instead of many, higher status and less problematic paths. Her passion frequently led her to be on the fringe of ordinary academic life. She had a vision so different from the world view of her time that she was derided as being "unscientific" in approach and eventually left the academy. I hasten to affirm that her proclivity enabled her to see a whole new world and was at the heart of her great contribution. Remember that my analysis concerns only possible costs from a psychological standpoint and raises questions as to her access to resources that might have offered additional protection from some of the pain. Her beloved creation, the "Movement, Culture, and Women" project, was "designed to break barriers between fields." The face of a device that breaks a barrier takes the brunt of the blow.

In developing this paper, many "sensory fragments" from my own path were elicited. In high school, I never thought twice about selecting physical education as a college major. It was my favorite class! I had an intuition of its special importance for girls and women although it was virtually denied to us. My algebra teacher (an ambitious woman, rare for the time as she had been a successful corporate business woman before choosing to return to teaching) approached me after class one day to scornfully chide me "Carole, you can do so much better than that."

The derogation of women, sport, and exercise, by mainstream feminists, was particularly painful to me. In 1978 I was a principal organizer of an event designed to focus public attention on the "National Women's Conference" in Houston, TX. The conference was preceded by 50 statewide conferences for the preparation of a "women's agenda" in virtually all areas of private and public life. My colleagues and I devised, and carried out, a torch run in which a torch was literally carried/run 2 miles per person, 50 miles per day from Seneca Falls, NY, to Houston. We, sportswomen, began the run two months before the conference, with little or no funding and in relative obscurity. By the time the torch hit "the Big Apple," on time and lovingly carried by little girls in pigtails, pregnant women, elder women, diverse colors and shades of girls and women, it was the symbol of women's dreams and potential. The press/media adored the torch run. We should have confirmed that our issues for the "Women's Agenda" were secured while the torch was still out on the road. When the torch run was completed, and the "real conference" begun, the concerns of sports women and health/physical educators were deemed too trivial to be added to the deliberation.

In a similar vein but differing context, I was called one summer, a month into a sabbatical year, by a highly placed university administrator who codirected women's studies at my university. As part of the prolonged tensions between the university president and the women studies faculty, the president had agreed to name a woman faculty member to an honorary, one-year research/scholarly post. She would have no responsibility, at full pay, other than to do her work for a year. The codirector was offering me the position. First, I felt a rush of pleasure but then she went on to recount that the women's studies executive had determined to offer me the post because my work "was so different . . . all of us are so comparable in what we do; in order to avoid competing among us, we decided to offer this to you."

While in these and other incidents I could recount, there is no particular fault of mine that is shameful, I definitely felt shame hearing the perceptions of others whose opinions I valued. I also felt foolish as, over and over, colleagues behaved in these ways and I never seemed to learn to expect it. They unfailingly "surprised me" with their unquestioned assumptions and interpretations.

Stories of Arja also seem to include her surprise at negative emotions engendered by some of her work involving Movement, Culture, and Women. These bring back to me more "fragments": of rejected abstracts, withering assessments by senior male scholars of early papers offered in department research seminars, sport science conferences that only mirrored men's views of sport and the world. Looking back now, it is not surprising at all that I harbor these fragments. What I feel surprised about and grateful for, is that I was so wounded but came back to final success on my terms.

So, who is it that so ultimately hurts us? Women colleagues whom we expect to understand; male colleagues who are gatekeepers in realms we wish to enter; even our beloved students! I smile when I hear of Arja's penchant for giving room for students to be equal persons, on par with her. It has been said that she transformed high-flown theory to that which was everyday and could be understood with relative ease. Yes, I tried to achieve these same goals. I see these intentions as strengths. I refuse to affirm status hierarchy because I define such a stance as an important tenant of feminist philosophy. However, my ego has been crushed and self-confidence battered by students taking me for granted. Because I reduced status distance between us and other (usually male) colleagues enhanced distance, these others were perceived as "more important to listen to and court." These other individuals were often cited in the student's papers submitted to me and my work was not cited although it would have been completely appropriate given their topic.

These can seem such small, insignificant occurrences. Who possibly cares whether one is cited in a term paper submitted in a graduate class? Who possibly can remember the dismissive and disparaging words, the patronizing tone of a senior male colleague spoken more than 30 years ago in a dingy conference room filled with departmental colleagues during a faculty seminar devoted to prepublication critiques of one's work? I can. I remember sensory fragments of these events vividly. For a long time, I experienced the increase in heart rate, the spreading facial blush of shame and embarrassment not only in the context of these events. Such emotions had to be overcome when there was anticipation that my work would be ill-received. When we posit a calendar of days, multiplied by the months and years of life filled with omissions, injustices, slights, cuts, wounds, and losses then we begin to realize that, without amelioration, the result can be traumatic loss of self, career, or health.

TRANSFORMING PERSONAL TRAUMA

Psychology literature is beginning to suggest many positive antidotes to the experiencing of pervasive stressors and little t trauma. Perhaps that is the plus side of observing so much of it. Of great aid is the presence of social support. The creation of an organization like VFA speaks anecdotally to the benefit of being able to surround oneself with others of like-mind. For sport feminists, global organizations such as WomenSport International and the Women's Sports Foundation of the USA can offer respite and healing. What has been called an "external validation of the reality of a traumatic experience" (VanderKolk, McFarlane, & Weisaerth, 1996, p. 25) is a vital aspect of prevention and treatment. Simply belonging to an organization with feminist goals is not enough, however. In my experience, the sport feminist requires a conscious awareness of the particular dimensions of a psychic wound she has experienced. She needs (a) an opportunity to reexperience the event with an empathetic other(s); and (b) opportunity to dialogue the event with the intention of evaluating the experience and assessing its meaning. This dialogue occurs within mainstream understandings but, importantly, includes the context of one's own world view and commitments.

A second potential healing step for sport feminists is so-called action therapy (Williams & Sommer, 1994). Research has shown that traumatic abuse is visited upon all aspects of self. The "physical body" is important to include in healing. Sport and recreation contexts, sweat lodges, massage, and questing tasks have all been utilized as adjuncts to trauma therapy. In my own life, without conscious awareness of the use of exercise to heal trauma, I have consistently participated in action therapy. Daily exercise regiments of jogging distance, roller-blading, lifting, and stretching have served me as distractions from anger, opportunities to replay and assess events of the day and to regain capacity. These regimens have served as crucial confirmations of my core capacity to do and endure. Sport feminists, in my opinion, can never afford to become "too busy" to remember and re-create their bodies.

One last antidote I wish to address is something I have no empirical support for asserting. I can only say "it worked for me." This is finding a way to write about the agonies. Several of the experiences I have recounted here appear as anecdotes in articles I have published.

In several recent papers, I have addressed the marginalization of women sport science pioneers whose work preceded my own (Oglesby, 2001a, 2001b; Oglesby & Shelton, 1992). It has been "therapeutic" for me to do so. My reading in family-systems work assures me it is natural to "want to be remembered" and to fear that one will not be (Boszormenyi-Nagy & Ulrich, 1981). Nagy (1981) observed that our own fears and concerns (stressors) for our legacy can be productively reduced by demonstrating trustworthiness in recognition of authentic contributions of foremothers and fathers. Indeed, it has been the case for me that I have felt more secure, less anxious, about what (if anything) of "mine" is lasting, as I have worked on behalf of the recognition of deserving others. In the spirit of that commitment, I have attempted to illuminate a possible interpretation of Arja Laitinen's life. She may have experienced events which, momentarily, froze her in her tracks. She well may have experienced fears, timidity, and vicious conflict for scarce resources. Surely this life is a light to those who knew her personally. We learn that we need not be immobilized by trauma.

REFERENCES

Boszormenyi-Nagy, I., & Ulrich, D. (1981). Contextual family therapy. In A. Gurment & D. Kniskern (Eds.), *Handbook of family therapy*. New York: Bruner/Mazel.

Ceballos, J. (2002, April). *Veteran feminists of America newsletter.*

Heide, W. (1978). Feminism for a sporting future. In C. Oglesby (Ed.), *Women and sport: From myth to reality* (195–203). Philadelphia: Lea & Febiger.

Lazarus, R. & Folkman, S. (1984). *Stress, appraisal, and coping.* New York: Springer.

Meek, C. (1990). *Post-traumatic stress disorder: Assessment, differential diagnosis, and forensic evaluation.* Sarasota, FL: Professional Resource Exchange.

Nathanson, D. (1998). *Locating EMDR: Affect, scene, and script.* Unpublished presentation, EMDRIA Annual Conference, Baltimore, MD.

Oglesby, C. (2001a). Intersections: Women's sport leadership and feminist praxis. In S. Freeman, S. Bourque, & C. Shelton (Eds.), *Women on power: Leadership redefined* (pp. 441–454). Boston: Northeastern University Press.

Oglesby, C. (2001b). Leaving it all on the field: Journeys of growth and change in women's sport. In C. Cohen (Ed.), *Women in sport: Issues and controversies* (pp. 441–454). Oxen Hill, MD: Alliance for Health, Physical Education, Recreation, and Dance.

Oglesby, C. & Shelton, C. (1992). Exercise and sport studies: Toward a fit, informed and joyful embodiment of feminism. In C. Kramarae & D. Spender (Eds.), *The knowledge explosion: Generations of feminist scholarship* (pp. 181–190). New York and London: Athene Series, Teachers College Press.

Seligman, M. (1992). *Helplessness.* New York: Freeman.

Selye, H. (1974). *Stress without distress.* New York: New American Library.

Shalev, A. (1996). Stress vs. traumatic stress: From acute homoeostatic reactions to chronic psychopathology. In B. VanderKolk, A. McFarlane, & L. Neisaeth (Eds.), *Traumatic stress: The effects of overwhelming experience on mind, body, and society* (105–138). New York: Guilford.

Sue, D. W., & Sue, D. C. (1990). *Counseling the culturally different.* New York: Wiley & Sons.

VanderKolk, B. (1984). *Post-traumatic stress disorder: Psychological and biological sequelae.* Washington, DC: American Psychiatric Press.

VanderKolk, B., McFarlane, A., & Weisaeth, L. (1996). *Traumatic stress: The effects of overwhelming experience on mind, body, and society.* New York: Guilford.

Williams, M., & Sommer, J. (1994). *Handbook of post-traumatic therapy.* Westport, CT: Greenwood Press.

Chapter 6

Feminist Utopias and the Patriarchal Shadow: A Restrospective Look at a Feminist Project

Sabine Kröner

From 1989 to 1996 I directed a comprehensive and complex women's research project and presented the results in a series of publications (Kröner, 1993a, 1993b, 1995, 1997, 2000). Five years have now passed since the end of the project, and—inspired by the memory of Arja LAITI-NEN, *a feminist sister*—I am motivated to take a new look at this project with a particular emphasis on the theme of conflict with the leadership and between generations. Giving rise to this renewed attention are the by now internationally well-known and numerous reports about feminist projects foundering on the problematics of the *mother-daughter* conflict/struggle. All too often, the price of this conflict is that the accomplishments of the mother-generation—the generation of pioneers of the new women's movement—are left to languish without recognition. Taking a closer look at this phenomenon amounts to a political necessity: first of all, in order to save the collective feminist memory, and secondly, *also* in order to reclaim from the regions of taboo the destructive potential, which obviously exists between the generations. For only when feminists become aware of their own patriarchal shadow, when they thematize it and also individually work to change it, can progress be made in a direction that promises an alternative to the patriarchal constitution of society and its actual modes of behavior. Against this well-known background of failed feminist projects, I no longer conceive of certain events in my own project as singular and strange, but shall present them thematically in the second part of this paper. First, however, I outline the project's main features.

INTRODUCTION

More than 30 years have passed since the emergence of the new women's movement. The social and political movements of 1968 had of course fought for greater social justice and democracy in the former Federal Republic of Germany, but had always failed to address the anti-democratic features of the practiced order of gender relation. Changing this, therefore, was the declared goal of the women's movement from the 1970s on. The concepts of how to achieve this goal were extremely varied as far as politics, strategies, and specific contents were concerned. A multitude of theoretical and practical projects "saw the light of day." Aside from long-term structural changes and intellectual shifts in our thinking, the women's movement also succeeded in creating ties of emotional solidarity among women. The slogan adopted from the American women's movement—*Sisterhood is powerful!*—was held up as the idealistic basis for women's relations among themselves. The majority of the followers of the new movement belonged to a single generation, were in their 20s and 30s—and were thus "social sisters" in a concrete sense.

Within the framework of my doctoral dissertation in sociology at the University of Giessen and my work as an assistant lecturer in the Faculty of Sport Science, I was confronted with the spectacle of women's movement and soon joined in. I actively helped found the Women's Center in Giessen and, against this political background, devoted my research to the question of gender-specific socialization patterns in sports. Needless to say, this topic had remained a desideratum in the academic landscape. This background in women's politics and gender research has ever since shaped and determined my academic career.

WOMEN IN SPORT SCIENCE LEARN NETWORKING

In the 1980s I helped found a network of women doing research in sport science in West Germany; we were joined by politically active women in sports federations, trade unions, and autonomous groups. All of them wanted to transform sports in its structures and contents, to make it more attractive to women and more egalitarian to women. At an international congress in Jyväskylä (Finland) in 1987, these national groups and their activities were to be continued at an international level. From my perspective, it was there that a *broad* network of internationally active women in sport science was first formed. It continued to function far into the 1990s and made the present book possible. The above-named conference created a strong sense of solidarity among feminist women active in the science of sport through the scientific debates and many discussions that took place there. We traded information back and forth about current and planned projects, about their various successes or lack thereof, and felt strengthened in our research and teaching. Our Finnish colleagues considerably helped this exchange along, but no one more so than Arja Laitinen. One of the central questions that we had brought up again and again was: How can the dominant male-oriented movement culture of sports be changed into a women's-oriented culture for women, and indeed not just on the level of content but in its deep structures? Striving for equal chances and equal rights in a mixed-gender sports league or in the classroom had up to that point brought little progress in the Federal Republic. What we needed was a major change of strategy on our way to greater equal opportunity. Against this background, a decidedly women's-oriented and women's-centered perspective gained more and more importance in the discourse of research and politics in sport science. And for me as well.

FEMINIST DAUGHTERS BECOME ALLIES

My research into women's and gender-related issues underwent a praxis-oriented change as a result of that congress in Jyväskylä. It became more recognized—in tune with the spirit of feminist political goals—that women's research in sport science also had to be at the service of social change. Thus scientific reflection on sports and analysis of gender relations had to develop correspondingly innovative projects.

In 1988 I outlined and published a proposal for a feminist culture of movement and communication that found a strong echo among the groups mentioned above. A Women's and Girls' Center for Movement and Communication was founded to implement this concept. The center was located in the country about 40 kilometers from the University of Münster and was affiliated with my department of sport sociology within my home faculty of sport science. I was able to involve several young, feminist-oriented sport scientists, teachers, students, movement therapists, and dance instructors in this practical research project. Some of them had experience in the feminist politics of physical education and sports, others had done feminist research in sports, yet others were involved in continuing adult education courses. But we had one common goal: to try out and scientifically evaluate an alternative to the dominant culture of physical movement and communication in sports. Financial support for the initial, model-building phase and the second, continuing phase of the project came mainly from the junior partner of the German Sports Federation, the Youth for German Sports (translated from the German title *Deutsche Sportjugend, DSJ*).

THE WOMEN'S AND GIRLS' CENTER FOR MOVEMENT AND COMMUNICATION: AN ALTERNATIVE DESIGN

Between Autonomy and Institution

The project's coworkers and I (as project director) were under enormous pressure to succeed, since we had gathered to do nothing less than to plan and test an alternative design to the dominant culture of sport. All the women involved set themselves to the task at hand with extreme optimism, even euphoria. Though my concept of a feminist center provided a basic sort of blueprint, getting there still required endless new steps and pauses for reflection. Using anti-hierarchical, grassroots democratic organization as our guiding principle, we cast our teamwork in the spirit of the women's movement and of Theme Centered Interaction (TCI). The financial support I managed to secure and the (hard won) private space at our disposal allowed us a high measure of *autonomous* room to maneuver.

The *project sponsor*, the DSJ, was organized as a strictly hierarchical system, but was open to structural and thematic reforms. The Deutsche Sportjugend, (DJS) had itself launched a program promoting girls and young women and therefore expected tangible results from our project that could be successfully integrated into their own concerns.

In the *Faculty of Sport Science* the reactions were varied. A few female colleagues showed good will and curiosity; several, especially male professors, turned out to be indifferent, suspicious and/or aggressive. The sitting dean at the time proved to be obstructive; for example, he hindered our ability to rent space favorable to our work. At this point the failure of our project seemed inevitable.

The task confronting me, as the project director, was how to balance institutional obligations and more personal, autonomous goals centered in the project. On the one hand I had to adapt myself to the hierarchical conditions of university life and fulfill the duties of a professor. On the other hand it was just these hierarchical structures that I wanted to minimize in the project; democratizing the ways in which women dealt with each other would serve the goal of participation and self-determination. Balancing acts were also necessary in bargaining for financial and ideational support from the DSJ, itself a part of the insulated, hierarchical sports system. One had to make the project comprehensible, and above all avoid falling victim to nonfeminist clichés that would have sunk it entirely.

The Theoretical Concept of "Brochterbeck"

In 1989 the Women's and Girls' Center for Movement and Communication opened in Brochterbeck as an experimental model for reflective research into the practice of sports. It was first a matter of implementing the projected movement-and-interaction-based didactics for women in the spirit of Theme Centered Interaction (TCI). A good prognosis for success was ensured by a women-friendly organizational framework and the participatory nature of the leadership. Within the project's six-year run there was a full range of theoretical and practical tasks to accomplish, with corresponding data to be developed. I will now outline the most important research guidelines and results.

TOWARD A FEMINIST UNDERSTANDING OF RESEARCH

Maria Mies formulated basic methodological postulates for feminist research in 1977–1978. She outlined not only intellectual premises, but also a frame for research that made it possible to grasp the emancipatory elements of theory and practice. In the course of our own research we owed a great deal to the foundation laid by her postulates. I shall limit myself to two that increasingly determined our work during the project.

CONSCIOUS PARTIALITY INSTEAD OF VALUE-NEUTRAL OBJECTIVITY The word partiality again and again evokes, particularly in scientific discourse, the idea of irritation and contradiction, but also challenges one to engage in fruitful argumentation. What, then, should we understand by the term women's partiality within our context? Collectively, women and girls often lack their own cultural space, particularly the cultural room needed for movement. If a change is to be made here, then research has to create the preconditions for bringing forth innovations. We had taken a first step in creating conditions auspicious to women by renting the former Brochterbeck School.

CHOOSE A VIEW FROM BELOW Science, including social science, as a rule adopts a view *from above* and *from without,* theories tending to emerge with only a tenuous link to social reality. This often leads to political and pedagogical measures that sail past their target, and to changes that fail to take place. If providing spaces for women's and girls' physical activity is to lead to improved chances for collective and individual self-determination, then next to such structural preconditions we also need to consider innovative contents and themes. Therefore a women's perspective has to be based on their actual, everyday life circumstances and address women thematically on that basis. In this way women are brought into the research process as *subjects.* This is how "the view from below" is to be understood. Both postulates—*women's partiality* and *the view from below*—were central preconditions for a feminist research practice, without yet having attained the status of concepts.

A WOMEN-CENTERED APPROACH TO RESEARCH IN PRACTICE

The two projects carried out since 1989 in the Women's and Girls' Center for Movement and Communication in Brochterbeck had different research objects and goals.

THE FIRST PROJECT: THE MODEL PHASE The first project from 1989 to 1992 could be characterized as a model phase. It was essentially concerned with the founding of the Cultural and Educational Center for Body, Movement and Sports for Women and Girls (thus the title of the project application). The goal was both to experiment with a women's space organized exclusively by and for women, and to develop and test a concept of movement pedagogy oriented toward women and girls—a concept essentially geared to reach those women who had no desire join sport clubs. The upshot of this model phase was the successful realization of our goals. This comprised offering various sports and movement exercise classes based on recipients' expressed needs, the dialogical approach to learning and teaching, and the teamwork for which the leadership and administration had been striving. Our success was due to the group-procedure of TCI that underlies all action. TCI enabled us to build up a considerable reservoir of trust as the basis for cooperative action on all levels. At the same time this approach drew all the researchers involved into an intensive, personal learning process. And for me it was no different.

I chose TCI as the framing concept for the project because it provides more practical guidelines than feminist utopias up to now have been wont to do. TCI's understanding of leadership is based on the premise that whoever takes over this role has to enter into the working and learning process not only mentally, but emotionally as well. In this sense she (or he) is a practicing member of all group events and dynamics. In the awareness of TCI's two precepts—"Be your own chairperson" and "Disturbances have right of way"—all group members can act as coleaders. To this extent the TCI method is a concept that encourages and supports autonomy, responsibility and shared decision making.

THE SECOND PROJECT: THE IMPLEMENTATION The goal enshrined in the *second* project, the continuing education project from 1992 to 1995, was to develop a forum for continuing education and consultation that would correspond to the critera of the *first, model project*. In other words, continuing education aimed not only to transmit exercise techniques or teaching concepts to future participants, but to offer recipients the possibility of developing their personality by means of movement exercise and body training. TCI provided the framework. Accordingly, the continuing education concept (referred to in the following as the Integrative Brochterbecker Approach) combined three aspects: personality building through body, movement, and sports, the open dialogue of all participants, and women's partiality.

Our work is based on the recognition that a system can only support its own longterm changes if, next to these changed structures, the people regulating and controlling the system learn to live those innovations. To this extent the Integrative Brochterbecker Approach empowers women by offering them the opportunity to *use their self-perception as a stepping-stone to greater self-confidence and thus more self-determination*. The women targeted in the continuing education seminars and consultation work were *pedagogues* in adolescent services and social work, in physical education and sports clubs, at universities, as well as *functionaries* in organized sports at the local, county, state, and federal level.

RESEARCH QUESTIONS

Next to the didactic and movement-oriented level of the research project, the organization and daily administration of the center was a decisive factor in the success of this counterproposal. In this respect there were no role models that we could follow: we were on untrod terrain. We also could not foresee the extent to which our center would draw in the rural female population. Our prognosis had made allowance for maybe 50 women and girls who would be interested in checking out our experiment. But at the beginning there were 200, and later as many as 500 women and girls who used the center. The coworkers' delight over this high turnout was soon overshadowed by the question: How will we ever hope to master such a challenge? Especially our personnel resources were not sufficient. We had to develop a high level of creativity in order to manage the unexpected numbers with the personnel at our disposal (one full-time, two part-time positions). A host of volunteer positions (about 25 women) for courses and supervision had to be coordinated in the end.

The *central question* accompanying me/us from the start and throughout the multilayered research process, was: *How do women interact with women in a center reserved exclusively for women and girls?*—on the level of the individual course, through the course leadership and on to the level of management. In the following remarks I single out the management process and reflect upon this against the dual background of feminist utopias and TCI's understanding of leadership.

FEMINIST UTOPIAS AND THE THEMATICS OF LEADERSHIP

As mentioned above, highly motivated, young feminist women were engaged in the project. Aside from me and the TCI supervisor for the courses—both of us in our mid-fifties—all the women were between 25 and 35 years old. As far as I was concerned, generational difference played no role at first. In accordance with the project application, the organizational development of the center was explicitly based on the participatory model of TCI. I was bound to this and silently assumed that all my coworkers were, too. Beyond that my mind was full of the maxims of egalitarian sisterhood. A discussion of principles and explicit agreement about the manner of our work together, especially in the management team, did not occur in the beginning phase of the project work. We started out with more or less heterogeneous feminist utopias of cooperation and participatory leadership. At this point I shall deal with two of these particular utopias in greater detail.

WE-ARE-ALL-EQUAL This notion abstractly reflects the collective history of women as one of oppression and victimization. But it degenerates into a merely *horizontal ideology* if actually existing differences are denied, fought against, or simply ignored (Knapp 1991, p. 126). At the beginning of the new women's movement, the postulate of equality had its meaning, was resonant with the strength of solidarity, and contained a real political punch. Even today, autonomous projects still partly hang on to the ideology of undifferentiated sisterhood—and frequently fail when they informally reactivate those same hierarchies, with the same corresponding patterns of competition that they wanted to abolish in the first place. The tensions generated between an implied equality of all women, on the one hand, and the actual battles waged against hierarchical structures, on the other, frequently exhaust women's autonomous groups and lead to their downfall.

WE-ARE-ALL-DIFFERENT The developments of the last 30 years have seen women acquire a broad range of power, competence, and influence. This has not only changed the collective reality of women, but also has consequences for the debate on equality. With [the German translation of] their book, *Wie weibliche Freiheit entsteht* (Libreria Delle Donne Di Milano, 1988), Italian women at the end of the 1980s set new critera for political practice. While I cannot go into this book in detail here, I would like to single out one aspect that is relevant for us. The Italians emphasize, in contrast to the feminist ideology of equality, the *vertical* dimension of relations among women as their hierarchical differences. By doing so they refer both to the necessity of having pedagogical masters and to women's need for positive authority—so long as they live their lives as an experiment in freedom and want to found their being as women upon this (Knapp, 1991, p. 120). Since the idea of a feminine genealogy underlies this concept, a central role is played by the *symbolic mother* as a loving authority and guide in the world, from whose hand the growing *daughter* receives orientation.

Equality, or rather similarity and difference, are not mutually exclusive terms for me, but complementary categories of thought. In other words, next to symbolic sisterhood there is the symbolic mother/daughter relation, whose inner tensions remain to be explored (Knapp, 1991, p. 126). I now wish to *explore concretely* the dynamics, positive effects, and problems encountered in the team-work with the women of the center during the project.

ON THE DIFFICULTIES OF REALIZING A COUNTER-MODEL

The First Project: the Model Phase (1989–1991/92)

THE ORIENTATION OR CONSENSUS PHASE

Under the premise of partiality for women, the team wanted to build up an organization at the center whose regulation would be as self-determined as possible. The projected conceptual framework of TCI offered guidelines for action in our weekly team meetings as well as in the monthly supervision days. Everyone was equally busy with current demands such as the development of the program, preparations for the opening celebration and the acquisition of sports equipment and furniture. These tasks were all successfully completed. Work tended to be divided on a personal basis, depending on who was most interested, most professionally qualified, and had the most time. Since all the decisions were shared, the coordination of the work was an outcome of our agreement as to what was most necessary. All in all, the process was distinguished by a high degree of consensus. Defending the exclusivity of the center as a place for women against critics in our rural area proved to be an excellent source of solidarity among us. Supervisory meetings constructively helped along the team process at this stage in matters of structure and by clarifying personal relations.

THE PHASE OF COMPETITION AND DISSENT

In this phase the team was beset more and more often by competing themes. It had to do with the manner in which an organization such as the center's is built up and how it is administered. The controversy revolved around the choice of a process-oriented method of decision making and acting, or the contrary model of a structurally oriented method—by which is meant the designation of specific work topics or rubrics with permanently responsible facilitators who would prepare decisions for the various team committees in a competent and time-saving manner. Not by chance, the protagonists of both camps were the academic coworkers whose involvement in a particular task predisposed them to favor one way over the other. On the one hand, the colleague for scientific evaluation (H.) wanted to research in a process-oriented way; but the colleague in charge of business affairs (A.) was continually reminded of the project's institutional ties and obligations. Her contact people belonged to highly structured institutions such as the university, the Youth for German Sports. Both viewpoints have their advantages and disadvantages. Only their integration brings out their best features, but at that point in time they were competing against each other. A further controversy was closely related to this: How large should the center be in order to work meaningfully within the project guidelines? Should our efforts be directed toward a more scaled-down research project with few courses and course leaders, or should we—given the overwhelming public response—try to build up an academically focused educational institute?

In this context the question was raised: Who makes these decisions, how binding are they for all involved, and who bears responsibility for them? And so the theme of leadership was pushed into the foreground. As the director I of course bore ultimate responsibility for the realization of the project and its fundamental orientation. However, given my understanding of participatory leadership coupled with the precepts of TCI, I delegated a high degree of decision-making powers to individual women in the group. The organizational profile of the center took features from hierarchical institutions of an established type, where the paths of decision making are strictly mapped out, and from autonomous projects where decisions are made throughout the process, but often at the price of a certain discontinuity or instability. Thus the center's hybrid nature was a challenge to everyone, questioning as it did habitual ways of viewing leadership. Consequently there was criticism—more covert than open—of my leadership style. It stood in ideological contrast to autonomous claims of the type *We-are-all-equal*. The official opening celebration of the center in February 1990 was symptomatic of these *problematics of hierarchy*. Some women from the team presented public talks, others worked more in the background based on their roles and qualifications. At this point, too, the difference between valuable and less-valuable contributions on the part of team members was brought up for the first time. Though this topic was discussed in the following supervisors' meeting, there was no satisfying solution in sight.

THE PHASE OF IRRITATION AND SUDDEN EXIT

About a year later, the team—thanks to budget appropriations from the city—could be enlarged by four extra positions for pedagogy. The initiative for this action came from the colleague for business affairs. Despite the objective relief this meant for our work conditions, the measure at first had no chance of contributing to a constructive solution of old problems. On the contrary, they seemed to become even more serious and to receive new impetus from the expansion of our team personnel. The hiring of the additional four women ultimately favored turning the center into an educational institute. The consequences—which by then had affected the personal relationship of the two main antagonists in the matter—were discussed during one of the supervision days. This discussion took place—at the request of one of the two women—without the presence of myself and the TCI supervisor. (We were both on vacation at the time.) The team supervisor let herself be drawn into this constellation (thus committing a serious error of professional judgment). The upshot was that on this day there was no discussion of the topics "Competition Among Women" or

"Winning and Losing," but instead the simmering structural *conflict* was conjured up and projected onto the two of us who were absent, so that— as it later turned out—we were made responsible for it. No one spoke of this supervisors' meeting to us for a long time; an open confrontation was not desired.

Upon returning from vacation, I was struck by the fact that H., the colleague for scientific evaluation, behaved in a withdrawn manner and then became sick. Only in the next supervisors' meeting, in which we had a full quorum, did this colleague finally let go of her pent-up rage—first against the TCI supervisor and then against me. She gave her resignation. In the meantime she had made allies among the research assistants assigned to her. These three women also resigned.

It took me a long time to understand what had happened and to overcome emotionally this sudden exit of women's solidarity. In order to deal with a loss of influence and power, the women who had left the project could not do without an emotional slight projected upon the director. Withdrawal, illness, forming cliques behind the back of the leadership, and *abandoning the field* (giving notice) are passive behaviors of presumably powerless people. They are typically feminine strategies for overcoming conflict, well learned during years of socialization. It is doubtful that there was any emancipatory gain arising from this. Up to this point in time we had hardly succeeded in critically examining patriarchal behavioral patterns or in meaningfully integrating the TCI principles *Be your own chairperson* and *Disturbances have right of way* into our organizational work. The remaining women on the team used this crisis as an opportunity for a constructive change.

THE PHASE OF INTEGRATION

In this phase there was a pronounced consensus to continue the systematic development of our so far positive approaches to a women and girls-oriented organization. And we succeeded in many areas of our teamwork and administration in applying the principles of TCI. The postulate regarding "disturbances" was also honored insofar as we faced head-on any murky areas of personal relationships or thematic concerns. Our style of interaction became increasingly more tolerant and accepting. Summing up, by the end of the model phase a secure infrastructure of shared decision making had become visible and showed results not only internally, but also externally. The center was accepted and highly appreciated by the rural population, especially by the women.

Lessons from the Model Phase: How Do Women Interact with Women?

Measured against the phases and crises in the development of all groups, our team's behavior was *normal* (Rubner, 1991). As Rubner (1991) points out, the typical succession of closing phases moves from group trust to group farewell. Both of these phases marked the second half of our project.

Beyond these general remarks, it is interesting in our context to observe how women concretely shape their relationships to one another in an organization that they have built up and directed themselves. I would like to underscore a few points here from a position of women's partiality. In a relatively short time we had managed to establish an organization devoted to movement culture for women and girls that was unique in its kind. This was made possible by the way in which the participating women mutually supported, nourished, and learned from each other in ever more effective ways. From a more critical but nonetheless women-supportive perspective, I would also like to mention those behaviors that obstructed the process.

One expectation that is inseparably part of a woman's role is that she takes care of relationships. Accordingly she is often educated to empathize with others and show concern for their well-being, especially when they are faring badly. These qualities—if they have been attained by women—distinguish them and are the source of their strength, among other things. If the course participants and visitors at the center regularly praised the good atmosphere there, then this evidently has to do with the strengths mentioned above. But what happens in a women's environment—like this one—when the (usually high) expectations of empathetic concern are not fulfilled every time? In the project team this problem expressed itself as follows.

The thus affected coworkers frequently reacted by manifesting an inhibited approach to their work, according to the (unconscious) motto: "I feel bad, you're not giving me enough" (Streit, 1989). The pressure of this usually nonverbalized expectation awakened guilt feelings in the other team members and often led to the hoped-for display of tender empathy on the part of some or all the women present. These tentative *mothering games* led to mutual dependencies and were scarcely suited to fulfill emancipatory goals, at least not as understood by the precept of chairpersonship. At the same time they blocked the desired interplay between the levels of the personal *and* the professional, which is the only way to realize a common aim and to satisfy the individual woman.

The maxim that, in a women's project, *everyone is equal and everyone is sitting in the same boat* (that of the oppressed victims) was meaningful at the beginning of the women's movement (in the 1970s) and helped foster strength in solidarity. In the meantime, however, a complex process of differentiation has taken place among women. This is also true of the personnel in our project. A research project like the one in question here can neither be successfully applied for nor carried out without a qualified director. Coworkers with all their varied qualifications bring something of great value to the creative development of an innovative project. To have knowledge, to be competent, to be widely informed, and to know influential people—all this means to have power. In our project, women had various degrees of power, some more, some less. And this was the root of the dilemma. On the one hand, it was crucial for the project's development that women on the team increase their power in order—for example—to gain more influence in the various sports leagues. On the other hand, it was precisely this growth of individual power in the sense of expanded influence that became problematic for many women on the team. A certain tendency became visible to regard women who stood out as particularly successful with skepticism and ill will. A drive for power was supposed to be lurking everywhere, and particularly where I, the project director, stood. Only mediocrity can flourish in such a repressive climate, for women are not challenged to go to the limits of their intellectual or mental capacities. Thus is revealed how women contribute to their own oppression.

A further problem is closely connected to the above. Holding oneself back, refusing to stand out, or preventing others from excelling (in the sense of stepping forth from the crowd, appearing unique), brings no progress, because then being average becomes the norm. But if women bear (aloft) their own differences, accept the diversity of personal qualifications, then heterogeneous ideas and concepts—regarding an organization advocating for women, for example—can come together, as ultimately happened in our case. In this sense there should and must be a space for fair competition to arrive at the best solution of the issue at hand. A condescending or belittling stance toward those who think differently, or complaining, fussing and passively withdrawing, are not progressive reactions. In the end such behaviors only swamp creative energies in senseless opposition.

In the course of time the team recognized that when women do not learn to deal constructively with conflicts, they not only hinder their own ability to take the lead, but hinder other women through their leadership example. Beyond that, women must still learn elementary lessons of solidarity with powerful and influential women: To support them at the right moment, to applaud them on occasion, and, on occasion, to enter into fair competition with them. This would give all of them that sense of sovereignty and strength that they urgently need for the task of creating structural change through feminist politics, and not least of all in the realm of sports.

Implementing the Second Project (1992–1995)

The team members' evolution as sketched above shows us what strengths and weaknesses women have to contend with among each other in an organizational setting. But all in all it was an exciting, lively, and creative process, both for the individual woman, for the team, and the project in its entirety. At the end of the model phase, therefore, the team was ready to carry on the successful job in a continuing education project for future movement-exercise trainers, a process that we called "transferral."

Meanwhile, after two-and-half years, the center was well achored in the community. The coworkers were growing more and more secure and confident in their tasks. Although a few tight corners with personnel hiring and shifting had to be navigated at this phase, the team succeeded in intensifying its cooperative working style. *The phase of trust* (Rubner, 1992) in our relations carried our message of an alternative culture of movement and communications for women further afield, and we received ever more inquiries from groups and institutions. Since our concept was sound, the continuing education seminars in the region and nationwide were well attended and appreciated. There was also international interest in our work.

And yet—even in this three-year project period there were renewed *leadership problems*, this time with the business manager (A.). She was the only one of the coworkers who had a full-time position. Her job—carried out in constant consultation with me—involved applying for funding along with administering and overseeing these funds. Because of this position she was the one who spent the most time at the center. Often she fulfilled managerial and technical duties as my deputy when I was unavailable because of my teaching load at the university. It was necessary for me to confer with her alone, beyond the regular team meetings, especially when technical financial matters were involved. Thus she deeply shared the responsibilities of directorship. I can no longer exactly name the point in time when A. terminated our overwhelmingly cooperative and trusting work relationship. I became aware after a while that we had differences of opinion more and more often, and our discussions began to turn into a strain. She seemed to have different ideas of how the directorship had to function. These ideas remained vague to me, so that in the supervisory meetings I deemed it necessary to reaffirm my role as the ultimate arbiter of guidelines for the project. Because of her skills in finance she had evidently come to have persistent fantasies of being the director. In the framework of the supervisors' meetings the necessary strategies for conflict-resolution could be worked out, but they had only a passing influence. The longer the project went on and the closer its end grew near, the more this conflict weighed on both of us. After an interval in which she left the work process due to illness, A. began her offensive phase. She worked against me, neglected her duties, tried to discredit my leadership style and sought allies outside of the circle of our project members, i.e., among my colleagues in the faculty of sport science at the university, in which she partly succeeded. A doctoral student who had been my dissertation protegée of many years refused to continue her loyal and orderly work with me and instead finished it with a male supervisor. Finally A. tried to discredit the good name of the center. She returned the performance evaluation that I had written not long after the project ended and demanded that I rewrite it to suit her. After convening the personnel board, she put me under intense pressure when I did not comply with her wishes. For its part, the personnel board expressed its total surprise at A.'s venture, since it considered the evaluation to be excellent. After this the psycho-terror against me came to an end.

(FEMINIST) MOTHERS AND (FEMINIST) DAUGHTERS: A CASE OF PATRIARCHAL CONFLICT

As you can see, there were conflicts over my directorship in both phases of the project, and in both cases the conflicts were with colleagues who were particularly important for the project and whom I had particularly promoted. They shared with me a vision of women's solidarity for the purpose of gaining enough power in patriarchal society to finally abolish it. Only the question of *how* this goal was to be attained in praxis— in our segment of patriarchal reality—opened a cleft of dissenting views between them and me. They had also been ready to follow me in my feminist visions as their intellectual mentor, their feminist mother. But in reality there were conflict-laden arguments over the research process facing us, the feminist paths to organization building and continuing education. On the face of it, everyone seemed to agree with the course worked out in the supervisory discussion rounds. But *behind our backs* the conflict continued to smolder for many coworkers. Those strategies for overcoming conflict so well practiced by women in patriarchy—hidden violence (psycho-terror, mobbing) or stepping out of conflict's way (illness, giving notices)—were also practiced with destructive consequences by our coworkers H. and A. It is simply not enough to have a vision of a more just, more comradely society in one's head. It must be proven practically, in cooperative forms of living and working that can also withstand conflict. Looking back at the work of the project has strengthened my insight that a solid feminist sisterhood has to be based on just this kind of mother/daughter relationship, if women are to develop an alternative to a patriarchy that is destructive on all fronts. Patriarchal social relations are distinguished by envy, competition, and rivalry among women. Particularly the elementary bond between mother and daughter is consciously destroyed in patriarchy, engendering psychic hatred between the generations. Matriarchal social order (Göttner-Abendroth, 2000) is, in contrast, based on the cohesion of generations and on sisterhood. These forms of collective life do exist, and they do not have to remain utopian.

LOOKING BACK TO THE FUTURE—TOWARD SOLIDARITY BETWEEN THE GENERATIONS

What is the significance of this experience for today's historical situation—beyond the context of sports? It seems to me that one unavoidable precondition for finding a way (back) to cooperative forms of living and working, is the necessity for women to clarify their relationship to their own mother and, simultaneously, to their intellectual mother/mentor. Bound up with this task is the mental work of feminist daughters who must take notice of, and appropriate in their own way, the theories and political convictions of their feminist mothers and teachers. This critical appropriation should be marked by fairness and recognition of the historical accomplishment of each woman. Their successes could in this way become visible as the historical basis of a knowledge that is anchored in the consciousness of all members of a society—but especially in the consciousness of women. This knowledge can strengthen women as a collective and create a historical continuum that helps to expand women's power. For their part, feminist pioneers and mentors must be ready to see their theories and political convictions put to the test.

In order to approach these goals on a broad collective front, it is emotionally indispensable that (feminist) mothers and daughters clarify their relationship to one another. This process of clarification is meaningful if it takes into account the emotional and social (de)formation of mothers and daughters in the patriarchal family and society. It is a (de)formation that often goes hand in hand with devaluation, humiliation, and restricted chances for autonomous growth. Since social change is inseparable from personal change, women cannot be spared the confrontation with injuries and indignities they may have experienced in the course of growing up. To *per*ceive (and not simply to *re*ceive) the blighted experience of the past, to work on it, to make room for feelings of mourning in order to let them go, offers a chance to acquire an autonomous identity. With this comes the probability that women would not have to turn their rage against other women (and men). Mutual respect and understanding would also have a chance to flourish between the generations. This is the way that I urgently recommend each woman to take in order to become free. The vision of global strength and empowerment can then realize itself in the everyday relation of mutually fortifying togetherness.

ACKNOWLEDGMENTS

I would like thank Walter Allmand (USA) lector at the University of Magdeburg (Germany) for translating this chapter.

REFERENCES

Göttner-Abendroth, H. (2000). *Das Matriarchat II, 2. Stammesgesellschaften in Amerika, Indien, Afrika*. Stuttgart, Berlin, Köln.

Knapp, G. -A. (1991). Zur Theorie und politischen Utopie des 'affidamento' *Feministische Studien* 9(1), 117–128.

Kröner, S. (1993a). *Annäherungen an eine andere Bewegungskultur*. Pfaffenweiler.

Kröner, S. (1993b). Zwischen patriarchaler Realität und feministischer Utopie: Frauen in Leitenden Positionen im Sport und in der Sportwissenschaft. In P. Gieß-Stüber and I. Hartmann-Tews (Eds.). *Frauen und Sport in Europa*. Sankt Augustin: Academia Verlag.

Kröner, S. (1995) and project group (ed. Deutsche Sportjugend). *Mädchen- und FrauenparteilicheBewegungs- und Kommunikationskultur: Projektbericht*. Frankfurt/M.

Kröner, S. (1997). "Hier dagegen ist das anders." Bilanz einer innovativen Praxisforschung. In U. Henkel and S. Kröner (Eds.), *Und sie bewegt sich doch!* Pfaffenweiler.

Kröner, S. (2000). Für eine andere Bewegungs- und Kommunikationskultur: Das Projekt Brochterbeck. In M. Buschmann and S. Kröner (Eds.), *TZI bewegt—bewegende TZI. Neue Wege bewegungszentrierter Gruppenarbeit in Weiterbildung und Sozialarbeit mit Frauen*. Mainz.

Libreria delle Donne di Milano (1988). *Wie weibliche Freiheit entsteht: Eine neue politische Praxis*. Berlin.

Mies, M. (1984). Methodische Postulate der Frauenforschung. *Beiträge zur feministischen Theorie und Praxis*, 11, 7–25.

Rubner, E. (1992). *Störung als Beitrag zum Gruppengeschehen*. (Reihe: Aspekte Themen-zentrierter Interaktion.). Mainz.

Streit, M. (1989). "Mir geht es schlecht—du gibst mir nicht genug!" Symbiose, Opfermentalität und Masochismus in Beziehungen zwischen Frauen. In R.Burgard and B. Rommelspracher (Eds.), *Leideunlust: der Mythos vom weiblichen Masochismus*. Berlin.

Chapter 7

Fight or Flight?: Experiences of Sexual Harassment among Female Athletes

Kari Fasting

INTRODUCTION

During the last five years my research area has been sexual harassment and abuse in sport. However, starting this project was not a result of a long period of planning. In some ways one can say that it happened by accident. As part of a larger project, run by the Norwegian Olympic Committee (Fasting, Brackenridge, & Sundgot-Borgen, 2000), I was asked by a colleague to survey Norwegian elite female athletes' experiences with sexual harassment and abuse inside and outside the sport setting.[1] When I started to review the research in this area I soon realized that the literature focused mainly on the prevalance of sexual harassment and abuse in the educational institutions and the workplace, but our knowledge concerning sexual harassment in sport was very scarce (Stockdale, 1996). Reading the relevant literature is often an eye-opener, and it definitely opened my eyes. Analyzing the studies on sexual harassment and interviewing female elite athletes who had been harassed have made me reflect upon my own past experiences as well as upon what happens around me today. I now notice incidents of sexual harassment both at formal meetings and in other situations; particularly verbal comments that make me and other women uneasy. My studies in this area have been like putting on new lenses, and I now reflect upon past situations in a different way than before (Bem, 1993). In one such situation, which happened many years ago, Arja Laitinen was the central person. My "new lenses" have made me reinterpret and rereflect upon that situation.

I, as most of the contributors to this book, participated in "The International Congress on Movement and Sport in Women's Life," in Jyväskylä in August 1987. During this conference Arja gave a presentation titled "On Movement Culture by and for Women: A Process-Oriented Approach to Research" (Laitinen, 1991). Presenting her paper required great courage. The main purpose of the paper was "to give a short overview of the Finnish women's research in sport sciences" (p. 208) based on empirical work mainly from her own institution. She showed the gendering process of science, talked about "research on men, by men and for men" (p. 210), and revealed the "masculine images of a culture of science" (p. 211). In addition, Arja analyzed "the gendering process of scientific work organizations" and demonstrated how the "hierarchy of scientific professions" (p. 212) and the hierarchy of decision making in science influenced the "women's work culture" which she called "a grass roots level of scientific culture," (p. 214). Under her third theme, "the gendering process of research work," Arja described how androcentric research teams and the "hidden mechanisms of gendering process" (p. 216) evolve in scientific institutions (p. 215). Her last focus was on "women's research," and she talked about the experiences of "research by women in the high culture of science," and the "slight transformation from sex to gender analyses." I believe that many of the people in the audience, independent of gender, experienced her speech as "a radical critique," which also was one of her own conclusions (p. 219). She closed the paper with the following statement:

> In Finnish sport sciences a Marxist critique became manifest in the 1970's, not as Marxist research, but as a "left-hand" radical perspective in research. Now women's perspectives in sport research can be seen as a second wave of a critique in sport sciences. The "re-action" to the waves of critiques has been different. The leftist radical wave "died" and the group disappeared; for the second wave an international congress was arranged to develop the research field. Whether the women's perspective is going to be one of the research areas of Finnish sport sciences in a larger scale is hard to predict. The future will show. (p. 219)

My task here is not to analyze the later developments of Finnish sport sciences. It is my opinion, however, that sport sciences definitely lost a major contributor when Arja Laitinen, after a relatively short time, left the university and the area of sport research. What I will try to describe here is the atmosphere in the auditorium during her talk. First, it changed as the minutes went by. The audience became very silent, so silent that apart from her soft voice, one could have heard a pin drop. At the same time one could feel admiration, surprise, excitement, frustration, and aggression in the air, particularly when she gave the following examples of what she called "micro-inequities":

- plans for the department are discussed in small informal groups of men before the meetings for the whole department;

- women are not invited to the meetings where the departmental research projects are presented to a visiting professor;

- during the visits by professors women are not invited to the lunch where the latest news from the scientific work culture are discussed;

- women are not informed about the scholarships unless the information is sent to the office of the department;

- women do not get financial support for new areas of research, but the following year a male colleague applies for a grant to research the same topic and gets the financial support. The research money is then used for his own or his assistant's research project;

- in the licenciate seminar (a post graduate research seminar) a female researcher is told that her topic will not make a worthwhile research study. A couple of years later a thesis is published about these phenomena;

- women are not presented to the new students among the staff of the department. While the men's positions are mentioned, the women's positions are left unmentioned. The women are presented only with their first names while the men are presented with their titles and their full names. (Laitinen, 1991, p. 225)

Arja Laitinen's presentation pictures a very chilly climate for female researchers in Finland at that time. Today, with my knowledge of sexual harassment, I understand that the atmosphere in the auditorium during and after her presentation certainly can be characterized as a gender and/or sexually harassing climate.

WHAT IS SEXUAL HARASSMENT?

According to the United Nations, sexual harassment and intimidation at work is defined as violence. The definition of violence should be understood to encompass the following: "Physical, sexual and psychological violence occurring within the general community, including rape, sexual abuse, sexual harassment and intimidation at work, in educational institutions and elsewhere, trafficking in women and forced prostitution" (UNIFEM, 2001).

Sexual harassment is a difficult term to define and therefore deserves some clarification. There is no universally accepted definition of sexual harassment. Central in all definitions is, however, that it is unwanted sexual attention. This is evident particularly in gender harassment. Gender harassment consists of generalized sexist remarks and behavior not designed to elicit sexual cooperation but to convey insulting, degrading, or sexist attitudes about women; seductive behavior that is unwanted or inappropriate; and offensive sexual advances that all include subjective elements. Sexual harassment will vary with culture and environment, and it occurs often in situations where one person has power over the other. This is not limited to an individual level (male professor and female student), but exists also on a more structural level, as Arja described in her presentation. The personal and psychological impact of the same kind of sexually harassing behavior may be vastly different depending on the individual's background and perceptions. It is important to notice that the same behavior can be experienced and interpreted differently by women and men, and that the same woman, depending on the situation can provide a different interpretation of the situation.

One example of a European definition of sexual harassment is by the Netherlands' Olympic Committee and Confederation of Sport (1997): "'Sexual harassment' is any form of sexual behaviour or suggestion, in verbal, non-verbal or physical form, whether intentional or not, which is regarded by the person experiencing it as undesired or forced" (p. 3). In New Zealand sexual harassment is defined as "any unwelcome behaviour of a sexual nature." This definition also contains an additional, important aspect: In most cases, sexual harassment is "an attempt by one person to inappropriately exert power over another person. Harassment ranges from mild conduct such as gestures or comments to conduct which may be physical, forceful and violent" (p. 9). Examples of behavior covered by such broad definitions are:

- Derogatory or demeaning jokes and comments of a sexual nature
- Nonverbal behavior such as whistling, sexual staring or leering
- Unwanted sexual suggestions about one's body, clothes, or private life
- Unwanted telephone calls, or letters with sexual content

- To be shown or to receive pictures or things with unwanted sexual content

- Ridicule or sexist jokes about women in general

- Repeated unwanted sexual proposals or invitations concerning sexual behavior

- Unwanted touching of a sexual nature

- Pinching

- Attempted kissing

- Unwanted body pressing and body contact

- Forced sexual acts

- Attempted rape or rape

It is difficult to distinguish between sexual harassment and abuse—there is definitely a gray area between them. While some authors make a clear distinction between the two terms, others see the concept of sexual harassment including sexual abuse. The definitions from the Netherlands and New Zealand are examples of such an "inclusive" definition. Some researchers (Brackenridge, 1997) conceptualize a continuum from sex discrimination to sexual harassment to sexual abuse. Thinking of a continuum may be very useful when we try to understand what sometimes goes on between coaches and young athletes, or between professors and students. The process of "grooming" someone for sexual abuse means that one slowly gains the trust of a child or youth before systematically breaking down interpersonal barriers. It can begin very innocently by the coach offering a ride home or offering other special privileges to the athlete. The young athlete or student can become totally trapped, because compliance is assured by using threats such as being cut from the team, bad marks, and/or giving or withholding privileges.

As suggested earlier sexual harassment and abuse are normally not about sex, but about control. The motivation behind sexual harassment is often power—the harasser having or wanting to have power and control over another individual. This issue of power is particularly problematic in the sport environment and in sport science institutions, where the most powerful positions are held by men and where coaches, other leaders, and professors hold considerable power over young people.

Some authors (Paludi, 1998) differentiate between the legal and the empirical definitions of sexual harassment. In the United States, there are two kinds of legal terms for sexual harassment: *quid pro quo* and "hostile environment." *Quid pro quo* exists when benefits are granted or withheld as a result of an athlete's willingness or refusal to submit to the sexual demands of a person in authority. A coach, for example, could cut an athlete from the team because she refused sexual advances. A hostile environment exists when a coach, another athlete, or another person in a power position exhibits conduct that is so pervasive or so severe that it disturbs the athlete's ability to perform. A hostile environment can affect more than just the targeted person. For example, a team member who witnesses repeated incidents, even if they are not directed at her or him, may be considered a victim of sexual harassment (WSF, 1994). In the situation described by Arja there seemed to have been a hostile environment in the department(s). Fitzgerald and her colleagues (1997) have proposed a classification of harassing behavior, which also consists of three related but distinct dimensions: gender harassment, unwanted attention, and sexual coercion. They link these categories to the legal constructs just mentioned. They further state that both gender harassment and unwanted sexual attention, which according to research coexist, constitute two aspects of a hostile environment (Fitzgerald, Swan, & Magley, 1997). Fitzgerald, Swan, and Magley (1997) conclude that gender harassment "refers to a broad range of verbal behaviour, physical acts, and symbolic gestures that are not aimed at sexual cooperation but that convey insulting, hostile and degrading attitudes about women" (p.10).

Empirical definitions of sexual harassment are derived from students' and employees' descriptions of their experiences of harassment. Frank Till (1980) classified the responses to an open-ended sexual harassment survey of college women and derived the following five categories of generally increasing severity:

Gender harassment
Seductive behavior
Sexual bribery
Sexual coercion
Sexual imposition or assault

Gender harassment would probably best fit the situations Arja described in her talk. Arja's examples of her daily experiences as a female sport researcher made an impression on all of us because of their negative content. But we were also impressed that she dared to present the results in front of the people who were a part of her everyday research culture. This had a huge impact on the discussion that followed her presentation. She was verbally attacked by her male professors and colleagues through their questions and comments. I don't remember the details, but I remember afterward that many of us (the female participants) were very upset. Everything, however, happened relatively fast and there was not much time for the discussion. As a consequence, many women didn't get the chance to present their comments. Now, years later when I have my sexual harassment lenses on, I understand that not only was Arja's working environment hostile, but the way the discussion was run afterward created a hostile environment at the Congress. We had all, along with Arja, experienced gender harassment. I don't know what the personal and political aftereffects were for Arja, but for many women they can be severe. I also wonder that if some of us in the audience had more knowledge about issues of gender harassment, would we have reacted differently during the discussion or had we even written to the scientific committee or the university to complain? I don't know. However, during the last 10–15 years our knowledge about sexual harassment has increased.

I came to know Arja as a sport sociologist, though later in her career she left the area of sport research. In memory of Arja as a sport sociologist and our shared experience described above, I will first present a review of the prevalence of sexual harassment in sport in this chapter. Second, I will discuss some results from a Norwegian interview study of 25 elite-level athletes who had experienced sexual harassment. I focus on two areas from this study: the consequences of sexual harassment, and the characteristics of the harassing sporting milieu as described by these athletes. Although I would have liked to include research regarding sexual harassment in sport science institutions in my chapter, to my knowledge, no such research currently exits.

The studies on sexual harassment in the workplace and educational settings, however, indicate that sport organizations and perhaps the sport sciences represent cultures in which sexual harassment can easily occur, because gender ratios, sexualized atmospheres, and organizational power have been found to influence both the incidence and maintenance of sexual harassment in the workplace and in academia (Hotelling & Zuber, 1997). Research also indicates that the prevalence of sexual harassment is the highest in workplaces where women traditionally have been underrepresented (Gutek, 1985), and the lowest in workplaces dominated by women (Grauerholz, 1996). Since men, masculinity, and traditional male values heavily dominate most sport organizations and most of the sport sciences, sport and sport science institutions might be particularly risky locations for sexual harassment. I hope that the more knowledge we can gain in this area, the better prepared we will be for developing strategies to prevent the kind of scientific environment described and experienced by Arja and many other women around the world.

PREVALENCE OF SEXUAL HARASSMENT

Research on sexual harassment was first undertaken in the workplace and in the educational system. According to Fiztgerald (1993), different surveys indicate that half of all women will be subjected to some form of harassment during their academic or working lives. This indicates that harassment is the most widespread of all forms of sexual victimization. Very few large-scale quantitative studies have been carried out to explore the prevalence of these experiences in sport and or in a sport science academe.

In the first-ever national-level survey of sexual harassment and abuse in sport was administered to the total population (N = 1,200) of Canada's high performance and recently retired Olympic athletes by Kirby and Greaves (1996). Twenty-two percent of the 266 respondents replied that they had had sexual intercourse with persons in positions of authority in sport. Nine percent reported they had experienced forced sexual intercourse, or rape, by such persons. Twenty-three respondents were under 16 years of age at the time of the sexual assault and, therefore, they had experienced child sexual assault. Another Canadian study of 1,024 female and male student athletes (Holman, 1995) found that 57 % had experienced some form of sexual harassment. Most of these experiences could be defined as gender harassment, like sexist jokes or comments, but also seductive behavior, coercion, or physical intrusion/assault was reported. A Danish study (Toftegaard, 1998) of 250 male and female college sport science students found that 25% either knew about or had themselves experienced situations where a sport participant under the age of 18 years had been sexually harassed by the coach. Four of these reported having been sexually abused. Using a screening questionnaire of 2,118 Australian athletes Leahy (2002) found that 31% of the female and 21% of male athletes reported experiencing sexual abuse at some time in their lives. Of these, 41% of females and 29% of males had been sexually abused within the sports environment. However, it is difficult to compare these quantitative studies because of their different definitions, samples, ethics, and consent procedures, validity and reliability, and underreporting/nonresponse. Both Kirby and Greaves's (1996) and Leahy's (2002) surveys had low response rates (22% and 19% respectively), which can result in underreporting and bias in the data. However, these studies can be seen as benchmarks for further investigations.

The studies referred to here have all taken place in Australia, North America, or Scandinavia. What then about the rest of the world? Many sad individual stories concerning both physical and sexual violence toward female athletes have been told at women's conferences in sport, but systematic research is lacking. In Asia a string of sexual harassment cases over the past few years has shocked the Japanese sports world (www.asahi.com 7.11.02). As a result, the first criminal trial on a charge of sexual harassment started in July, 2001 when a former teacher and manager of a track-and-field club was arrested in August, 2000 on suspicion of indecent assaults. This trial is on-going as the case has been moved to a higher court in Fukuoka, Japan. In Africa, sexual harassment and abuse also seem to be barriers for girls' and women's involvement in sport. Prisca Bruno Massao (2001) carried out interviews with 13 Tanzanian leaders from different sport organizations, 10 women and 3 men. Her interview guidelines did not contain any questions about sexual harassment, but the theme came up in the interviews as a barrier toward girls' and women's involvement in sport. She concluded:

> Although the issue of sexual harassment was not the major theme at the beginning of this study, through the interviews it reoccurred to the extent of indicating it is one of the important experiences for women in Tanzanian sport. It was presented that sport was a distrusted institution for girls and women due to sexual harassment suspicions. This situation is said to be the reason that many parents and husbands do not allow their daughters or wives to participate in sport. (p. 87)

A Norwegian research project *Females, Elite Sports and Sexual Harassment* was a part of The Norwegian Women Project that was administered by the Norwegian Olympic Committee during 1995–2000. The study consisted of two parts. Part one was a survey of all Norwegian female elite athletes. Part two dealt with elite athletes who had experienced one or more forms of sexual harassment in a sport setting. Twenty-five of these athletes were interviewed (Fasting, Brackenridge, & Sundgot-Borgen, 2000). A total of 660 female athletes aged 15–39, representing 58 sport disciplines, were invited to participate in the study. Once the structure of the female athlete sample was known, a control group from the general population was defined and matched by age. A total of 572 athletes (87%) and 574 controls (73%) answered the questionnaire. The results show that there were no significant differences between the athletes and the controls concerning prevalence of male sexual harassment and abuse as 47% of the controls and 45% of the athletes had such experiences. There was no difference between the athletes' experiences in a sport setting with the controls' work/school experience, but both groups had experienced more sexual harassment and abuse from settings outside of sport or outside of school and work. Concerning these experiences the athletes have experienced less sexual harassment than the controls. This is particularly true for the oldest athletes (above 23 years old). Based on the results, the elite female athletes in Norway are not exposed to sexual harassment and abuse more than other female groups in society (Fasting, Brackenridge, & Sundgot-Borgen, 2003). It is interesting that among the oldest participants fewer athletes than controls have been exposed to sexual harassment outside a sport setting. We found that the controls (20%) had been exposed to much more serious forms of sexual harassment and abuse than the athletes (4%) such as forced rape, attempted rape, or "forced into sexual behavior" (Fasting, Brackenridge, & Walseth, 2000). Bart (1981 cited in Finkelhor, 1986) found that strength and athleticism is associated with women's successful rape avoidance. We could argue that as the female elite athletes grow older, they become more adept at protecting themselves, and are thereby able to avoid or escape potentially dangerous harassment situations in nonsport settings.

However, being an elite female athlete in a sporting environment can also be looked upon as a risk factor. More athletes had experienced sexual harassment from an authority figure in sport (28%) than nonathletes had from supervisors or teachers (16%). The number of athletes with these kinds of experiences increases with age, from 17% among the youngest (15–19 years of age) to 42% among the oldest (23–39 years of age). This indicates that authority figures in sport exhibit behavior toward athletes that is not tolerated or accepted at a workplace or in an educational institution. It is possible that the best athletes are more likely to be in the older group and spend more time in the company of authority figures during travel and/or competition. These situations seem to constitute the main risk situations (Kirby & Greaves, 1996; Cense & Brackenridge, 2001). We could also argue that as the athletes become older, they become more aware of what behaviors can be defined as sexual harassment or sexual abuse.

The studies above report harassing behavior by male harassers. This doesn't mean that female perpetrators are nonexistent. However, very low rates of female sexual exploitation have been found in mainstream studies (Brackenridge, 2001). The Norwegian project discussed earlier found that 15% of the female top-level athletes had experienced harassment from another woman compared to 21% among the control group.

CONSEQUENCES OF SEXUAL HARASSMENT

Gutek and Koss (1993) find that it is difficult to define the exact impact of sexual harassment on the individual. Rather there are many different consequences that depend on the domain examined and the point in the process of sexual harassment where the assessments are made. These authors argue that, in addition to the impact of the sexual harassment itself, the aftereffects are often influenced by disappointment to the way the others react to the situation. In addition, the stress of harassment-induced life changes such as forced moving from place to place or job to job, loss of income, and the trauma of litigation can have an impact on the individual's life. Garlick (1994) claimed that as many as 90% of sexual harassment victims suffered from a significant degree of emotional stress and Koss (1991) wrote that, depending on the severity of the sexual harassment, between 21% and 82% of all women reported that their emotional and/or physical condition deteriorated as a result of their experiences. She stated further that "experiencing sexual harassment transforms women into victims and changes their lives. It is inevitable that once victimized, at minimum, one can never again feel quite as invulnerable" (p. 37).

The sexual harassment can have on impact on individual's somatic, physical, and psychological/emotional health, well-being, worklife and career development. For example, one might be forced to change her job assignment, lose her job, experience decreased job satisfaction, and experience damaged interpersonal relationships at work. Experiencing sexual harassment has led university students to drop courses, change majors (main subjects of study), change academic departments and programs, or alter their career intentions. Psychological and somatic outcomes include negative effects on self-esteem and life satisfaction, low sense of self-confidence, negative effect on a woman's relationship with other men, anger, fear, anxiety, depression, feelings of humiliation and alienation, a sense of helplessness and vulnerability, headaches, sleep disturbance, weight loss or gain, gastrointestinal disturbances, and nausea (Gutek & Koss, 1993; Fitzgerald, 1993).

What, then, is the impact of sexual harassment in a sport setting? What are the consequences for athletes? Are they similar to those in the workplace or in educational institutions? Being an athlete is often associated with a strong feeling of self-esteem. Does this mean that athletes' experiences and coping strategies differ from those who experience sexual harassment outside sport?

Greaves and Hankivsky (2000) write that the outcomes for the athletes who were victimized by sexual assault or attempted sexual assault were serious in both short and long term:

> For many, it changed how they behaved in sport and in their day-to-day lives. Athletes found ways to take care of themselves by not associating with the perpetrators, by changing the training routine, by changing personal behaviour to become more professional, or by changing the situation or location so they would be less at risk. Several athletes continue to have long-term personal problems. They sought psychotherapy/counselling, refused media interviews, lost interest in sport and/or remained unable to deal with the experience and are now "violent and temperamental." (p. 96)

In addition to these serious impacts, sexual harassment in sport seems to affect the athletes' lives not only in a sport setting but also during their daily lives. For example, the analysis of the consequences of sexual harassment among the Norwegian female athletes revealed that four of the athletes had left sport because of sexual harassment. The athletes also felt that the sexual harassment episodes had damaged the coach-athlete relationship, and led to changes in behavior toward the coach. Others felt that it was difficult to concentrate when the harasser was at the same place, for example, at an event even when the harassment had happened some years before. These athletes reflected the incident(s) continually and many felt anger, irritability, confusion, and anxiety. Experiencing sexual harassment affected their self-esteem and their body image. Some also thought it changed their behavior toward other men and coaches (Fasting, Brackenridge, & Walseth, 2002).

Coaches are normally trusted by the female athletes who may become emotionally dependent on their coaches (Gutek & Koss, 1993). Behavior or incidents that lead to a breakdown of this trust may have devastating effects. These findings are echoed by Quina (1991) who showed that women victims suffered longterm aftereffects from sexual harassment. She further argued that sexual harassment violated trust, especially when the harasser was in a position of authority, which is the case almost always in sport and in academia.

Four of the elite athletes had opted to change sports and also knew other athletes who had left the sport because sexual harassment. Since these athletes are survivors in elite sport, we can assume that many more girls and women leave sport due to sexual harassment. Sexual harassment, therefore, might contribute significantly to girls' dropout from sport, which takes place around or just after puberty. Similar to students who drop out or change their academic courses because of sexual harassment, the female athletes feel a "chilly climate," which is often expressed as "ridicule" not welcoming them into some sports. These reactions parallel taking a sick leave or quitting a job because of sexual harassment in work life. The latter is, however, often more difficult, because most people are economically dependent on their jobs. For some professions, like in academia, it is not that easy to change to another academic institution.

According to Larkin (1991), men's harassment of women takes on a male interpretation, when women's direct experiences of sexual harassment are viewed through a patriarchal lens. The sexually harassing behavior that is degrading, demeaning, humiliating, infuriating, and disempowering to women is redefined as a joke, natural male-female behavior, a misinterpretation, or just a bit of fun. It is, therefore, difficult for women to accuse someone of sexual harassment. Accordingly, it was not surprising that none of the athletes in this study complained about their sexual harassment experiences to any authorities, or even to their parents, although some of them had talked to girlfriends about what had happened to them. In her study about sexual harassment and coercion in education, Cairns (1997) was surprised to find a very high frequency and intensity of confusion, self-blame, guilt, and shame by female victims of harassment. She criticized the university community for not having worked to reduce sex-role stereotyping, and not having effective workplace equity programs. Today most universities have such programs and in Norway sexual harassment in educational institutions has just been prohibited by law. Fifteen to 20 years ago when Arja carried out her study this was probably not the case.

"—YOU JUST FIND YOUR PLACE IN THE CULTURE" – THE HARASSING SPORT MILIEU

What, then, characterizes the Norwegian female athletes' sporting milieu? How do they describe it themselves? Many athletes noted on the numerical domination by males, which created a milieu dominated by boys' and men's humor and ways of behaving. As a consequence, the sport environment was dominated by heterosexuality. This was particularly evident in the use of sexist language. In addition, the athletes observed that their sport was not acceptable for girls and women, but many also seemed to take for granted the harassing culture as "that is just the way it is" (Fasting, Brackenridge, & Walseth, 2002). Similar to other studies (Cense and Brackenridge, 2001; Robinson, 1998), alcohol was often a precursor for sexual harassment and was often related to parties. The sport milieu was often small with a dominant, powerful coach.

As mentioned before, there is a lack of research concerning sexual harassment and abuse at sport science institutions. However, in her study of women in medical professions Nicholson (1997) shows how women as a group have almost no influence on either the structure or the culture of medical practice. She writes that the medical culture exists in "a toxic organizational context" (p. 35) where sexual harassment and discrimination are accepted. According to her "they are taken for granted as part of the culture of medical school and the professional clinical experience" (p. 35). One may wonder whether women in sport science also become socialized into such a culture. Did we women silently accept the sexually harassing behavior in the audience when we, in the audience, listened to the critical questions that Arja received, without reacting?

CONCLUSIONS

The studies I discuss here demonstrate clearly that the structural and material conditions of an organization contribute in the experience of sexual harassment. The parallels between sport organizations and sport science institutions seem obvious, primarily because of the domination of males combined with a hierarchical structure. Some such conditions were described and documented by Arja Laitinen in her presentation. These conditions, however, can be addressed. For example, the gender distribution of organizations as well as of academic institutions can be changed by the use of targets, quotas, minima, rule changes, cochairing, and a host of other mechanisms. Changing the organizational culture of sport, the sport science departments, and sport institutions is a more difficult challenge, but can nevertheless be addressed through shadowing, mentoring, educational work, and the use of sanctions for poor practice and rewards for good practice.

If sexual harassment in sport organizations and sport science institutions is ever to be reduced or abolished then a range of interventions and strategies is needed, both at structural and cultural levels. Research can assist in this task by describing the different milieus and by establishing how individuals respond to them. There also needs to be the political will from those in positions of authority to bring about cultural change. However, without collective political action from women in sport and sport academia the scope for effective resistance does not materialize. In this sense, Arja Laitinen was a brave individual voice of resistance. Now 15 years later I realize that we, as an audience, were not politicized enough to act right there and then after Arja's talk and we didn't manage either in the auditorium or after her speech to take any action to help her. However, we could look upon her as our role model for a more collective use of agency in sport sciences.

It should be clear from the overview of the research on sexual harassment in sport, that more knowledge is needed. There are many rumors and few facts based on research in this area. We don't, for example, have any research on sexual harassment within sport science institutions from the perspectives of the female students or female staff. What about the departments of physical education or kinesiology and the culture of the sport sciences? Do they represent a gender harassing culture? And what about the flirting and seductive professor? Does he also exist in our field? These are important questions that should be answered through future research. It is important to develop more knowledge so that both sport organizations and academic sport institutions can be safer places for women. Only then can women fulfill their potentials and perform optimally, either as athletes or as scientists.

NOTE

1. One of the reasons that I accepted the invitation was the encouragement I got from my friend and expert in this area, Celia Brackenridge from UK. We are still working together in publishing the data from this research project (Brackenridge & Fasting, 2002; Fasting, Brackenridge, & Walseth, 2002; Fasting, Brackenridge, & Sundgot-Borgen, 2003).

REFERENCES

ASAHI (www.asahi.com 7.11.02).

Bem, S. (1993). *The lenses of gender, transforming the debate on sexual inequality.* New Haven: Yale University Press.

Brackenridge, C. H. (1997). He owned me basically. Women's experience of sexual abuse in sport. *International Review for the Sociology of Sport,* 32, 115–130.

Brackenridge, C. H. (2001). *Spoilsports, understanding and preventing sexual exploitation in sports.* London: Routledge.

Cairns, K. V. (1997). 'Femininity' and women's silence in response to sexual harassment and coercion. In A. M. Thomas & C. Kitzinger, (Eds.), *Sexual harassment: Contemporary feminist perspectives* (pp. 91–113). Buckingham: Open University Press.

Cense, M. & Brackenridge, C. H. (2001). Temporal and developmental risk factors for sexual harassment and abuse in sport. *European Physical Education Review,* 7, 61–80.

Fasting, K., Brackenridge, C. H., & Sundgot-Borgen, J. (2000*). The Norwegian women project. Females, elite sports and sexual harassment.* Oslo: The Norwegian Olympic Committee and Confederation of Sports.

Fasting, K., Brackenridge, C. H., & Walseth, K. (2000, July). Sexual harassment in and outside sport. Forms of sexual harassment experienced by female athletes and non-athletes. Paper presented at the *XXVII International Congress of Psychology,* July 24–28, 2000, Stockholm Sweden.

Fasting, K., Brackenridge, C. H., & Walseth, K. (2002). Coping with sexual harassment. *The Journal of Sexual Aggression,* 8, 37–49.

Fasting, K., Brackenridge, C. H., & Sundgot-Borgen, J. (in press). The experiences of sexual harassment and abuse amongst Norwegian elite female athletes and non-athletes. *Research Quarterly for Sport and Exercise.*

Fasting, K. Brackenridge, C., & Walseth. K. (2002, July) ". . . you just find your place in the culture:" Sport milieu and women athletes' experiences of sexual harassment. Paper presented to a *Symposium of the International Sport Sociology Association the International Sociology Association Congress,* Brisbane.

Finkelhor, D. (1986). *A Sourcebook on child sexual abuse.* London: Sage.

Fitzgerald, L. F. (1993). Sexual harassment. Violence against women in the workplace. *American Psychologist,* 48 (10), 1070–1076.

Fitzgerald, L. F., Swan, S., & Magley, V. J. (1997). But was it really sexual harassment?: Legal, behavioral, and psychological definitions of the workplace victimization of women. In O'Donohue (Ed.), *Sexual harassment. Theory, research, and treatment* (pp. 6–29). Boston: Allyn and Bacon.

Garlick, R. (1994). Male and female responses to ambiguous instructor behaviors. *Sex Roles,* 30, 135–158.

Gutek, B. A. (1985). *Sex and the workplace.* San Francisco: Jossey-Bass.

Gutek, B. A. & Koss, M. P. (1993). Changed women and changed organizations: Consequences of and coping with sexual harassment. *Journal of Vocational Behaviour,* 42, 28–48.

Grauerholz, E. (1996). Sexual harassment in the academy: The case of women professors. In M. S. Stockdale, (Ed.), *Sexual harassment in workplace. Perspectives, frontiers and response strategies* (pp. 29–51). Thousand Oaks, CA: Sage.

Hearn, J. & Parkin, W. (2001). *Gender, sexuality and violence in organizations.* London: Sage.

Holman, J. M. (1995). *Female and male athletes' accounts and meanings of sexual harassment in Canadian interuniversity athletics.* A Dissertation submitted to Michigan State University in partial fulfilment of the requirements for the degree of Doctor of Philosophy.

Hotelling, K. & Zuber, B. A. (1997). Feminist issues in sexual harassment. In O'Donohue (Ed.), Sexual harassment. Theory, research, and treatment (pp. 99–112). Boston: Allyn and Bacon.

Kirby, S. & Greaves, L. (1996, July). Foul play: sexual harassment in sport. Paper presented at the *Pre-Olympic Scientific Congress,* Dallas, TX.

Kirby, S. & Greaves, L., & Hankivsky, O. (2000). *The dome of silence. Sexual harassment and abuse in sport.* Halifax: Fernwood.

Koss, M. P. (1991). Changed Lives. The psychological impact of sexual harassment. In M. A. Paludi (Ed.), *Ivory power, sexual harassment on campus* (pp. 73–92). Albany, NY: State University of New York Press.

Leahy, T., Pretty, G., & Tenenbaum, G. (2002). Prevalence of sexual abuse in organised competitive sport in Australia. *The Journal of Sexual Aggression,* 8, 16–37.

Larkin, J. (1991). Sexual harassment: From the personal to the political. *Atlantis,* 17 *(1),* 106.

Laitinen, A. (1991). On movement culture by and for women: A Process-oriented approach to research. *Proceedings of the Jyväskylä Congress on Movement and Sport in Women's Lives,* August 17–21, 1987. The Press of the University of Jyväskylä,Vol 1, 208–228.

Massao, P. (2001). *Women in sport: The feminist analysis of the sport development policy of Tanzania.* Unpublished Master Thesis, The Norwegian University of Sport and Physical Education. Oslo: Norway.

Netherlands Olympic Committee. Netherlands Sports Federation (1997). *Sexual harassment in sport. Code of conduct.* Arnheim: The Netherlands.

Nicholson, P. (1997). Gender inequality, sexual harassment and toxic organization: The case of medical women. In A. M. Thomas & C. Kitzinger (Eds.), *Sexual Harassment. Contemporary Feminist Perspectives* (pp. 32–49). Buckingham: Open University Press.

Paludi, M. A. (1998). *The psychology of women.* NJ: Prentice Hall. Quina, K. (1991). The Victimization of Women. In M. A. Paludi (Ed.), *Ivory power, sexual harassment on campus* (pp. 93–101). Albany, NY: State University of New York Press.

Robinson, L. (1998). *Crossing the line: Sexual harassment and abuse in Canada's national sport.* Toronto: McClelland and Stewart.

Stockdale, M. S. (1996). *Sexual harassment in the workplace: Perspectives, frontiers, and response strategies.* Thousand Oaks, CA: Sage.

Till, F. J. (1980). *Sexual harassment: A report on the sexual harassment of students.* Washington, DC: Government Printing Office.

Toftegård, Nielsen, J. (1998). *"The Forbidden Zone" About intimacy, sexual relations and misconduct in the relationship between coaches and athletes.* Unpublished Master Thesis, Department of Sport: University of Copenhagen.

Women's Sports Foundation (1994). *Prevention of sexual harassment in athletic settings: An educational resource kit for athletic administrators.* New York: Women's Sport Foundation

UNIFEM (United Nations Development Fund for Women). *The Trustfund in support of action to eliminate violence against women.* Internet 2001. http://www.unifem.undp.org/trustfund.

PART III

The Feminist Sport Researcher:
Multiple Selves

Chapter 8

Time Out—Managing Research and Managing Myself

Celia Brackenridge

Everyone knows that academics can become rather passionate about frog warts, the techniques of Mayan architecture, or whether Bacon actually wrote some of Shakespeare's sonnets. Yet the potential for emotional upheaval and personal attack is much greater in the field of violence against women. Researchers must learn how to control or channel their own emotions. Particularly if they are women, they are sure to be challenged, attacked, ridiculed, sexualised, or accused of being lesbian (as if this is relevant) at the same time that they are literally mad with frustration at the events they are studying.

—(Schwartz, 1997: x)

My acquaintance with Arja Laitinen was fleeting, at the 1987 International Congress of Movement and Sport in Women's Life in Finland, but she impressed me deeply as a committed, caring, and able woman working in a chilly—some might even say hostile—male environment. She had the courage to speak out against their discrimination and was taken to task after the conference for having done so. As someone who suffered professional and personal pain but faced both of these with stern resolve, she was a model to the rest of us.

149

In this chapter I take a metaphorical "time out" to turn to a personal, reflexive account of my research on sexual exploitation in sport in order to illustrate some of the power relations involved. In doing this, I hope to expose some of the subjectivities that characterize the research process and, perhaps, to challenge any lingering view that this research is based on or in objectivity. I examine different ways of managing the research role. In so doing, I offer some personal evaluations of the challenges faced during my previous investigative research on sexual abuse in sport (Brackenridge, 1986, 1987, 1991, 1997a and b, 1998a). During my 15 years working on this "sensitive topic" (Raymond Lee, 1993) I have compiled an intermittent research diary and a continuous archive of written correspondence and other material. These texts now constitute a case study of the ways in which an individual researcher can both act upon and be manipulated by the broader social and political systems within sport. They not only trace my journey as an advocate of harassment-free sport but also record the stumbling blocks, changes of direction, and major breakthroughs in my intellectual journey toward a better understanding of sexual exploitation in sport. My archives comprise material from several different countries but are predominantly British so most of my reflections are set within this cultural context.

Many researchers have worked in dangerous or sensitive settings for years and have developed their own ways of handling personal conflicts, pain, or emotional burdens (Kelly, 1988; Sugden, 1995; Stanko, 1997). I do not claim that my research is necessarily distinctive in this regard nor do I claim any special expertise. The primary purpose of this chapter is simply to reflect on the subjectivity of a lesbian engaged in a gendered research process. In particular, I will use my own research experience to explore strategies for personal survival as an investigator and to propose a framework for self-management, which I hope other researchers might also find helpful.

The chapter begins by examining the reasons why I have come to adopt a reflexive approach at this juncture and how this relates to the wider reflexive project in the social sciences (Richardson, 1990; Sparkes, 1995; Fine, 1998). I discuss how I have (or have not) situated myself in my various writings on sexual abuse in sport. I also examine the question of "othering" and where and how my research participants have been situated in the work. The major part of the chapter interrogates the idea of "managing myself" using three different meanings of the term, each incorporating the subjectivity of a lesbian engaged in a gendered research process. The first meaning, managing myself, addresses how I have coped with the strains and stresses of the research. The second meaning, managing (by) myself, explores my sense of being alone in the research. Finally, managing my self or selves, explores which of several possible selves or agendas—the personal, the scientific, or the political—I am addressing at any given time. The chapter concludes with a review of how I have attempted to maintain focus as a researcher in the face of internal doubts and external pressures.

SITUATING MYSELF AND OTHERS

Reflexivity is becoming an increasingly important research skill: it helps the researcher to locate herself within the power dynamics of the research relationships (such as researcher/researched or researcher/funder). Pearsall (1998, p. 1559) defines reflexive thus " . . . (of a method or theory in the social sciences) taking account of itself or of the effect of the personality or presence of the researcher on what is being investigated." There is a long and respected tradition in social science (Becker, 1967), and in feminist social science in particular (Oakley, 1981; Finch, 1984; Hagan, 1986), of examining questions of allegiance and reciprocity. One purpose of this chapter is to recognize the reciprocal effects of the research process on me, the investigator, and on my participants, of researching those who have experienced sexual abuse in sport. In adopting such an approach I am, however, conscious that it does not meet with the approval of certain members of the academy and that, in some fields of study, it has been met with downright skepticism. Indeed, Okely (1992) explores how criticisms of reflexivity as narcissistic confuse self-adoration with self-awareness. There is certainly a danger that, in attempting to situate oneself within research writing, the individual writer somehow, falsely, stakes a claim over territory that has been collectively trod for years by others. The individual approach of autobiographical writing could also be argued to sit uneasily with the collectivist commitment of some feminisms while at the same time giving expression to the imperative that the "personal is political."

Coming to terms with an autobiographical approach within the sociology of sport is particularly difficult for those, like myself, with positivist origins. The sociology of sport, like any other branch of the parent discipline, is currently experiencing poststructuralist challenges to the conventions of its various traditional perspectives, whether functionalist, symbolic interactionist, critical, or feminist. Both Sage (1997) and Dunning (1998) have expressed the view that, within the highly practical world of sport, the postmodern tendency to deconstruction seems to pose even greater threats than elsewhere. For example, the theoretical deconstruction of gender brought about by queer theorists (Butler, 1990) and some radical feminists seems to present an almost impossible practical dilemma for an institution that has been built on sex segregation. I consider that, whereas in the 1970s the practice of sport was only weakly aligned with theory, in terms of scientific understanding and social explanation, social theory is now so distant from practice that it is in danger of becoming irrelevant.

Qualitative researchers are nowadays acutely conscious of the issue of representation, giving voice or what Sparkes (1995, p. 160) describes as "How . . . people get written in and out of the account." In my own papers, whether to broadly scientific audiences or to practitioner groups, I have typically adopted a combination of two modes of authorial voice. The first is the disembodied, pseudoscientific, *positivistic authority* where I present "data" "theoretical models" and "explanations" of the "risk factors" and dynamics of sexual abuse in sport (Brackenridge, 1997a; Brackenridge & Kirby, 1997). The second is the voice of *experiential authority*, in which I draw heavily on quotations from research participants to illustrate the social processes and personal consequences of abuse (Brackenridge, 1997b). In both types of representation, I am absent-as-person. But, under the post structuralist critique of such texts, there has to be a view from somewhere (Richardson, 1990, p. 27); there can be no context-free voices. It therefore seems important to acknowledge my own voice within my writing to avoid Geertz's accusation of producing what he calls "author-evacuated texts" (1988 cited in Sparkes 1995, p. 160). As Okely (1992, p. 3) says so succinctly, "Autobiography dismantles the positivist machine." I can hardly press a claim for autobiographical work on sexual abusers and not turn the autobiographical spotlight on my own work.

I am an agent in the research inasmuch as I play a political role, lobby actively for policy change in sport, and try to help my research participants in their struggles to seek support, counseling and/or redress. My interpretations of findings, my own sense of self, and the lives of many of the people who have assisted me in this work have been irrevocably altered by the experience of doing this research. Influences are therefore reciprocal, even if not consciously so.

Part of the reflexive project of modern sociology is to acknowledge the influence of our gender and sexual identities within the research landscape and, in particular, to account for the ways in which personal agendas map onto and shape scientific ones. I am engaged here in a reflexive account of a white, middle-class lesbian engaged in sensitive research about (largely) female oppression in a (largely) male-dominated world. Two stimuli provoked this exercise: the first was a personal legitimation crisis brought about by serial failure with grant applications and the second was a growing sense of burnout from the many reverses that I had experienced since starting work in this field (Brackenridge, 1998c). Confronting all this led me to articulate the previously taken-for-granted rationale for my research and to recognize more clearly the social, political, and historical contingency of the work.

My own sexuality was constructed and realized largely through my personal and professional involvement in sports. It guides my epistemological decisions—what I regard as problematic and why, how I decide to investigate particular issues, how and where I choose to present my work, and how I value myself as a researcher and as a person. It took me (too) many years to realize this and to begin to see that, not only is scientific knowledge socially constructed but it is also highly personal: what I know, then, shapes who I am just as who I am shapes what I know.

In trying to position myself within the power relations of the research, I recognize that I am more powerful than my research participants yet less powerful than the agencies that I am trying to influence. There is, of course, a danger of attempting to become "more reflexive than thou" (Marks, 1993, p. 149) and becoming trapped inside a circular reflexivity. Nonetheless, I have found it helpful to adopt reflexiveness as a coping strategy. Marks (1993, p. 140) suggests:

> The attempt to encourage reflection and to instigate change in practices represent(s) the clash between (post-modern) concerns to construct systems of meaning as contingent, positioned and partial with (modern) liberatory concerns to challenge social inequalities.

I feel caught up in this clash. However, I suggest that the shift of emphasis from modern analysis of "inequality" to postmodern analysis of "difference" has barely impinged on the lived reality of male violence against women and children, violence that finds particular legitimation in sport. I consider that political challenges to this violence may well be impeded by undue emphasis on relativism.

In the discourses of sexual abuse in sport, "othering" is frequently encountered as a mechanism for: assuaging guilt ("it's not my fault it's *theirs*"); denying responsibility ("it's not my problem, it's *theirs*"); and claiming innocence ("we must keep *them* out of *our* sport"). As Kelly et al. (1995) point out, there is also the possibility that the language used to describe sexual abuse (instead of sexual exploitation) and sexual abusers (as paedophiles) exacerbates this tendency to other, since both abuse and paedophile are such emotionally charged terms and because they play upon fears of stranger danger.

Richardson (1990, p. 65) sees writing as a site of moral responsibility, saying "How and for whom we write lives matters." I have tried to use my "skills and privileges . . . [to] . . . give voice to those whose narratives have been excluded from the public domain and civic discourse." (Richardson, 1990, p. 28). What Fine describes as the "clean edges" of the narratives presented by me as researcher, in conference papers, journal articles and speeches, contrast starkly with the "frayed borders" (Fine, 1998, p. 136) of the Other, the testimonies of my research participants. However, my interpretations of my participants' accounts can never come close to matching their actual experiences; the experiences they have recounted to me have been lived, then relived, then told by them, then are retold by me. Despite my efforts to observe ethically sensitive protocols, I quote selectively from their words, I frame their concerns and, through my writing, I lobby on their behalves. All this, then, reinforces my view of their (other) worlds. Very few of the participants in my earliest study on sexual exploitation accepted my invitation to comment on written work emanating from their interviews. Most of them wanted to exit the research scene and to reclaim anonymity. My concerns about (mis)representing and othering them remain especially acute.

This concern about othering the survivors of sexual harassment and abuse in sport is compounded by the realization that I am certainly distorting the experiences of those who agree to be interviewed and even, perhaps, making their lives more miserable than they are already. It is difficult *not* to become cast, or indeed to cast oneself, as a kind of modern-day moral crusader or what Becker (1963, pp. 147–148) called a *moral entrepreneur* and, in the process, to lay claim to the emotional and political territory of my research participants. Fine reminds us that it is not good enough simply to write about those who have been othered. Instead, echoing Richardson's call for a practical ethics, she argues that we should ". . . engage in the social struggles with those who have been exploited and subjugated . . ." (Fine, 1998, p. 135) "unpacking the notions of scientific neutrality, universal truths and researcher dispassion" (Fine, 1998, p. 131). There is, then, a moral imperative that suggests that detachment should not lead to indifference. Below, I discuss how I have engaged in such struggles and the methods of self-management that this engagement has required.

MANAGING MYSELF

Managing my data, emergent theories, the various stakeholders in the research and, especially, the lives and preoccupations of my research participants, has proved difficult. On reflection, however, I realize that managing myself within the research has been far *more* difficult. Issues of research competence have confronted me throughout: for example, I have been criticized by different research colleagues as being unqualified for undertaking work in this field both because I am a lesbian and because I am not a clinical psychologist! I also made a rule for myself to advise undergraduates *not* to undertake empirical work on this topic with survivors, judging that the potential negative consequences for the survivors of poor research practice were simply too great. Yet I have often supervised student projects on homophobia, racism, and sports violence so why did I impose this exclusion? The ethical ground rules, research methods, and working practices that I adopted during this research have all been affected by processes well beyond conventional social science. As I discuss below, the "plural self" (Rowan & Cooper, 1998) has been a major feature of my research work. There was no easy way to disentangle the competing demands made by the research or, indeed, to find established codes of practice that answered all my own questions about how to proceed.

Managing Myself

Researching sexual abuse in sport has exacted a toll on me as an individual. This is not an uncommon experience for ethnographers and investigative researchers (Sugden, 1995; Lee, 1995) but I have not found it easy to deal with. This is ghetto research in the sense that: it occurs in the sport setting, which is often defined as nonserious and therefore not worth the scrutiny of researchers from its parent discipline; it is feminist in a male-dominated field of study; it is new with almost no context-specific literature; and it is about a sensitive, embarrassing topic. Learning to cope with the ups and downs of the research process is simply part of the job for all of us (Lee, 1995, pp. 12–13) but, for me, the messy conjunction of personal conviction and political resistance in this work has proved, at times, almost intolerable.

Some of the direct traumas or stressors that I have experienced during this research include:

- personal insults and attempted blackmail from a coach;

- a threat of legal action from a sport organization;

- attempted recruitment into causes by my participants;

- hate mail and crank telephone calls following a television appearance;

- media harassment and misrepresentation by journalists wanting access to my data about individuals;

- isolation and ridicule by individuals and agencies about whom I have incriminating "evidence";

- rejection of grant submissions on the grounds that sport research allegedly has nothing new to say about sexual abuse; and,

- withdrawal of access by a major sport organization to an elite athlete sample for fear of what might be uncovered.

Indirect traumas have included the general emotional contagion of listening to and reading about dozens of cases of sexual exploitation and feelings of guilt or blame that I could or should have done more to prevent these. The consequences of such stressors are commonly experienced by other social scientists doing sensitive or dangerous research, especially where they adopt a dual researcher-advocate role. They include: anxiety; insomnia; political frustration and ineffectiveness; funding shortages; lack of primary data; publishing delays or rejection (with papers being judged as either too personal or too positivistic); and personal legitimation crises.

It is tempting for researchers in this area to be drawn into individual cases: sometimes, an aggrieved athlete will ask for direct help in bringing her persecutor to account. However distressing these individual cases may be, the researcher would be advised not to intervene but to refer the athlete to reporting mechanisms in their sport or organization. It is also advisable to have a list of counseling services available in case the individual needs professional help. No researcher should overstep the limits of her professional training or skills by giving counseling or advice that lie outside her competence. I worked with a qualified social worker before commencing my first set of interviews and Palzkill (1994) volunteered to go through therapy herself during her research to help her cope with the rigors of the experience. It is good practice to prepare in this way before embarking on potentially dangerous work where distress may be caused to the researcher and harm to the participants.

In addition to presenting personal challenges this work has also posed interesting and difficult methodological challenges. I have found it necessary to tackle these without a great deal of assistance from conventional research literature. For example, disclosure of "the famous," such as Olympic coaches, was an unanticipated outcome of the research but has burdened me with what Fetterman (1984) calls "guilty knowledge" (Brackenridge, 1997a). I have coped with this by following Sugden's advice "Never tell" (Sugden, 1995, p. 243) and deciding that, *in extremis*, I would rather face contempt of court charges than reveal my data sources.

As with many critical social researchers, I have felt the need to establish my own support systems in order to maintain some sanity and to protect myself at points of particular stress. My feelings have ranged, at different times, through mild annoyance, to anger and helplessness, to virtual paranoia and despair. Some obvious stress-management options available to me have been to stop the research, to change topic, or simply to learn to cope. Neither stopping nor changing topic are realistic options for me since the process of engagement has bound me inextricably to the political and personal struggles of my research participants. Some of them call on me regularly, asking for advice, technical information, referral locations, reporting procedures, and networks. A small number have elected to act as informal reviewers of my work, providing critical comments and ideas. For the most part, however, participants want to be left to get on with their lives. For them, learning to cope has been a long process.

Particularly in the earlier, inductive stages of my research, I found most of the scholarly codes of ethics that I consulted inadequate as sources of support and guidance. I therefore established a protocol that has helped to steer me through many of the ethically problematic situations that have arisen during the work. Following the advice of Miles and Huberman (1994), I set down my research rules, a step-by-step list of procedures that acted as my route map through the difficult terrain of contacting, meeting, interviewing, and attempting to support athletes who have been sexually exploited by their coaches. For me, writing out my research rules was an important coping mechanism. It meant that not only could I break down the work of each contact into manageable chunks, but I could also check that each person involved had been offered the same care (or omissions) within the same ethical boundaries. These rules were listed under a set of headings (see Table 1). They guided me through the sequence of: contacting participants; putting them at ease/gaining credibility; gaining trust/giving control; listening; checking emerging findings; following up and the various stages of data analysis and storage. When I first prepared this protocol I had no idea how helpful it would turn out to be. I now look upon this as a vital aspect of the qualitative research process.

Table 1
Research Rules Adopted for Collecting and Analyzing Unstructured Interviews on Sexual Exploitation in Sport

With Participants		
1 Contacting	a)	Start of the "snowball"—a contact asks the participant if they would be willing to meet me to talk
	b)	If they agree, send them, or give them my contact details (via the intermediary)
	c)	Once they have contacted me, by telephone or letter, arrange a meeting, at a time and place to suit them
	d)	Ask for oral consent to interviews (and later, to tape recording) to avoid participant having to write their name
2 Putting at ease/ gaining credibility	a)	On first meeting, find somewhere quiet and as discreet as possible
	b)	Begin by introducing myself, thanking them for coming, saying who I am, briefly sketching my background as an athlete, coach, lecturer, and researcher
	c)	Say what I am researching and why
	d)	Guarantee confidentiality and say that the raw material gathered will be stored in a location known only to myself
3 Gaining trust/ giving control	a)	Check if they're still happy to talk: say they can control the pace and content of the interview or leave if they wish . . .
	b)	. . . or contact me afterward to add/delete/change anything

(continued)

Table 1 (*continued*)
Research Rules Adopted for Collecting and Analyzing
Unstructured Interviews on Sexual Exploitation in Sport

With Participants (*continued*)

4 Listening	a) Invite them to "Tell me your story" b) Prompt on particular issues, if necessary (early interviews were unstructured: thereafter a semistructured schedule was used) c) Always end by asking "What would you like to see done?"
5 Checking emerging findings	a) (For the later interviews) Show the merging models and risk findings factors and ask for feedback on whether and how these fit their own experience b) Thank them, exchange any contact details not already known: offer to meet and/or talk and/or write again c) (For the early interviews) Take full notes if possible during the interview, with verbatim quotes on key points. (No tape recorder used to ensure trust and avoid scaring participant) d) (For the subsequent interviews) Tape record complete interview
6 Follow up	a) Write soon afterward to thank them b) Complete *pro forma* with descriptive details of the participant, their age and sex, age and sex of abuser, age at time of abuse, date and method of my first contact and subsequent contacts, whether parents knew of the abuse, whether and to whom the abuse had been reported, and any official consequences (legal charges, internal disciplinary enquiry, etc.) c) If participants wish, correspond afterward (some even exchanged comments/copies of my academic papers) d) If participants wish, send them details of counseling agencies and/or reporting procedures and/or NCF Codes of Ethics/ Practice and encourage them to use these e) Never get involved in reporting on behalf of a participant

With Data

7 Writing up	a) Write up notes, statement by statement on separate lines. Use upper case for my words and lower case for theirs/direct quotes b) Code each statement numerically: D (Direct case) N (number) /n (number of statement) Thus, D3/23 = third direct case interview, twenty-third statement c) Acknowledge the influence of my own verbal and nonverbal behavior on the interview, and of my "editorial" work d) Store the notes/tape and add any subsequent material, notes, or correspondence to the raw data case file e) Prepare an anonymized transcript (changing names, place names, dates, sport names, and any potential identifying features such as sport techniques or coaching jargon) f) Keep Research Diary to detail the research process and personal feelings about the work

(continued)

Table 1 (*continued*)
Research Rules Adopted for Collecting and Analyzing
Unstructured Interviews on Sexual Exploitation in Sport

With Data (*continued*)

---

8 Analysis	a) Read and reread all transcripts and case notes several times
	b) Brainstorm possible major codes
	c) List codes and subcodes as systematically as possible and number each one
	d) Go through each anonymized transcript line by line, coding each statement in the margin. (Avoid allocating more than one code unless absolutely necessary)
	e) Iterate between the list of codes and the transcript statements/meaning units until satisfied that the codes are distinct and accurate
	f) Prepare a matrix of participant numbers against major codes: allocate every number into each code to reveal gaps and clusters
	g) Open separate computer files for each code and allocate every statement to the appropriate code
	h) In the case of Code 2 (victim) and 3 (coach) there was so much data that subcodes were allocated
	i) Check the whole pattern of data against the emerging theoretical models to examine gaps, contradictions, and uncertainties
9 Storage	a) File all original material, case by case with a summary catalogue at the front recording basic descriptive details (age, sex, etc.)
	b) Compile one catalogue for Direct cases (from face-to-face interviews) and one for Indirect cases (from media, correspondence, and books)
	c) Include in the Direct case catalogue all letters, notes from meetings, and supplementary data plus the pro forma with basic information
	d) Include in the Indirect case catalogue detail of sources, press clippings, page references, etc., about each case
	e) Lock all files away in a location completely separate from other research material and keep this location secret. (Once data have been anonymized, papers may be kept in the public domain)
	b) Keep chronological Archive of all correspondence with other academics and interested parties, notes on telephone calls, press comments, papers from agencies, etc.

Research of this type is unpopular with sport organizations because it reveals a side of sport that is often denied or ignored. Cooperation from such organizations is therefore difficult to secure. Each researcher will find her own form of access to these agencies but, for the sake of those who follow, precise details of methods should always be written up and made public.

Managing (by) Myself

One of the major causes of the stress in this research has been the lack of collaborators with whom to share ideas, successes, and failures. Until the late 1990s, I had to manage almost entirely by myself because this was a relatively new subject of research in sport. Very few colleagues chose to engage with the subject, and researchers from the parent disciplines of sociology and psychology either failed to respond to my approaches for help or defined sport as insufficiently serious to merit their academic attention. For reasons of confidentiality, and the sanctity of my personal relationships, I decided long ago that my own significant others should not be burdened with my research concerns. Finding others to share with took many years. There is now, at last, an active international network of researcher-advocates in this field with whom I can exchange both technical and personal concerns.

As described above, research participants in this work have represented a considerable drain on my personal resources: they have often turned to me—but to whom could I turn? Even though I have not been using ethnography in the anthropological sense (Clifford, 1988), I have experienced similar feelings of aloneness in the field (Clarke, 1975 cited by Punch, 1998) and burnout (Horwitz, 1998). Adopting the research rules referred to earlier helped me, I believe, to maintain the necessary and genuine empathy with my research participants, while simultaneously establishing sufficient psychological distance to allow me to function as a researcher. This boundary issue has been addressed by other feminist researchers (Finch, 1984; Oakley, 1981) who have celebrated the subjectivity of feminist research *with*, rather than *on*, women.

Fine (1998, p. 152) suggests that "Those of us who do this work need to invent communities of friendly critical informants who can help us think through whose voices and analyses to front, and whose to foreground." I have adopted other self-protection methods such as keeping an intermittent research diary, seeking counseling and debriefing opportunities (discussed below), and establishing a network of allies. Research is a shared experience: without the willing cooperation and continuous support and feedback from athletes, their families, and friends, and of one particular journalist, it would not have been possible for me to sustain the necessary effort to keep my work going. All of this contributed to what Rutter (1987) calls "building resilience."

Managing My Self/Selves

A second protocol, adopted mainly for my own survival and sanity, arose from two days of intensive discussion with an informed adviser/friend. During a period of particularly intensive pressure to divulge sources, names and data to the media, I felt the need to share my excitement, concerns and frustrations about this research. I could not do this in my usual personal circles, for obvious ethical reasons. I also felt that I needed to confide in someone beyond my immediate circle of close professional colleagues. I therefore approached someone who had known me for many years and who had a wide range of facilitation skills. She agreed to work with me, in the role of counselor, on an as-needs basis. Our first meeting began with several tortuous hours, attempting to map the emotional and methodological spaces of the research. At her suggestion, I tried to separate my approach to the work into three different missions—the personal, the political, and the scientific—each with its own written aims and objectives. This led me to recognize that I was driven by overlapping personal, political, and scientific motivations and that it was not always easy to see which I was privileging at any given time.

PERSONAL SELF

Gill Valentine (1998) has described eloquently, but terrifyingly, how a systematic campaign of anonymous, homophobic hate mail undermined her own, previously "unhyphenated, asexual academic identity with a sexual signifier" (Valentine, 1998, p. 307). Reading her account of the exclusionary discourses she experienced in her own subject (geography) made me reexamine my own positionality within sport and leisure studies and within my relations with my research participants. For example, whereas my status as "out" lesbian is well-known within my professional community, I never mentioned it in interviews, meetings, or correspondence with my research participants. Why? It is certainly not of concern to me in other contexts. But, in making a conscious decision to lay out my credentials as a former athlete, coach, and researcher and *not* to mention my status as feminist, lesbian, or activist, I have steered a particular path through the space that lies between interviewer and interviewee. I do not know whether the responses I elicited would have been any different had my sexuality been declared. I have exercised self-censure on my sexual identity (is this auto-homophobia?) for fear that interviewees might, as many others do, conflate (homo)sexual identity with sexual perversion and, as a result, choose to retreat from the interview. My judgment, then, was that disclosure of my lesbian identity might have affected the willingness of the participants to engage with the research. In retrospect I realize that I denied them an opportunity to make such a judgment for themselves.

POLITICAL SELF

At the same time as struggling to address these discourses within the worlds of research and policy, I have been making ever-widening connections with the world of practice and advocacy, through delivering presentations, seminars, and training workshops on sexual abuse and athlete protection. My office has become a *de facto* clearing house for advice, referral, or information, because there is, as yet, no official conduit for such inquiries. Another level of engagement in this research has been, of course, with athletes themselves and, occasionally, with their parents or close friends. I have given dozens of newspaper and radio interviews, written many short articles for magazines or newsletters, and appeared in television documentary programs in England, Australia, and Denmark. All this has been done because of my determination to bring the issue of sexual abuse in sport to wider public attention in the hope of stimulating policy development and implementation from the major sport agencies in Britain and beyond.

The quick response, sound-bite approach of most journalists rests very uneasily with the requirements of painstaking research. I have had to adopt my own personal guidelines to avoid being pushed too hard into "naming and shaming." I do not divulge names or other identifying features of athletes or their coaches; I do not even name their sports yet, since the evidence base about differences between sports is so limited. At the same time, I weigh the benefits of media coverage (reaching a wider audience, encouraging athletes to come forward and talk, perhaps giving athletes or their parents the confidence to seek help from someone else) against the disadvantages of ill-informed, exaggerated coverage. In all my political activity, self-surveillance-as-lesbian is ongoing. Will my work be discredited as the rantings of a man-hater? Will I be rejected by informants who judge me to be hijacking their misery to pursue my own feminist goals? How should I dress to meet interviewees? How do I answer questions about female sexual abusers in sport? How do I prevent the constant confusion of (homo)sexuality and sexual predation? Herein lies food for further thought and research.

SCIENTIFIC SELF

When in doubt about which "self" is at work I remember the advice of my counsellor/friend "Keep going back to your desk." In other words, unless the scientific work is good, the political and personal missions can never be realized. But this exhortation implies a) that there is only one science and b) that the scientific self is somehow privileged over the other selves. Feminist, more especially poststructural/feminist, critiques of traditional science have destabilized conceptions of "good science" (Barrett & Phillips, 1992). Under these kinds of descriptions the concept of truth is problematized. Although theory development is my scientific ambition, the kind of work I do meets very few of the criteria for conventional/malestream social science (Spender, 1981; Brackenridge, 1995a) yet it also fails to engage substantially with the politics of difference. I have chosen, in the main, to adopt the relative safety of social-psychological language and methods because I judge that this is "where sport is" (Brackenridge, 1998b) and this kind of science is most likely to effect leverage and bring about change in practice. However, in making such a choice, and as I waver between positivism and varieties of feminism (Renzetti, 1997), I risk satisfying neither structuralists nor poststructuralists.

Part of my scientific self is my self-as-teacher. The pedagogical and the emotional can easily become tangled when teaching about sexual exploitation. Stanko (1997) describes vividly how teaching students about sexual abuse, for example, challenges her own emotional resources as they bring into the public domain their own experiences, frightened silences, and angry denials. As one of the world's leading researchers on sexual violence to women for almost three decades, she gives the following advice to lecturers and research supervisors (Stanko, 1997, pp. 84–85):

1. share your personal emotions;
2. anticipate the need for providing emotional support to fellow researchers, and especially to students;
3. be prepared to be baited.

The articulation of my different selves with their different missions has proved enormously helpful in unscrambling problems with the research. Feminists have long claimed that the "personal is political" and consequently have striven to avoid depoliticizing debates about individual and organizational power. Despite this, I justify my conceptual separation of selves as both a device to help clarify my motives and as a framework to help guide my research strategy.

MAINTAINING FOCUS

During the course of my intellectual journey I have come to face several crises, some of representation (of others) and others of legitimation (of self-as-researcher). My greatest challenge in learning to manage myself has been how to maintain focus in the face of internal doubts and external pressures. The exhortation to keep going back to my desk, that is to do good science, is a very important voice in my head when I am being pulled one way by the power of the media and another by the selfishness of personal ambition. It also helps me to focus on what I call my "long game" by which I mean the investment in the painstaking accumulation of evidence and the tortuous process of theory development. In this respect, at least, my research ambitions—to predict and then to control—are shared with those of many other traditional social scientists. Yet I am constantly faced by questions about what might distort my data or make the work "bad science." For example: only volunteers come forward; they reproduce (possibly false) memories; they have vested interests; theirs is only one side of the story; I cannot verify what I am told; I rarely meet athletes who have dropped out of sport because of the abuse; those who survive, stay in sport and choose to speak out may be atypical or unusually strong. I have also realized very late in the research that my silence on matters of sexuality must have influenced the research process and that it certainly has influenced the (hostile) reception of my work in certain quarters of both the practical and academic sport domains.

CONCLUSION

My research work on sexual abuse in sport has developed largely through feminist perspectives but with strong clinical undertones. It uses a mix of both theoretical approaches and research methods. Whether this work is "biologically determinist" or "culturally determinist" is for others to judge. I prefer Mary Midgley's (1978) position, which is that "No set of causes alone can be 'fully determining.' That, surely, is the weakness of all forms of hyphenated determinism—economic, social, physical or, indeed, genetic" (pp. 63–64). My main concern is that my work should pass the test of scientific rigor in order meet the needs of political action.

In this chapter I have used my personal experience of researching sexual abuse in sport to explore strategies for personal survival as an investigator. Acknowledgment of the interrelationship of researcher and researched, a part of the reflexive project in sociology, is a step toward positioning myself as researcher. In the process, I have "discovered" evidence of missing dimensions in the research, notably those concerning my own sexuality and the sexual politics of investigative social science. It might be argued that another missing dimension is that of female-to-female oppression. My response to this is that, while it should certainly be added to the list of under-researched issues, and contextualized very broadly within debates about homophobia and gender politics, it is neither a statistical nor political priority.

The framework of self-management—coping with stress, coping with being alone, and privileging the personal, political, or scientific self—is, of course, an artificial one. As someone once said, reality just *is* messy: my "selves," of course, are in constant dialogue, seeking consensus through conflict. For me the personal *is* still political. Nonetheless, there have been moments when this framework has helped me to practice mental hygiene and to survive as an investigator simply by offering a set of optional routes toward the same destination.

ACKNOWLEDGMENTS

This chapter is adapted, by permission, from C. Brackenridge, 2001, *Spoilsports*, Routledge, 281–309.

REFERENCES

Barrett, M., & Phillips, A. (1992). *Destabilising Theory: Contemporary Feminist Debates*. Cambridge: Polity Press.
Becker, H. (1963). *Outsiders*. New York: Free Press.

Becker, H. (1967). 'Whose side are we on?'. *Social Problems*, 14, 239–247.

Brackenridge, C. H. (1986, December). Problem? What problem? Thoughts on professional code of practice for coaches. Paper presented to the Annual Conference of the British Association of National Coaches. Bristol, England.

Brackenridge, C. H. (1987). Ethical problems in women's sport. *Coaching Focus*, Summer, 6, 5–7.

Brackenridge, C. H. (1991). Cross-gender coaching relationships: Myth, drama or crisis? *Coaching Focus*, Spring, 16, 12–147.

Brackenridge, C. H. (1995a, March). "It's alright if you marry them afterwards isn't it?" Some thoughts on sport science and the coach-athlete relationship. Keynote address to the Annual Student Conference of the British Association of Sport and Exercise Sciences, Cheltenham and Gloucester College of Higher Education.

Brackenridge, C. H. (1997a). Researching sexual abuse and sexual harassment in sport. In G. Clarke and B. Humberstone (Eds.), *Researching women in sport*. London: Macmillan.

Brackenridge, C. H. (1997b). "He owned me basically": Women's experience of sexual abuse in sport. *International Review for the Sociology of Sport*, 32, 115–130.

Brackenridge, C. H. (1998a). *Child protection in British sport: A position statement*. Cheltenham, UK: Cheltenham and Gloucester College of Higher Education.

Brackenridge, C. H. (1998b). Healthy sport for healthy girls? The role of parents in preventing sexual abuse in sport. *Sport, Education and Society*, 3(2), 59–78.

Brackenridge, C. H. (1998c, July). Casting a shadow: The dynamics and discourses of sexual abuse in sport. Paper presented to The Big Ghetto: Leisure, Gender and Sexuality, Leisure Studies Association International Conference. Leeds Metropolitan University, England.

Brackenridge, C. H. (1999a). In my opinion . . . , *Sports Law Bulletin*, March/April, 2, 2:2.

Brackenridge, C. H. & Kirby, S. (1997). Playing safe? Assessing the risk of sexual abuse to young elite athletes. *International Review for the Sociology of Sport*, 32, 407–418.

Butler, J. (1990). *Gender trouble: Feminism and the subversion of identity*. London: Routledge.

Clifford, J. (1988). *The predicament of culture: Twentieth century ethnography, literature, and art*. London: Harvard University Press.

Dunning, E. (1998, November). Sociology of sport in the balance: Critical reflections on recent and more enduring trends. Paper to the Annual Conference of the North American Society for the Sociology of Sport. Las Vegas, USA.

Fetterman, D. M. (1984). *Ethnography in educational evaluation*. Beverley Hills, CA: Sage.

Finch, J. (1984). "Its great to have someone to talk to": Ethics and politics of interviewing women. In C. Bell & H. Roberts (Eds.), *Social researching: Politics, problems, practice*. London: Routledge.

Fine, M. (1998). Working the hyphen: Reinventing self and other in qualitative research. In N. K. Denzin & Y. S. Lincoln (Eds.), *The landscape of qualitative research: Theories and issues*. London: Sage.

Hagan, T. (1986). Interviewing the downtrodden. In P. D. Ashworth, A. Giorgia, & A. J. J. Konig (Eds.), *Qualitative research in psychology.* Pittsburgh, PA: Duquesne University Press.

Horwitz, M. (1998). Social worker trauma–building resilience in child protection social workers. *Smith College Studies in Social Work*, 68 (3), 363–377.

Kelly, L. (1988). *Surviving sexual violence.* Cambridge: Polity Press.

Kelly, L., Wingfield, R., Burton, S., & Regan, L. (1995). *Splintered lives: Sexual exploitation of children in the context of children's rights and child protection.* Ilford, Essex: Barnado's.

Lee, R. M. (1993). *Doing research on sensitive topics.* London: Sage.

Lee, R. M. (1995). *Dangerous fieldwork.* Qualitative Research Methods Series No. 34. London: Sage.

Marks, D. (1993). Case conference analysis in action research. In E. Burman, & E. I. Parker (Eds.), *Discourse analytic research: Repertoires and readings of texts in action.* London: Routledge.

Midgley, M. (1978). *Beast and man: The roots of human nature.* Brighton: Harvester Press.

Miles, M. B., & Huberman, A. M. (1994). *Qualitative data analysis: An expanded sourcebook,* 2nd Edition. London: Sage.

Oakley, A. (1981). Interviewing women; a contradiction in terms. In H. Roberts (Ed.), *Doing feminist research.* London: Routledge & Kegan Paul.

Okely, J. (1992). Anthropology and autobiography: Participatory experience and embodied knowledge. In J. Okely & H. Callaway (Eds.), *Anthropology and autobiography.* London: Routledge.

Palzkill, B. (1994). Between gym shoes and high heels: The development of a lesbian identity and existence in top class sport. *International Review for the Sociology of Sport*, 25, 221–234.

Pearsall, J. (1998). *The New Oxford dictionary of English,* Oxford: Clarendon Press.

Punch, M. (1998). Politics and ethics in qualitative research. In N. K. Denzin & Y. S. Lincoln (Eds.), *The landscape of qualitative research: Theories and issues.* London: Sage.

Renzetti, C. M. (1997). Confessions of a reformed positivist: Feminist participatory research and good social science. In M. D. Schwartz (Ed.), *Researching sexual violence against women: Methodological and personal perspectives.* London: Sage.

Richardson, L. (1990). *Writing strategies: Reaching diverse audience.* London: Sage.

Rowan, J., & Cooper, M. (1998). *The plural self: Multiplicity in everyday life.* London: Sage.

Rutter, M. (1989). *Sex in the forbidden zone.* Los Angeles, CA: Jeremy Tarcher.

Sage, G. H. (1997). Physical education, sociology, and sociology of sport: Points of intersection. *Sociology of Sport Journal*, 14, 317–339.

Sparkes, A. (1995). Writing people: Reflections on the dual crises of representation and legitimation in qualitative inquiry. *Quest*, 47, 158–195.

Spender, D. (1981). *Men's studies modified: The impact of feminism on the academic disciplines.* London: Pergamon Press.

Stanko, E. (1997). "I second that emotion": Reflections on feminism, emotionality, and research on sexual violence. In M. D. Schwartz (Ed.), *Researching sexual violence against women: Methodological and personal perspective.* London: Sage.

Sugden, J. (1995). Field workers rush in (where ethnographers fear to tread): The perils of ethnography. In A. Tomlinson & S. Fleming (Eds.), *Ethics, sport and leisure: Crises and critiques.* Brighton: CSRC Topic Report 5, Chelsea School Research Centre.

Valentine, G. (1998). "Sticks and stones may break my bones": A personal geography of harassment. *Antipode, 30,* 305–332.

Chapter 9

Sophie—Reconstruction and Deconstruction of a Female Icon

Gertrud Pfister

CAUSE FOR REFLECTION

Although I seldom met Arja, I felt a close attachment to her. I was impressed by her spontaneity, her frankness, her curiosity, and her integrity as well as by the courage she showed in striking out along new paths in academic studies and (women's) politics. She was a feminist who neither raised an admonishing finger nor always thought she knew better, and she explored women's lives together with the women she interviewed. She was proof that the unity of private life, academic research, and political action is not an impossibility.

Her method of biographical research, now carried on by her friends and colleagues in Finland, caused me to reflect on my own identity as an academic and on my own historical studies. After lectures by Arja or in discussions with her, but above all during the work on this article, I was confronted over and over again by questions about the sense and purpose, the methods and motives of my academic work: What does my research have to do with myself and my life? Why and how do I carry out, interpret, and evaluate my research into historical developments? Why am I interested in biographies? What messages are important to me? Inquiring into my own research amounts ultimately to inquiring into my own person; the choice of topics, theoretical approaches, and methods says a great deal about myself and my view of the world.

In my chapter I will attempt to trace the fascination that certain topics and human beings hold for me, to decipher the research process and, finally, to discover my own involvement in and with history and historiography. When I carry out research into events that took place in the distant past or into figures who died long ago, the active exchange with the objects of my curiosity is impossible; nevertheless, there are reciprocities that I would like to describe, taking as my example a biography: the biography of Sophie Eliott-Lynn.

THE BACKGROUND—THE SUBJECT OF WOMEN'S SPORT

My interest in the topic of women and sport began in the 1970s when I was a newly recruited research assistant in the sport history department. While writing a thesis on a topic of ancient history, I discovered that in the literature of sport history women played no more than a marginal role. What I first regarded as a rewarding, hitherto unploughed field of research quickly developed into a vocation. I felt personally affected when women were given no mention at all in the literature or when they were depicted as the "weaker" sex and so I decided to examine more closely the myth of female weakness.

When I then began to look specifically for women in sport history, for aims and contents, attitudes, policies, and evaluations as well as structures and organizations, I found myself confronted again and again with the fact that the "players," those who were involved in one way or another in the development of sport, all seemed to be men. And in the "naïve" phase of sport historiography the description of these men and their achievements were the focus of (his)stories.[2] The more I delved into sport history, the more I felt that I had to take up the challenge of (re)constructing women's roles in sport and combating the innumerable prejudices that existed. I collected material for the (re)construction of women's physical activities,[3] and I searched in particular for women who played an active role in the development of sport and/or expressed their views in debates on sport science or sport politics. Like other scholars of women's studies in the 1970s and 1980s I was taken by the women's movement's slogan "Hidden from History – Discovering Herstory." "Her story" was at that time mostly "compensatory" history; that is, it was a matter of reconstructing the work of notable women in order to fill in the gaps of research in traditional history studies (see, among others, Hausen, 1983). This approach poses the following questions: Which women are missing in historical accounts as well as in popular fan literature, in which the ephemeral glory of today's or yesterday's sports stars is kept alive? What have these women achieved and what effects have their achievements had in the area of sport as well as in society as a whole? I wanted to use the biographies of "notable" women as arguments against the marginalization of women as the "second sex." Women like Sophie, who fought the myth of the "weaker sex" in both words and deeds, seemed like weapons in the struggle against the stereotype of women as silent victims, a symbol of women's potentials, possibilities, and achievements. Through women like Sophie I felt more highly valued and motivated at the same time; she seemed—at least according to the initial information I had about her—to be living proof that women were able to achieve everything they set themselves to do.

At the same time I was well aware that, in answering the above questions, exceptional women would be highlighted—or even "token women"—with the result that the experiences and the (his)stories of the "average" female population remained invisible.[4] Moreover, achievement and success as well as influence and power would be measured according to male standards, along with the demand that women adapt to the male world instead of changes being made in society. The problems of compensatory women's research are also the problems of my biographical studies; and I am aware of this without being able to offer any solutions.

PIONEERS, PILOTS, AND FEMINISTS—THE SUBJECTS OF MY RESEARCH

The "invisibility of women" in sport history referred to above prompted me more than anything else to take up biographical research. I had always loved reading biographies; I was always carried away by the exploits of my heroes and heroines, and in my imagination I filled in all the gaps that had remained in the depictions of their lives.

The 'players,' both male and female, that I encountered during my sport history research aroused my curiosity, too, and enticed me to further research, the results of which could often only be mentioned in a footnote. For about 30 years now I have collected biographical data ranging from full biographies to newspaper articles and pictures, and I archive the material—some of which is the product of long hard research and some of which I have stumbled across by chance—in files that in the meantime almost fill a whole set of bookshelves. Some of the material I have already used in biographical texts; the rest is there waiting for my retirement.

In the preparatory work for this article I searched through my list of publications and was surprised at the number of biographical texts in it. Most of the biographical research I have done was my own free choice; nobody had asked me to write about these individuals and often it was by pure chance that I came upon an interesting person and had the opportunity of finding out more about her life and publishing a biographical text.[5] Thus, the choice of subject says a lot about my interests. Who were the individuals and which were the topics, then, that attracted my attention to such an enormous degree that I devoted a great amount of time and energy to researching and writing about them?

With the exception of a small number of brief texts that I was commissioned to do, all my biographical studies are about women, and this has to do with the main areas of my research; that is, the development and the situation of girls and women in sport, as well as with attitudes and aims that I have already referred to above. My first biographical studies were published in 1980 in the reader "Women and Sport," in which I collected texts written by women on women's sport. At the same time I collected biographical and autobiographical material for a book on "Women and Adventure," which, unfortunately, never materialized. I used some of the material later for my book about female pilots, in which I tried to combine (auto)biographical texts with the history of flying and described the attitudes and actions of the pilots against the background of the social and gender orders.

Although it was never a conscious decision or a plan systematically pursued, when I looked at the list of the biographies that I have written, I discovered that my work concentrated on two types of women: the female adventurer and the 'feminist' sports leader. Among the former were pilots like Marga von Etzdorf, Antonie Straßmann, and Sophie Eliott-Lynn; among the latter were the president of the Fédération Sportive Féminine Internationale, Alice Milliat, as well as the presidents of the International Association for the Physical Education of Girls and Women, Dorothy Ainsworth, Marie-Thérèse Eyquem, and Liselott Diem.[6] But the choice of women as subjects was not only a political decision, it is also explained by my curiosity about the lives of other women in other times and in other cultures and by my fascination for adventure, achievement, and (political) power. For me, the most fascinating life stories were those of women pilots whose eccentricity, technical intelligence, courage, and lust for adventure I admired and who seemed to disprove quite plainly the myth of female weakness. I became aware that it was, and still is, quite impossible for me to confront the "objects" of my scientific desires in a neutral and unemotional way. On the contrary, the individuals whose lives I studied forced their way into my life. They also caused me to reflect on my studies and their theoretical and methodological bases.

In this contribution I wish to describe the construction and deconstruction of "life courses" along with their ambiguities and complexities. In doing so, I intend not to exclude feelings, even if the greatly differing and often ambivalent relationships between me and my research subjects can be neither operationalized, standardized, nor argumentatively explained.

Biographical work is a process, a process that progresses between coincidence and systematic research, without any fixed beginning and with an open ending, and with fluctuating degrees of intensity. In the course of this process I was overtaken by postmodernism and the debates on history studies as narration; the discussions on theories and their significance caused me many a sleepless night. Should I write a novel about Sophie or give up the work on her biography completely? In the end I decided to put my new insight to use in a largely traditional study. As an example of my historical research I have chosen the biography of a woman who in many respects can be looked upon as a role model, who arouses contradiction and criticism and whose tragic failure preempts any idolization.

Sophie was, among other things, an athlete, an author, a pilot, and vice-president of the International Women's Sport Federation (FSFI); and she was looked upon as a feminist (Pfister, 2001b). In the course of her life her maiden name, Peirce-Evans, changed to Eliott-Lynn, to Heath, and finally to Williams. These names were the names of her different husbands and the changes, not unusual among women, did not exactly make the research into Sophie's life any easier. Each new name signaled a new phase of her life. Taking the known fragments of her "life course" as an example, I would like to describe not only my interest and my feelings but also the research process along with the methodological and epistemological problems connected with biographical research.

SOPHIE. PART ONE: THE PIONEER OF FLYING

In my research into the first women pilots I repeatedly came across the "Flying Ladies" from England, the Duchess of Bedford, Lady Bailey, and Lady Heath, who alone because of their titles were given a special role in the popular press. All three of them were excellent pilots.[7] In my book on pioneering female pilots I devoted a chapter to the Duchess of Bedford, not only because she left to posterity a very informative autobiography but also because she had taken the test for her pilot's license when she was over 66 years of age, thus clearly giving the lie to stereotypes of age as well as femininity. I only made brief mentions of Lady Bailey and Lady Heath, the one having flown from London to Cape Town and the other from Cape Town to London—apart from this, I was first unable to discover much else about either of them. What had greatly impressed me, however, was the frequently printed photograph of Sophie Mary Heath on her arrival in England.[8] She was wearing a fur coat and a black, tightly fitting straw hat adorned with a brooch. Smiling, she was swinging one of her long, silk-stockinged legs out of the open cockpit. Everything about her was big and powerful: her body, her features, her teeth. Although Lady Heath did not belong to the close circle of women pilots profiled in my book, I collected every piece of information about her that I could lay my hands on. In the course of my searches, among other places in the bibliographies of the few books published on women pilots, I came across a book coauthored by Lady Heath and Stella Wolfe Murray (Heath & Murray, 1929), which, when I finally managed to get hold of a copy through the university library after months of waiting, not only provided me with information about every single leg of the long-distance flight but also gave me an insight into the early flying career of Sophie Eliott-Lynn, who only became Lady Heath in 1927 on marrying Sir James Heath. My curiosity was aroused and I began a more systematic search for information about Sophie in libraries, archives, and museums. At the same time I got into contact with experts on aviation history. From a myriad of mosaic stones I was finally able to piece together a picture of Sophie, the pilot.

Sophie had discovered her enthusiasm for flying as a passenger on a flight to Prague. (I later learned that she had flown there in her capacity as vice-president of the FSFI.) In the same year she obtained a pilot's license at the London Aeroplane Club—the first woman to do so—and decided to make a career out of flying.

Unfortunately for her, women were barred from piloting passenger airplanes by the regulations of the International Aviation Association, which are reproduced in full in "Woman and Flying," the book she coauthored with Stella Wolfe Murray. This induced Sophie to initiate all kinds of activities, among them being a letter to the International Aviation Association in which she cited herself as the best proof of women's physical and mental health, enumerated her achievements in sport, and offered to have herself physically examined and professionally tested on a regular basis. Finally, she obtained permission to take part in a training course for pilots of passenger planes, and in the summer of 1926 the regulation barring women from flying planes with paying passengers on board was rescinded (Heath & Murray, 1929, pp. 36ff). Sophie was the first woman ever to obtain the so-called "B licence" of the International Commission for Air Navigation. In the meantime, in her personal affairs, she had burned all her bridges and invested all her capital in aviation. During her training she made her living by working as a stunt pilot and giving exhibition flights. In 1928, after her return from South Africa, she was engaged by KLM as a copilot, flying 70,000 miles for the company, she recorded, between Amsterdam and London. As a matter of fact, she did not have to fly all these miles since, after marrying the wealthy Sir James Heath in October 1927, she became the owner of four airplanes and could go about demonstrating to the world the abilities of women pilots. For this she chose a spectacular but not all too dangerous route, which, running as it did over land for most of the way, allowed for the necessary refueling stops. In 1928 she made her famous flight from Cape Town to Croydon (London), an undertaking that took three months and attracted world attention. It was the first flight from an overseas colony to England. She gave a detailed account of her experiences and adventures in her book. In December 1927 she had set sail for South Africa with her husband

and an airplane. Arriving there, she undertook demonstration flights in many towns, gave lectures, and campaigned for the building of airports and the scheduling of regular flights between them. Her long-distance flight itself was a mixture of work and pleasure; besides lots of spare parts, the standard equipment included an evening gown and a tennis racket. And on some of their many stops they would pursue one of their most exciting hobbies—big-game hunting. The story of the flight, whose most thrilling episodes involved a bout of sunstroke and a rifle fired at her plane, cannot be told here. After the flight she sold her plane to Amelia Earhart, the first woman to fly solo across the Atlantic in 1932 (albeit in a different plane).

In 1928 and 1929 Sophie demonstrated her flying skills in many European countries.[9] She tested airplanes, took part in flying demonstrations and competitions, and set new records; for example, two altitude records for light aircraft in 1927. She also regarded as a record the fact that she had flown 1,300 miles around England in a single day, making 79 stops. By her own account she won 143 cups and medals in flying competitions. In 1929 she traveled to the United States, where, as "Britain's Lady Lindy," she was celebrated as one of the best women pilots of the day. Unlike many other women pilots, she took an interest in aviation technology: besides obtaining a license for instrument flights and making herself familiar with navigation techniques (Boase, 1979) she also acquired an aviation mechanic's license from the United States Department of Commerce in 1929—the first woman to do so. She was undoubtedly one of the best women pilots of her day.

There are numerous other records of Sophie's flying activities, which can no longer be put into an accurate chronological order but which all took place in the brief, three-year period of her piloting career. On an Irish stamp, for instance, Sophie is described as the first woman parachutist.[10] Although this may not be true (the first woman to make a parachute jump was Elisa Garnerin in 1814), Sophie no doubt undertook parachute jumps herself. In addition, she performed aerobatics such as looping and she also mastered the art of gliding, which had been invented in Germany in the early 1920s.

She published her ideas and her achievements in numerous publications, among other things in her own column in the magazine "Popular Aviation.[11] Moreover, she gave countless talks and lectures to thousands of listeners. She particularly enjoyed taking passengers for so-called "joyrides" in order to convince them of the advantages of flying.

In August 1929 she had a serious accident while training for a competition in Cleveland, USA. She suffered serious head injuries from which she never managed to recover properly.[12] No further information was to be found about her. Much later I stumbled upon a letter dated 1936 in which she noted that 2,679 flying hours and 76 different types of aircraft were recorded in her logbook (Buffington, 1978, p. 20).

FACTS, REALITY, AND THE PROBLEM OF SOURCES

The nature of the sources with data about Sophie that were available to me at that time raised many questions but gave few answers. Even if one considers that the information was taken from sources dealing with aviation history and thus illuminated her life from only one angle, I was still faced with the fundamental difficulties of biographical research, namely the superficial and one-sided nature of the sources as well as, in general, their limited information value. As a historian I am totally dependent on sources since they determine the contents, the color, and even the brush strokes of my picture. If little information is available, and if this little information is related mainly to Sophie's flying achievements and adventures, then the other aspects of her life and, what is more, her personality remain invisible. Nevertheless, the information about Sophie gleaned from the sources seem, at first glance, to be based on facts; they seem to mirror reality and constitute the truth.[13] In spite of this, I ask myself what "reality" means in connection with Sophie's biography. Is it simply a matter of the quantity and quality of the sources that enables me to depict reality and tell a "real" story about Sophie's life?

Of course, I know that history is not reality, and that a biographical text, even if it is based on numerous primary sources, can never be a picture of "real life." Why is it that the so-called hard facts are not as hard as they seem to be? Why can't I simply collect and present the facts?

I think that most of us would agree that there *are* historical facts and events—like Sophie's participation in the Nottingham Flying Meeting in July 1927 or her obtaining the aviation mechanic's licence in February 1929. There is no need to go into any detail about the different types of facts and realities, which can range from very simple facts to a complex network of facts, influences, processes, and structures. That Sophie boarded a plane on May 18, 1927, together with another famous pilot, Lady Mary Bailey, as a passenger is a fact, but the significance of this action can only be understood if one takes into consideration a combination of many other facts. Boarding the plane was the beginning of a flight in which Sophie set a new altitude record for light airplanes, and this is a far more complex reality; it was organized on the basis of a great number and variety of complicated rules and regulations. And the significance, aims, opportunities, and dangers connected with flying an airplane at that time, especially as a woman, can only be understood if one takes many other different social, economic, and political factors into account. The technical specifications of the plane as well as the commercial interests of the aircraft industry have to be considered, just as much as the safety regulations, which had been introduced for women, as they had been in other occupations.

Further, in order to sense the importance and the meaning of this record for Sophie, one has to know a lot about her personality and her biography. Sophie seems to have collected records like other people stamps; she seems to have been addicted to them, as it were. As already mentioned in a letter from 1936 she stressed that she had received 143 cups and medals for her achievements in flying (Buffington, 1978, p. 20). But then the question arises as to why Sophie was so obsessed by medals and records?

Even a simple fact like Sophie's boarding a plane can only be passed on to all those who were not actual eye-witnesses by means of symbols, mostly by means of language. And language is *per se* interpretation: it focuses the view, it structures the perception, it constructs meanings, and it is dependent on the context.[14] Language constitutes the spectacles through which we see the world around us and provides us with the categories and patterns that we use to interpret what we see. According to Booth (2002), "language determines consciousness, and ultimately being, by virtue of facilitating, or excluding from consideration, certain ways of thinking about experiences and by framing actions. In this sense, linguistic structures are said to shape social structures and cultural practices and therefore to constitute history" (p. 3). The rules and regulations of knowledge and meaning are connected with the power relations of social groups and societies.[15] Sophie's "correct" form of address, Lady Mary Heath, already indicates her social rank and points, furthermore, to England's hierarchic social structure. In addition, the language of the sources, especially that of the numerous newspaper articles, mirrors in many ways the existing gender order. Sophie, for example, was called "Lady Lindy" and thus compared with Charles Lindbergh. He is the standard by which Sophie, the exceptional woman, is measured. And precisely because Sophie was presented as an exception, the traditional gender roles are reaffirmed. The more I thought about my work on Sophie's biography, the more I became aware that language and culture were inextricably interwoven and therefore language—the language of the source, but also my language—could never be a mirror of reality. It also became clear to me that the historian's object of study was not a directly or personally experienced reality but text; and thus the (re)construction of events or "life courses" is only possible by means of an analysis of "'realities' which are recorded in language as texts" (Straub, 1993, p. 146), whereby "texts" is meant to denote more than merely written sources.

A further difficulty lies in the way in which the sources originated, for example, in the question of what the authors knew, or could know, and how they reported the information at their disposal. This depends on a variety of factors such as their interest, their experience, and their competence; but it also depends on the audience they are writing for and what this audience regards as important. While in aviation journals the reports contained numerous technical details about Sophie's airplanes and previous attempts at breaking records, with exact heights and times; for instance, the journalists of daily newspapers focused on the pilot's dress and appearance.

What is the significance of mentioning Sophie's fur coat? What might be interpreted as extravagance appears in a rather different light when one knows that Sophie flew a plane with an open cockpit. What do the types of airplane flown by Sophie tell us, say, about the pilot's flying skills? And what could the producers of the sources know about the technical details of the planes; what were they able to understand and describe?

Referring to Oriard's interpretation of American football, Booth (2002, p. 13) emphasises that "no single reading can represent the diversity of responses that readers assign to texts" and that "there are limitless possibilities for spectators interpreting a sporting text," for example, a football game or a pilot's record flight. Thus, information is always filtered through the eyes of the informant; sources always select and condense information. A flight that took several months can be reduced to one sentence: "Lady Mary Heath Flies from Cape Town to London." A further problem was the fact that most sources contained not only descriptions but also evaluations that were related to the experiences, the emotions, and the perspective of the informant.[16]

In my search for information about Sophie's life I came across many contradictory and even incorrect assertions. In many of the sources even her name was wrongly spelled, which did not make the research any easier. In many cases it can be clearly seen how one author has simply copied false information from another without taking the trouble to check it. A number of assessments in the sources are nothing less than condemnations, although Sophie sometimes had the opportunity to "hit back." Sophie was frequently at daggers drawn with the press; and when, for instance, in April 1931 the headline appeared: "Lady Mary Heath Jailed as Drunk; Fails to Appear," she countered with another headline: "Lady Mary Says She Can't Get 'Looped' on Two Glasses of Beer" (Buffington, 1978, p. 20). I will discuss below to what extent Sophie herself added color to an ideal picture of her personality in order to cover over certain "dark spots."

SOPHIE. PART TWO: THE ATHLETE

While I was trying to learn more about Sophie the pilot, I was not at first aware that her name was already to be found in another of my various filing boxes. In my research into the "Women's Olympics" in Monte Carlo, the International Women's Sport Federation (Fédération Sportive Feminine Internationale, FSFI), founded in 1921, and the Women's World Games organized by the FSFI I came across lists of competitors in which Sophie's name was included. In 1923 she had taken part in the "Women's Olympics" in Monte Carlo, winning third place in the javelin, third place in the pentathlon, and third place in the high jump, and in 1926 in the second World Games for Women in Gothenburg, where she won fourth place in the javelin (both hands) (FSFI, 1928, p. 25).

At that time, though, I was more interested in the organizers than the athletes. But when I discovered an interview with Sophie the pilot, published in 1930, in which she highlighted her athletic achievements, I searched my files—and subsequently books and statistics on women's athletics in England—and, lo and behold, there she was: Sophie, the world-class athlete who took part in numerous contests and international competitions; for example, in the annual international athletic competition in Paris in 1923 (second place in both the javelin and the hurdles) or in Sweden, where an international competition was held between Swedish and English athletes in 1926. Here, Sophie and a Swedish woman tied for first place in the high jump (Webster, 1930, p. 24).

Since best times and distances were not always clearly defined and recorded in the early days of athletics and since Sophie's best discipline, throwing the javelin "with both hands," disappeared from international contests, the following information is "unofficial." In 1922 and 1923 she was English champion in the javelin throw "with both hands" (i.e., the two throws, one with the right arm and one with the left arm, were added together) and in 1924 she held the British high-jump record. Together with an American athlete she even held the world record in the high jump in 1923.[17] In 1924 she held the European record in throwing the javelin. She reported proudly in an article that she had won 200 medals for her achievements in athletics and aviation.[18]

The name Eliott-Lynn appears frequently in Webster's book on women's athletics published in 1930, along with photographs showing her using techniques that were no longer in fashion in the second half of the 20th century. She is shown, for example, gripping the rear end of the javelin and using the "scissors" in the high jump. It can be said that Sophie was an all-round talent in athletics, the high jump, javelin, and hurdles being her strongest disciplines.

Sophie was evidently proud of her sporting achievements but it was impossible for me to discover much more than this about her life as an athlete. She was a member of the ladies' section of Kensington AC, one of the first athletic clubs that had opened its doors to women. But what was it like to be a member of such a club in those days? How often did she have to train? What was it like in the early 1920s to travel abroad as a young woman? Sophie seems, however, to have been more than a 'mere' athlete: she was, at any rate, one of the two women selected by men who had encouraged the development of women's sport in England to play a role in the founding of the Women's Amateur Athletic Association (WAAA) in 1922 and was entrusted with the office of Honorary Secretary and Treasurer.[19]

SOPHIE. PART THREE: THE SPORTS OFFICIAL

My research into the International Women's Sport Federation was much more intensive and persistent than my research into Sophie's life (Pfister, 2000a). The federation played a crucial role in the development of women's sport, in particular women's athletics. Unfortunately, however, it has not been possible so far to locate the archives of the organization, which was forced to discontinue its activities in 1936 under the pressure of the IOC and the IAAF. Alice Milliat, its president and the driving force behind the federation, subsequently "vanished into thin air" and historians are currently trying to discover more about her life and the FSFI's activities (Leigh & Bonin, 1977). My own research was in some respects unsuccessful. Archive material is allegedly stored in a Paris museum, inaccessible to the public and even academics, but the letters and requests that I have sent to the museum's director have remained unanswered. The activities of the FSFI, however, are mirrored in the minutes of IOC meetings in which the FSFI's demands must have been, at least, discussed.

In the documents I found on the FSFI in the Carl and Liselott Diem Archive (the most important of which is a brochure that contains the statutes, the names of the office-holders, and the member countries) the name Lady Mary Heath appears as vice-president (FSFI, 1928). Sophie's role in the FSFI can only be reconstructed against the background of the history of this organization.

The FSFI had unanimously demanded first of all the inclusion of women's track-and-field events in the Olympic program, a demand that met vigorous opposition from most IOC members, in particular from Pierre de Coubertin. Right up to the end of his life de Coubertin held the view that women should only play one role in the Olympic Games and that was to adorn the winners with the victory garlands (Leigh, 1974; Pfister, 2000a; 2000b).

After the participation of women had been discussed at several IOC meetings after World War I, the "women's issue" was then put on the agenda of the Pedagogical Congress in Prague in 1925.[20] Here, the debate largely focused on the question of whether women could or should practice what in French were called "sports violents." The only woman to take part in the congress was the vice-president of the FSFI, Sophie Eliott-Lynn. At the age of 28 she was probably also the youngest participant and the only athlete. She was a member of the Medical Committee, which was drafting a declaration and, in addition, she presented two statements to the Congress participants in which, on the one hand, she stressed the right of women to take up sporting activities but, on the other, upheld numerous stereotypes and ideals of femininity. For her, too, being able to bear children was the standard by which women's sport had to be measured. Thus, it is no surprise that the Prague Congress's "resolution on women's sport" contained nothing new: boxing, wrestling, and rugby were rejected as sports for women; on the question of track-and-field events the Congress was not willing to commit itself because of the lack of practical experience and scientific research; and feminine demureness was to remain the guiding principle of women's sport. The inclusion of women's track-and-field events in the Olympic program had not even been discussed but the resolution had no concrete results.

Nevertheless, in the second half of the 1920s the IOC and the IAAF had to make concessions to popular taste. In Germany, for instance, women's championships in track-and-field disciplines had already been held since 1920 and the Women's World Games organized by the FSFI were gaining increasing significance and acceptance (Fischer, 1983; Bernett, 1987, 1988; Pfister, 2000a). In the 1928 Olympics in Amsterdam, in order not to lose its influence on women's athletics, the IOC allowed women to enter five track-and-field events "on a trial basis." In the run-up to the games, however, there were heated debates within the FSFI on whether five track-and-field events were enough and whether one ought not to demand a "full program" for women. While the majority of FSFI members were in favor of taking part in the Olympics, Sophie asserted "that the Ladies' Games had been a great success, that in the majority of countries men-and-women meetings were avoided, as parents were adversely disposed towards them, and that women had nothing to gain by participation in the general Olympic Games" (quoted in Webster, 1930, p. 99). Accordingly, English women athletes did not attend the 1928 Games—with the single exception of Sophie, who took part as an official.

Her arrival there was quite extraordinary. The "African World" (11th August 1928, p. 119) reported:

HOW LADY HEATH SAW OLYMPIC GAMES

Lady Heath, the famous British airwoman, utilised her ability as a pilot in a novel way to secure admission to the Olympic Stadium at Amsterdam. When the British women athletes decided to stay away from the Olympiad, Lady Heath's name was erased from the register of officials, but she did not intend to miss the Olympiad and, finding there were no tickets, she set out in her aeroplane and circled above the Stadium. Then she dropped a note to this effect: 'I shall continue circling around until tickets of admission are left at the front office. When these arrangements are made, place coats in the shape of a cross in the centre of the Stadium and I will immediately make a landing and come along.' The request was complied with. Lady Heath returned to the Stadium by car, and has since acted in an official capacity.[21]

Sophie was evidently a born envoy. In the late 1920s she was president of the Women's International Aeronautical Association.[22]

TEXTS AND INTERPRETATIONS—OPPORTUNITIES AND CHALLENGES FOR THE HISTORIAN

With the addition of the sources on Sophie's role as an athlete and sports official I had completed the puzzle without, however, having gained any depth of focus. The pieces of information were so scattered that I have so far been able to provide only a mainly descriptive chain of facts and events. I cannot be content with this, though. As a historian I must endeavor to gain a synoptic perspective of Sophie by trying to combine facts, describe processes, and find correlations and explanations for her decisions and actions. Here, I am caught between the facts and events; the sources, which select, condense, and interpret; and my own way of looking at and interpreting things. What is more, I know only a few facts; and these facts and sources never speak for themselves; they have to be molded into a narrative. But lots of data are missing that could be used as pieces of a puzzle to put together a biography. I am also aware that through my sources and my information I have a certain power—the power to assert and propagate my view of Sophie. Robert Berkhofer (1995, p. 170) described the power of historians as follows: "Historians have authority over the past in the sense that they determine which voices of the past are heard through their expositions and thus which viewpoints are represented in their discourses." It also lies in my hands whether (and, if so, how) Sophie lives on as a more or less mythical figure.

Although relatively few sources were available to me at that time, I still had difficulty in selecting the information to use. From the great number of facts I was forced to *select* those I judged to be important. What were my criteria for selecting them? What kind of *screening* did I use to choose one piece of information and to ignore another? My definition, for example of "important," which depended on my perspective and my "taste" (I will discuss the subject of taste below), determined where the spotlight of attention was to be directed. And, like other authors before me, I considered Sophie's measurable achievements to be important whereas her poetic accounts of flights over Ireland were aspects that I thought might be left unmentioned. Due to the lack of space, moreover, I was forced to use methods of condensing the text, like summary and abstraction, even more than biographers usually have to. Instead of relating each or at least a number of Eliott-Lynn's speeches and lectures, I could only write briefly: "She gave numerous lectures."

All the problems connected with facts, objectivity, and truth, which I have already mentioned in connection with sources, also apply to my work as a historian. I try, as far as at all possible, to find out the truth by checking my sources using "state-of-the-art" techniques and eliminating contradictions and inconsistencies. If I wanted to reconstruct Sophie's life in detail and write a book about her, the many small but insoluble ambiguities, for which there was no place in my brief account of her life, would fill a great many footnotes. If I cannot capture the reality, I still feel obliged to adhere to the truth. Finding the truth is the central aim of all sciences but, without wishing to go into philosophical subtleties, there is never one single truth and, as I have already tried to explain, statements are not identical with facts. But if history claims to be a scientific discipline, then there must be an adequate correspondence between the information given in the sources and my narrative based on these sources. In my view a prerequisite of "truth" is that I make my selection and use of sources available and accessible to intersubjective control and communication.

I am aware that I have a selective perception and that the biography I write depends on my personal approach, my way of thinking, my more or less explicit theoretical assumptions, my evaluations, my political orientations—and my feelings toward the person upon whose life I have intruded. It is clear to me that, whether I like it or not, my attitudes and my basic convictions influence the selection of information and focus—in fact the whole perspective. And only by divulging these convictions, criteria, and feelings can I encourage the readers to find their own perspectives and their own truths. In the (re)construction of a "life course" perspective is decisive; and since there are not only two or three but numerous perspectives, many different biographies might be written about a single life. Perspective guides our attention and perception, our evaluation and, generally, our taste (in Bourdieu's sense of the term)—not only in history but also in our lives. Thus, my life, dreams, ambitions, and orientations are closely related to my perception of the world; and, therefore, the way I write Sophie's biography tells a great deal about myself, about my dream of flying, for instance, which I was never able to make come true.

The more I thought about it, the more I realized that my interest in Sophie and the picture I was painting of her were connected with my endeavor to experience and to describe women as the subjects of their history. However, the wish to have a heroine underpinning one's arguments, orientations, beliefs, and ideologies must not lead to misrepresentation. Other women authors who, like me, had evidently set out in search of "strong women" describe Sophie as a feminist, shoring up their assessment with a fitting quotation. However, after going back to the sources, I found out that Sophie's words had been taken out of context and that 'antifeminist' remarks of hers had simply been suppressed. What, then, is the "truth" about Sophie's feminism, which is repeatedly mentioned in the sources and the literature about her?

SOPHIE. PART FOUR: A FEMINIST?

It is an indisputable fact (for which there is much evidence in her writing) that in both words and deeds Sophie fought against prejudices that women faced in the world of aviation. Her key message was that flying is "safe and sane" and that women are able "to pilot their own planes" (Heath, 1929, p. 67). In her view there was not a single reason to bar women from flying professionally. She was the best example, she often said, that women could achieve (almost) everything in the air. Her quarrels with the aviation authorities and her arguments in the dispute about a professional pilot's license appear to be further evidence of her feminist stance. In lectures and articles (in the magazine "Aviation" she had her own column on "Women's Activities"), in taking women passengers for "joy rides" in her airplane and in founding a women pilots' scholarship Sophie did all she could to promote women in aviation.[23] Her activities in the International Women's Sport Federation and her book on women's athletics might also serve as evidence of Sophie's feminist leanings (Eliott-Lynn, 1925; see Hargreaves, 1979).

The joy of having found a woman like Sophie, who not only showed the myth of female weakness to be completely false through her many achievements but also stood up for the cause of women, suffered a serious setback when I read her book "Athletics for Women and Girls," published in 1925, which had lain unread on my desk for years since I had presumed it to be a dry, factual guide. In this book, however, as well as in a number of articles about flying which I subsequently reread, this time more closely, I discovered that she propagated a very traditional view of women and their abilities, roles, and destinies. Sophie was quite clearly of the opinion that women were first and foremost predestined for motherhood. In her "Athletics for Women and Girls," for instance, she wrote that a path had to be found between a too strenuous practice of sport that might be harmful to child-bearing on the one hand and leisure activities, which were of too little benefit for the body and health on the other (Eliott-Lynn, 1925, p. 18).[24]

Whereas she presented herself as a competent woman, capable of everything that men did, she depicted women generally as the weaker sex. For example, she spoke out strongly against the plans of various women pilots to undertake transatlantic flights. Women, she argued, were not cut out for such exertions and such dangers,[25] one of her arguments being that women were not in proper form during their periods and were even at risk of fainting. Women, then, should be content with becoming the mothers of future transatlantic pilots. But even in texts in which she emphasized that women were quite capable of flying airplanes she never failed to mention that flying was "absurdly easy" or, elsewhere, that it was "easier than driving a car." Sophie, labeled a "feminist" in her day, played only lip service to this role; although she thoroughly enjoyed her role as a rebel, she observed that her flying achievements had nothing to do with "daredevilry at all, nor yet rampant feminism" but with her striving for independence (Heath, 1929, p. 66).

SOPHIE. PART FIVE: HER PRIVATE LIFE

While I had recourse to a relatively large number of informative sources on Sophie's career in sport and aviation, there lay an almost impenetrable shroud over her private life. A brief newspaper cutting from 1929 reported her accident in Cleveland, Ohio, but for many years I could not find out whether or how she had survived the crash. Eventually, an article in the Pictorial Review of 1929 that I had ordered through the university library finally turned up in which there was a long interview with Sophie containing many references to her past.

Two years ago, moreover, I received an e-mail from an Irish journalist who was searching for information about the FSFI since—as I then learned to my great surprise—she was writing a book on Sophie. In several years of research she had ascertained numerous facts about Sophie's life and she was quite ready and willing to share her knowledge of Sophie with me. I sent her e-mails with my questions and was impatient to start up the computer next morning to look for the answers in my incoming mail. I have never met Lindie Naughton but I know that she is a sports journalist, that she writes well, and that she has published a book on gardening. After my 'virtual' discussions with her I had to revise many of my ideas about Sophie, which I had formed from Sophie's own accounts. The present chapter is largely based on what Sophie has told about herself with Lindie's additions and corrections.

In the interview mentioned above Sophie relates that she grew up in a small town in County Limerick in the Republic of Ireland. She was brought up by two maiden aunts and had a quiet (for her much too quiet) early childhood.[26] She made up for this during her schooldays: "As soon as I was sent off to school I went in most avidly for all forms of sport" (Heath, 1929, p. 66). She further reports that she studied agriculture in Dublin, was a motorcycle messenger for the Royal Air Force during the war, and ran her own coffee plantation in Kenya. Her mentioning the farm in Kenya reminded me of Karen Blixen and the film "Out of Africa" and the photo of Sophie, too, which accompanies the interview, conveys a hint of romanticism: elegantly dressed with a diadem-like bonnet, she stares into the distance, as if in search of something.

She had always wanted to overstep the boundaries of femininity, Sophie told the interviewer: in wild games as a child, as a motorcycle messenger during the war, as a sportswoman, and as a pilot. Independence and self-reliance were the character traits of which she was proud, as she never failed to emphasize. A large part of the interview is devoted to Sophie's flying achievements while not a single word is lost on parents, friends, or husbands. Sophie seems to have led a lonely life dedicated to her fame and glory.

Lindie's e-mails filled the gaps in Sophie's biography, putting her in an entirely new light. Sophie was born near Limerick in the Republic of Ireland in 1896. Her mother, an illegitimate child, was a domestic help and an alcoholic; her father, a farmer, was mentally ill and had been to prison for various misdemeanors. In a fit of mental derangement he clubbed his wife to death in 1897 and was put in a mental asylum, where he died in 1916.[27]

In that very year Sophie married William Davies Eliott-Lynn. In a short biography published in 1978 I discovered that in the year of their marriage Eliott-Lynn was 76 years old (Buffington, 1978, p. 20). I simply could not imagine what might have prompted Sophie to take such a step. But an email from Lindie was able to clarify this question at least: The age was a mistake and Sophie's husband was born in 1875, a soldier in the Royal Engineers, and was recovering from a motorcycle accident in Ireland. He was found dead in the Thames in 1927. Sophie really had studied at the Royal College of Science in Dublin and, after interrupting her studies during the war, obtained her degree in 1921. She then worked as a zoology demonstrator at Aberdeen University in Scotland, where she began her career in athletics.

Only a few months after her husband's death she married 72-year-old Sir Henry James Heath in October 1927. A wealthy man, he encouraged and supported her adventures in aviation, which ended, however, with her accident in 1929. In 1930 she divorced Heath in Reno but in 1932 she obtained a "proper" divorce in London. In 1931 she "unofficially" married her third husband, George Anthony Reginald Williams, in the USA. According to Lindie Naughton, Williams was a "Jamaican horse rider." The "proper" wedding took place after their return to Ireland in the autumn of 1932. From 1935 to 1938, together with her husband, she ran a small airline, named "Dublin Air Ferries," based at Kildonan Aerodrome north of Dublin.[28] The company trained pilots in its own school of aviation and carried out freight and passenger flights, mainly between Ireland and England.[29] During these years she founded or supervised several flying clubs. But competition from Air Lingus, which in 1936 had begun to establish international routes and which operated from different airports, forced Sophie and her husband to give up their small airline in August 1938. Kildonan aerodrome was closed down.

According to Lindie, Sophie was a highly intelligent woman, a born organizer, and an outstanding pilot. However, her egocentric self-praise (see Boase, 1979) did not exactly make her very popular and in the press she was called, among other things, "Lady-Hell-of-a-Din." Added to this was her alcoholism. In the sources there are numerous references to her addiction to drink and her dissolute lifestyle. Lindie wrote: "Wherever anything was happening, she was there, usually dressed to kill and smoking foul Turkish cigarettes" (e-mail, 12 June 2000). When her husband, who had been very attentive to her, left Ireland after their airline business had closed down, Sophie moved to London, where she increasingly took to drink. She was picked up by the police several times for being drunk and disorderly and was even gaoled more than once for offences related to drink. Shortly before her death she wrote in a newspaper article: "People wonder why I took to drink after I had been fearless and rose from a poor Irish girl to become a titled lady. It was the failure of my struggle for happiness. My frequent romances ruined my life" (quoted from an e-mail sent by Lindie Naughton, 21 October 2002). Now at last, she said, she wanted to make her childhood dream come true and become a doctor. Not long afterward, in 1939, she suffered fatal injuries after falling from a London tramcar.

Sophie's somewhat macabre humor stayed with her until the very end; in her will she had requested that her ashes be scattered from her airplane at midday, the hour at which Captain Curling, her archenemy, was known to take his daily walk. And when he came home on that day sprinkled with ashes, he is reported to have said, "There's that Peirce lady at it again. Will I ever be clear of her?" (quoted in Daniels & Tedder, 2000, p. 58).

AUTOBIOGRAPHICAL TEXTS

Sophie's autobiographical text "Why I Always Fly Solo," published in 1929, revealed to me in all clarity how Sophie wished to see herself. But it also made me realize how little autobiographical accounts could be trusted. Although the facts that Sophie reported all appear to be true, their selection and the omissions convey an entirely different picture from the one that I was beginning to draw with the help of Lindie's information. Sophie mentioned neither her parents nor her husbands. She attributed her achievements and successes solely to her abilities and her will power. "I do not remember when I was not used to relying on myself in whatever I undertook to do" (Heath, 1929, p. 66). After my correspondence with Lindie my fascination with the autobiographical text, which seemed to allow a clear and authentic insight into Sophie's life, turned into amazement. I realized that, while autobiographies certainly have their advantages for the historian, they also have definite drawbacks. On the one hand, Sophie is, of course, the most competent expert on her own life; on the other hand, autobiographies are in many respects unreliable, not least because the writers, Sophie included, usually wish to present themselves to the public or to posterity in a certain light. Sophie obviously wanted to take the credit for her successes herself.

But the portrayal of a life "as it really was"—even with the best of intentions—is virtually impossible, not only because the incredible number of events makes it necessary to select and condense but also because, retrospectively, people always construct and interpret the course of their lives by piecing together the numerous facts and events in order to form a coherent picture, thus molding coincidental and unrelated happenings and actions into a consistent, continuous, and logical process—a curriculum vitae (see, for example, Rosenmayr, 1979). "In their fundamental relations with themselves, most people are narrators . . . they love the orderly succession of facts . . . ; and the impression that their lives have a certain course leads them to feel somehow sheltered in the midst of chaos," Robert Musil observed in his novel "The Man Without Qualities" (Musil, 1978, p. 650). Bourdieu goes further than Musil, emphasizing that a person's "life" is a project and a construction; it is invested with a purpose and is related as a narrative with a starting and finishing point. According to Bourdieu (1990), this narrative is—apart from a person's name—one of the central institutions in the construction of ego as a unity as well as in the production of the self. Even if one does not accept this radical calling into question of the self and personal identity, there is not the slightest doubt that people are authors and ideologists of their own lives who select significant events and create connections between them. And, as authors, they are completely free to choose the kind of development and event they wish to highlight and which part of their person and their life they believe to be irrelevant—or wish to hide. And what right have I to change, or even demolish, the picture that Sophie wished to create of herself? Perhaps her story—a success story without men—and her self-portrayal as a person who has complete independence is her truth.

TOWARD AN EXPLANATION

Sophie believed that she had become what she was as a result of her all too sheltered childhood. She had rebelled against the restrictive upbringing of her two maiden aunts and, in doing so, had learned to be self-willed and self-reliant (Heath, 1929). As her biographer, I am not so sure about this seemingly plausible explanation of hers. As a historian my aim is not only to report facts, events, and processes or describe structures and institutions. I also try to relate facts, events, and processes to the underlying intentions, causes, and effects; in other words, my aim is to give explanations. And there are many different levels and possibilities for explanations. In the case of writing Sophie's biography, I have tried to find the reasons for and light up the backgrounds of the decisions she took as well as the events and developments that took place in her life. I assumed, for instance, that Sophie's obsession with records had to do not only with the time in which she lived (a time in which records held a fascination for the masses) but also with the fate of her parents. With her success she might have tried to compensate for her mother's origins and her father's crime. In one e-mail Lindie wrote that she suspected that Sophie's alcoholism was a result of the injuries sustained in the plane crash. Or had her mother's addiction to drink and her murder, which Sophie had experienced as a one-year-old infant (what effect would this have on a small child?), and the death of her first husband caused her so much distress and left such scars that Sophie wanted to use the alcohol as medicine? Or was it the end of her flying career that made Sophie take to drink? Anyone who has enjoyed a life in the limelight, as Sophie certainly did, finds it hard, later on, to come to terms with playing second fiddle. And what was the reason for her marrying James Heath, a man who was so much older than herself and who appeared small and inconspicuous beside the tall and athletic figure of Sophie? Was it her search for a father figure, the desire to have a title, or the prospect of being able to finance four airplanes and long-distance flights?

These examples demonstrate not only my attempt to relate different facts to each other and identify causes and effects but also that I have to use my own understanding of Sophie's motives, decisions, and actions. I would like to point out, moreover, that there are many problems connected with this "hermeneutic method" of interpretation but I cannot go into the details of this here. Röckelein (1993) has pointed out that it is impossible to write a biography without using psychological arguments. In her view, historians can only claim to work scientifically (in the sense of observing the principles of verifiability and coherence) if, instead of "wild analysis," they "make explicit reference to psychological or psychoanalytical theories" (Röckelein, 1993, p. 23). It belongs to the tenets of biographical research that social backgrounds and circumstances must be taken into account in each case, in other words, that the subject is "anchored" in a "social setting." This means, further, that Sophie's life should also be described using theoretical approaches pertaining to the gender order of a given society. For not only from her personal accounts but also from her own actions it can be inferred that the gender order was the backdrop and the questioning of traditional gender arrangements the mainspring of many of the decisions and developments in Sophie's life. However, in history studies there is great controversy over which theories may be made use of, and how.[30] In this question I advocate an instrumental use of theories proposed by Mommsen (1979) in order to achieve a more precise analysis and depiction of institutions, structures, and processes, which it is impossible to describe using hermeneutic methods. As far as I know, there is no debate on theory among authors of (sport) biographies.[31] We need intensive discussion and reflection on what theoretical approaches can achieve and on what role they might play in biographies. Dealing with the question of theories is essential—not least because we use theories every day without being open about it.

EVALUATIONS AND JUDGMENTS, STANDARDS AND PERSPECTIVES

Sophie's life was in many ways extraordinary. But what is ordinary? And, for that matter, what is right or wrong, or good or bad? The evaluation of facts and actions is relative and refers to a given standard that depends on the perspective. A special problem of "her story" is the use of double standards when characteristics, behavior, and situations are perceived and judged differently according to the class, race, or gender of the players. Thus, the participation of women in aeronautics was often interpreted as an abnormal and "unladylike" ambition, whereas the participation of men in dangerous air races and long-distance flights was interpreted as heroism.

The problem of evaluation (and there is no (re)construction without intentional or unintentional evaluation) can be clearly demonstrated using the example of the female pilots. On their famous flights, from London to Cape Town or across the Atlantic, they put their lives at risk, some of them dying in accidents like the most famous female pilot of all times, Amelia Earhart. The more risks the pilots took, the more fame there was to be earned. What should we think about this? I have to confess that I admire not only their courage and their will power but also their competence. But I know that the same pilots may be (and are) judged to be reckless or foolish.

RELATIONS AND EMOTIONS—WHO IS THE OBJECT, WHO THE SUBJECT?

Why am I interested in biographies? In addition to what I have said in the introduction, there are two answers to this question, one academic and one personal. First of all, biographies are important because they are able to create role models and provide identification. Besides, we should always bear in mind that historical situations, events, and processes are embodied in persons and that biographies can give an exemplary insight into experiences, developments, processes, and interdependencies between sport and society. According to Meier (1989), biographies also have a focus, "some kind of unity of object" (p. 108), which enables us to lessen the enormous complexity of history.

In many studies on biographical research reference is made to the special relationship that exists between biographers and their heroes. "Biographies on eminent figures in the arts or sciences often say more about the biographer than about the person or persons being portrayed," according to Röckelein (1993, p. 23; see also Reinharz, 1994). What, then, do the biographical texts that I have written about Sophie tell about me?

For one thing, it is important for me, as I have already mentioned, to make women and their achievements visible. For another, I am an inquisitive person and working on a biography is like looking through someone's keyhole. Moreover, Sophie led a life very different from my own, in some ways glamorous and exciting, in other ways very sad.

It is here that my own personal feelings come into play. Even though all scientists in their research must necessarily contend with their feelings and above all their feelings toward the people whose lives they explore, this is something that is rarely talked or written about; but, when it is talked or written about, emotions are regarded as problems since they influence both the scientist's portrayal as well as his or her appraisal. Refusing to allow feelings or ignoring them says something about the understanding that most historians have of both science and themselves: they believe that their professed objectivity is jeopardized by any acknowledgment of their emotions.[32] Some feminist authors, on the other hand, seem ready to admit the pains, joys, and dilemmas they encounter while working on biographies. They often describe understanding, empathy, even a "mysterious kinship" with their biographical subjects (Reinharz, 1994).

And this also holds true for me as well. In one way or another I admired all the women whose lives I have tried to describe; most of them I liked, to some of them I felt a strong attachment. I often sensed what other historians have described as the "mysterious alchemy" of author and subject (Reinharz, 1994). And, here, the question arises as to whether it is easier to work on a biography if one has positive feelings toward the person portrayed or if she or he is a role model or an idol. What is certain is that without some kind of empathy for the lives of one's subjects it is impossible to understand their intentions and their actions. At the same time, however, one must keep a certain distance and detachment (Meier, 1989).

In Sophie's case, curiosity developed into a kind of admiration and this transformed, in turn, into disappointment. The first traces of irritation I felt while reading some of her autobiographical texts because of the almost obsessive way she listed her achievements and records; after reeling off all the things that she was the first woman or even the first person to have achieved and all the exploits that were extraordinary and outstanding, there was little room for other topics or other people. I was disappointed at what she had to say about women's athletics and women as pilots since, although at first glance they appear quite feminist, on closer scrutiny they diminish women's abilities. Her own life was in no way reconcilable with the feminine ideals she propagated. And it was no doubt that because of her conservatism Sophie was able to succeed in a man's world. In many ways she played the role of the "enfant terrible" as well as that of the "token" woman and, in the process, developed what might be called the "queen-bee" syndrome. (Queen bees thrive and prosper because they are the only females and do everything they can to prevent other females from intruding on their territory.)

The ambivalence of accommodation and opposition, of the traditional and the progressive can also be considered typical of the WAAA and the FSFI, both of which Sophie joined as an active member. She vacillated between integration into the male world and segregation from it, between the demand for gender equality and concern for "true womanhood."

In the course of my research on Sophie I detected a different person—not the person I had initially constructed in my mind. And I began to see some of her actions and decisions in a different light. Even so, I still ask myself whether it is "fair" to measure attitudes, statements, and actions by my own standards.[33]

THE MEANS IS THE END—THE FASCINATION OF RESEARCH

In spite of my criticism of the opinions expressed in her texts and in spite of the mixed feelings I have about her views on feminism, there is no doubt that Sophie fascinates me as a person; and it is a wonderful feeling to have been able to save parts of her life from being forgotten. For me, just as for Reinharz (1994, p. 58), one of the fascinating things about working on a biography is the "magic moment of discovering the subject," even if, in Sophie's case, much has to be left to my imagination. During the work on a biography I can delve into the life of another person, in this case Sophie's; I can share her successes and feel sad about her failures. Sometimes I identify with her more or less; but I also have the opportunity of distancing myself, of becoming an observer and a scholar, looking at things through my "scientific spectacles." A large part of the fascination of working on Sophie's biography is the research itself; the search for sources is like detective work. I do not know what I will find and if I will ever be able to solve the puzzle. The open questions and the gaps in what I know about Sophie's life; the suspense and the sense of uncertainty while searching for information; and, not least, the hope of stumbling upon new sources—all this makes the work on a biography extremely exciting. It was such a wonderful moment, for example, when I found the book "Women and Flying" in a library or when I received Lindie Naughton's first e-mail. In addition to all this, the research on the various biographies I have written has taken me to many exciting places: I visited Antonie Straßmann's grave in a Berlin cemetery; I found newspaper clippings about her flight over Brazil in the Museum of Aeronautics in Rio de Janeiro; and I have worked for many, many hours in different archives. I love working in archives—the long rows of books and documents, the smell of old paper and the feeling that it is here that the secrets of history may be uncovered.

THE WAY FORWARD?

I hope that I have been able to show that, besides shoring up ideologies, history can also tear them down; for example, the stereotype of the weaker sex. Thus, it is not only important which facts are selected for a story (the biography of Sophie, say) but also how the facts are presented and interpreted. Sophie might be described by one author as an eccentric, always striving for publicity, or even as an alcoholic, thus sustaining the myth of women as the "second sex." A historian writing from a female perspective might describe these same attributes as a struggle in order to make her dreams come true and might interpret her story as a success story that highlights women's potentials. This perspective would reinforce the idea of female power; it would destroy stereotypes, provide role models, show strategies, and, as a whole, present a "lieu de mémoire," a place of remembrance, with which women today can identify. Thus, biographies are a contested terrain and it is a question of who has the power to determine the "right" questions, the "right" perspectives and the "right" interpretations.

At the end of this long text many questions still remain unanswered and many new questions have surfaced as well. This applies both to Sophie's life and to biographical research. I know very little about Sophie's personal relationships or about Sophie as a person. Did she want to have children or couldn't she have any? I suspect that she did not want children since they would neither have fit into her restless and unsettled life nor would they have been compatible with her image as a heroine. Why did Sophie divorce her rich husband? Did the mysterious Mr. Williams have a part to play in this? Did Sophie have any women friends?

Moreover, as far as biographical research is concerned, the main dilemma—the impossibility of writing real and true biographies—could only be discussed but not solved. Since facts can only be communicated by language and handed down in writing, and since these writings, including biographies, have in turn an influence on people and their "life courses," the question is raised by Raulff (1999), among others, of whether a "life without legend" (p. 139) is at all imaginable. Raulff regards it as an illusion to think that in biographical writing it is possible to uncover an "unknown quantity called life" (p. 139). He proposes that the processes and the histories of the "reception" of a person—how he or she has been subsequently remembered—be included in the biography so as to remove the distinction between life and legend, between biography and "reception." His motto is a self-reflective preoccupation with constructed lives. Whether or not this is a way forward, which biographers and readers will be able and willing to accept, I do not know. But what has become clear to me in the course of preparing this paper is that the personality of the author, along with his or her emotions, must find its way both into and out of biographical texts.

NOTES

1. The methodological parts of this contribution have been published also in other contexts.

2. On sport biographies as "hero-worshipping puff pieces" see, among others, Freeman (2001). On the lack of women in biographical research see, among others, Reinharz (1994). On (his)story, see Rowbotham (1976).

3. I use the term "(re)construction" because according to the terminology of "postmodern" historians reconstruction means reproducing the past as it actually was. This is, of course, impossible. According to Booth (2002), who follows Munslow (1997), the construction of history means "employ[ing] theory to mediate empirical evidence in the construction of the past; deconstructionists believe that historians can, at best, discover only one version of the past." See also Wehler (1979).

4. In spite of this limitation, this type of historical research can be justified since especially women who accomplished unusual feats provided different opportunities of identification, attracted public attention, and possibly contributed to a transformation of the female image and the destruction of the myths of femininity.

5. With few exceptions, the biographical texts that I have published are based, at least in part, on my own research.

6. See the various articles in Christensen, Guttman & Pfister (2001). See also Pfister (1989); Pfister & Niewerth (1999); Hall & Pfister (1999).

7. On female pilots see Boase (1979); Moolmann (1982); Lomax (1987); Pfister (1989); Schmitt (1993).

8. www.ctie.monash.edu.au/ hargrave/heath.html.

9. For the following see Heath & Murray (1929); Heath (1929); see also The 99 News, Oct. 1978, p. 20. Several sources are available in http://www.ctie.monash.edu.au/hargrave/heath.html.

10. http://www.limerick-leader.ie/issues/20010407/news03.html.

11. Cf. above all the book "Women and Flying", which she coauthored with Stella Wolfe Murray. The main part of the book deals with her flight from Cape Town to London.

12. See the newspaper report in the archive of the Luftsportverbandes [Aviation Sports Federation] Schleswig-Holstein; email from Lindie Naughton, 23.11.2000.

13. Cf. the discussions of methodological problems in Baumgartner & Rüsen (1976); Lorenz (1997); Iggers (2000); Booth (2002).

14. See, among others, Lorenz (1997, p. 40).

15. Here the ideas of Foucault about the development and the functions of discourses could be discussed.

16. Whereas in the past many historians believed that a fact was reported in the same way regardless of the individual who produced the source, there is now consensus that perception and interpretation depend on many different factors.

17. FSFI 1936, p. 17. In Pallett (1955) there is no mentioning of the high-jump record.

18. Heath 1929, p. 66.

19. Webster 1930, p. 33; Moon (1997, p. 91).

20. Premier Congrès (1925); see also Müller (1983).
21. I thank my colleague Floris van der Merwe for this information.
22. Smith (1967, p. 233); cf. The 99 News, Oct. 1978, p. 20; cf. e-mail from Lindie Naughton, 18.10. 2000. She was also the first president of the Irish Gliding Association (Haughton, 1999).
23. See the sources mentioned above; see also Haughton (1999).
24. For an evaluation see Hargreaves (1979).
25. Liberty 21 (1932), p. 51.
26. This and the following biographical information are taken from an interview printed in Pictorial Review, March, 1929, Vol. 30, pp. 66–67.
27. I thank the journalist and author Lindie Naughton for the information about Sophie Eliott-Lynn's origins; see also Daniels & Tedder (2000).
28. She flew for a short time in the Irish Aero Club in Baldonell, see Haughton (1999).
29. Cf. The 99 News, Oct. 1978, p. 20; Aviation in the Early Days, www.calrechampion.ie/01/oct/; cf. Houghton on the Kildonan aerodrome, http://indigo.ie.
30. Cf. the controversy in Kock & Nipperdey (1979).
31. A discussion on theoretical approaches, especially on postmodern approaches, arose at the annual convention of NASSH, 2002, in French Lick with papers by Douglas Booth and Murray Phillips. See also Freeman (2001) with an overview of the literature on biographical research.
32. On the problem of "Transference: The Biographer's Dilemma," see Edel (1984); Freeman (2001).
33. For a treatment of this problem see Reinharz (1994).

REFERENCES

Baumgartner, H. M. & Rüsen, J. (Hrsg.) (1976). *Seminar: Geschichte und Theorie. Umrisse einer Historik.* Frankfurt am Main: Suhrkamp.
Berkhofer, R. (1995). *Beyond the great story: History as text and discourse.* Cambridge, MA: Belknap.
Bernett, H. (1987). *Leichtathletik im geschichtlichen Wandel.* Schorndorf: Hofmann.
Bernett, H. (1988). Die ersten "olympischen" Wettbewerbe im internationalen Frauensport. *Sozial- und Zeitgeschichte des Sports, 2,* 66–87.
Boase, W. (1979). *The sky's the limit. Women pioneers in aviation.* New York: Osprey Publishing.
Booth, D. (2002, June). *The linguistic turn in sport history: Discourses, texts and narratives.* Paper presented at the Thirtieth Annual Convention of the North American Society for Sport History, French Lick.
Bourdieu, P. (1990). Die biographische Illusion. *Bios: Zeitschift für Biographieforshung und Oral History, 1,* 75–81.
Buffington, G. (1979, October 20). Lady Mary S. Heath. *The 99 News.*
Christensen, K., Guttmann, A., & Pfister, G. (Eds.) (2001). *International encyclopedia of women and sports.* Vol. 1–3. New York: Macmillan Reference USA.

Coubertin, P. de (1912). Les femmes aux Jeux Olympique. *Revue Olympique, Juillet 1912*, 109–110.

Daniels, S., & Tedder, A. (2000). "A proper spectacle". *Women Olympians 1900–1936*. Houghton Conquest: ZeNaNA.

Edel, L. (1984). Transference: The biographer's dilemma. *Biography, 7*(4), 283–296.

Eliott-Lynn, S. (1925). *Athletics for women & girls*. London: R. Scott.

FSFI (1928). *Fédération Sportive Feminine Internationale*. Paris.

FSFI (1936). *Fédération Sportive Feminine International*. (1936). Paris.

Fischer, H. (1983). *Der Weltverband für Frauensport und seine besonderen Aufgaben*. Unpublished thesis. Deutsche Sporthochschule Köln.

Freeman, W. H. (2001, September). *The problems of sport biography: Too-good buddies and fictional friends*. Paper presented at the Sixth Congress for the History of European Sport, Göttingen, Germany.

Gelderman, C. (1996). Ghostly doubles: Biographers and biographee. *The Antioch Review, 54*(3), 328–335.

Hall, A., & Pfister, G. (1999). *Honoring the legacy. Fifty years of the International Association of Physical Education and Sport for Girls and Women*. Nanaimo: North Isle Printers.

Hargreaves, J. (1979). *"Playing like gentlemen while behaving like ladies": The social significance of physical activity for females in the late nineteenth and early twentieth century Britain*. MA Thesis, University of London.

Hargreaves, J. (1994). *Sporting females. Critical issues in the history and sociology of women's sports*. London: Routledge.

Haughton, J. (1999). *Kildonan Aerodrome*. Retrieved December, 12, 2002, from http://indigie.ie.

Hausen, K. (1983). *Frauen suchen ihre Geschichte*. München: Beck.

Heath, S. M. & Murray, S. W. (1929). *Woman and flying*. London: J. Long.

Heath, M. (1928). Women as aviators. *The Living Age, 35*, 263–265.

Heath, M. (1929). Why I always fly solo. *Pictorial Review, 30*, 66–67.

Heath, M. (1932). Why I believe women pilots can't fly the Atlantic. *Liberty*, May, 48–50.

Honegger, C., & Arni, C. (2001). *Gender - die Tücken einer Kategorie: Joan W. Scott, Geschichte und Politik*. Zürich: Chronos.

Iggers, G. (2000). The uses and misuses of history and the responsibility of the historians. In A. Jolstadt & M. Lunde (Eds.), *Proceedings. Actes. 19th International Congress of Historical Sciences, University of Oslo* (pp. 83–92). Oslo: University of Oslo.

Kelly, J. (1984). *Women, history and theory. The essays of Joan Kelly*. Chicago: University of Chicago Press.

Kocka, J., & Nipperdey, Th. (1979). Theorie und Erzählung in der Geschichte. München: Deutscher Taschenbuch Verlag.

Leigh, M. (1974). Pierre de Coubertin: A man of his time. *Quest, 22*, 19–24.

Leigh, M., & Bonin, T. (1977). The pioneering role of Madame Alice Milliat and the FSFI in establishing international track and field competition for women. *Journal of Sport History, 4*, 72–83.

Lomax, J. (1987). *Women of the air*. New York: Dodd, Mead & Co.

Lorenz, C. (1997). *Konstruktion der Vergangenheit. Eine Einführung in die Geschichtstheorie*. Köln: Böhlau.

Lühe, I. von der, & Runge, A. (2001). *Biographisches Erzählen*. (Querelles. Jahrbuch für Frauenforschung, 6). Stuttgart: Metzler.

Mayer, O. (1960). *A travers les anneaux olympiques*. Genf: Cailler.

Meier, C. (1989). Die Faszination des Biographischen. In F. Niess (Hrsg.), *Interesse an der Geschichte* (pp. 100–111). Frankfurt: Campus Verlag.

Meran, J. (1985). *Theorien in der Geschichtswissenschaft. Die Diskussion über die Wissenschaftlichkeit der Geschichte*. Göttingen: Vandenhoeck & Ruprecht.

Meyer, H. P. (1988). *Die ersten "Olympischen Spiele" der Frauen 1921 in Monte Carlo*. Unpublished Thesis, Deutsche Sporthochschule, Köln.

Mitchell, S. (1977). Women's participation in the Olympic Games - 1926. *Journal of Sport History, 4*, 208–228.

Mommsen, W. (1979). Die Mehrdeutigkeit von Theorien in der Geschichtswissenschaft. In J. Kocka & T. Nipperdey (Hrsg.), *Theorie und Erzählung in der Geschichte* (pp. 334–370). München: Deutscher Taschenbuch Verlag.

Moolman, V. (1982). *Frauen in der Luft*. Amsterdam: Time-Life.

Moon, G. (1997). *"A new dawn rising": An empirical and social study concerning the emergence and development of English women's athletics until 1980*. Unpublished Thesis, Brunel University, London.

Musil, R. (1978). *Der Mann ohne Eigenschaften*. Reinbek bei Hamburg: Rowohlt.

Müller, N. (1983). *Von Paris bis Baden-Baden. Die Olympischen Kongresse 1894–1981*. Niederhausen: Schors.

Pallett, G. (1955). *Women's athletics*. Dulwich: Normal Press.

Pfister, G. (1980). *Frau und Sport. Frühe Texte*. Frankfurt: Fischer.

Pfister, G. (1989). *Fliegen - ihr Leben. Die ersten Pilotinnen*. Berlin: Orlanda Frauenverlag.

Pfister, G. (1990). Die andere Perspektive: Frauenforschung und Sportgeschichte. *Stadion, 16*(1), 143–169.

Pfister, G. (2000 a). Die Frauenweltspiele und die Beteiligung von Frauen an den Olympischen Spielen. In M. Behrendt & G. Steins (Hrsg.), *Sport(geschichte) in Museen und Archiven. Berichte und Materialen* (pp. 157–171). Berlin: Sportmuseum Berlin und Forum für Sportgeschichte - Fördererverein für das Sportmuseum Berlin.

Pfister, G. (2000 b). Umstrittene Geschichte: Der historische Diskurs über Frauen in der Olympischen Bewegung. *Vortrag auf dem Vorolympischen Kongreß in Brisbane 2000*.

Premier Congrès International Olympique Pédagogique de Prague. (1925). Prag.

Raulff, U. (1999). Inter Lineas oder Geschriebene Leben. In U. Raulff (Hrsg.), *Der unsichtbare Augenblick. Zeitkonzepte in der Geschichte* (pp. 118–143). Göttingen: Wallstein Verlag.

Reinharz, S. (1994). Feminist biography: The pains, the joys, the dilemmas. In A. Lieblich & R. Josselson (Eds.), *Exploring identity and gender. The narrative story of life* (pp. 37–83). Thousand Oaks: Sage.

Reulecke, A.-K. (1993). "Die Nase der Lady Hester". Überlegungen zum Verhältnis von Biographie und Geschlechterdifferenz. In H. Röckelein (Hrsg.), *Biographie als Geschichte* (pp. 117–142). Tübingen: Edition Diskord.

Rosenmayr, L. (1979). Lebensalter, Lebensverlauf und Biographie. In G. Klingenstein, H. Lutz & G. Stourzh (Hrsg.), *Biographie und Geschichtswissenschaft*. (pp. 47–67). Wien: Verlag für Geschichte und Politik.

Rowbotham, S. (1976). *Hidden from history. Rediscovering women in history from the 17th century to the present*. New York: Vintage Books.

Röckelein, H. (1993). Der Beitrag der psychohistorischen Methode zur "neuen historischen Biographie". In H. Röckelein (Hrsg.), *Biographie als Geschichte* (pp. 17–38). Tübingen: Edition Diskord.

Scott, J. (1991). Women's history. In P. Burke (Ed.), *New perspectives on historical writings* (pp. 42–66). Cambridge: Polity Press.

Straub, J. (1993). Zeit, Erzählung, Interpretation. Zur Konstruktion und Analyse von Erzähltexten in der narrativen Biographieforschung. In H. Röckelein (Hrsg.), *Biographie als Geschichte* (pp. 143–183). Tübingen: Edition Diskord.

Webster, F. A. M. (1930). *Athletics of to-day for women*. London/New York.

Wehler, H.-U. (1979). Anwendung von Theorien in der Geschichtswissenschaft. In J. Kocka & Th. Nipperdey (Hrsg.), *Theorie und Erzählung in der Geschichte* (pp. 17–39). München: Deutscher Taschenbuch Verlag.

Chapter 10

Transnational Feminism: Straddling the Academic Fault Line

Susan J. Bandy

There are times when I wonder how and why I came to live and work in Europe. I sometimes fear that I shall not be able to continue without sufficient language capabilities and the necessary understandings about cultures so very different from my own. When the autumn darkness comes to Scandinavia, I fear that I shall not survive the "white period" of winter, named so from years past when surviving the last months of winter depended on the white vegetables that lasted until March. One of my colleagues said that he "remembered the day when the first banana came to Denmark," and I tried to recall when I saw my first banana while growing up on a dairy farm in Georgia. And there are times, in these dark days, when riding Gladys, my bicycle, I fear that I shall entangle my scarf in the spokes of the wheel and suffer a fate similar to that of Isadora Duncan in the south of France, dying less accomplished and having lived a far less glamorous life than she.

On November 1 in Central Europe, people celebrate death in a way unknown to me, going to cemeteries in remembrance of the departed ones, somehow in a simultaneous celebration of life and death. The Hungarians take to the streets in droves on October 23 of every year to commemorate their insurgence against the Russians who killed 10,000 Hungarians in three days in 1956 and stayed thereafter to occupy their country for the next 40 years, again a celebration of both life and death. Standing in such a relation to life and death reveals the complexity of a culture, remindful of cultures of ancient times. The Hungarian sense of space and time is yet another difference; the way they move along the streets seems abrupt to me. I wonder why such a civilized people move in such ways. Is it because they lost almost 70% of their land in the Treaty of Trianon? Is physical space so important because they have lost so much of it? Coming from the South, which had lost so much over a century ago, I should understand such losses. And then, there is always time in Hungary.

There has also been the question about protocol and power and hierarchy that seem somehow also culturally specific. What is proper and how should one go about trying to accomplish one's work? How many different forms of democracy are there? I shall never forget being told by a former member of the communist party that I, as an American, should leave her country because I had violated very distinct and obvious matters of protocol and hierarchy when trying to plan a seminar to bring scholars from abroad. Moreover, I was power hungry, a liar, and antidemocratic. Where shall I go now was my immediate thought.

The obvious question is why would one choose such an existence? Even in retrospect, such choices are not clear. However, one thought always lingers—that often a life pattern can turn on one moment in a life, and that fateful turn may simply rest on one decision taken or one not taken or one made by someone else or even on timing, as the old belief about timing suggests. In my particular case, one fateful turn was the elimination of a university appointment that I held from 1980 to 1984 in the U.S. Although my life and career had not gone in strictly linear, predictable, and traditional fashion prior to the appointment, until the spring of 1984, they had seemed to have a certain direction, coherence, and purpose.

My education in physical education began in the late 1960s at a small liberal arts college in Georgia, one I chose because I could continue to compete in basketball. There, at Berry College, I studied physical education and literature, an odd combination during such times. I was trained to become a teacher and a coach. As I entered graduate school in 1970, physical education had entered a new phase in its development in the United States, one in which its academic and theoretical development began in earnest. Fortunately when I began my graduate work, the cultural study of sport had begun to emerge, first in the form of sport sociology, sport history, and sport psychology, soon to be followed by sport philosophy and sport literature. I eventually sought a combination of these subdisciplines as their collective perspectives engaged my interest. Of these, philosophy and literature came the nearest to offering answers to questions about the universal, timeless, and captivating mystery of sport.

After teaching and coaching for two years, I pursued the Ph.D. and by some synchronous miracle, I found a mentor in Robert G. Osterhoudt, a young and brilliant scholar who had studied with Earle Ziegler, among the first to pose serious philosophic questions about the nature and significance of sport and physical education and who thereby began the systematic and formal philosophic study of sport (Ziegler, 1968). The research and scholarship in sport philosophy, as well as sport history and sport sociology, entered what I consider to be its most creative phase, yet to be equaled in my view. In philosophy, Eleanor Metheny (1968) pondered the symbolic and representational movement forms, long before representation became the subject of much interest to sports scholars and with insights concerning the creative aspect of sport that most studies of representation and sport now exclude. That is to say, Metheny recognized the aesthetic and artistic possibilities of movement, sport, and dance. Similarly, Osterhoudt (1979), a Hegelian scholar, offered a humanistic and idealistic view, maintaining that sport, along with dance, comprise the movement arts. Howard Slusher (1967) brought forth the existential meanings of sport while Seymour Kleinman (1972) proposed phenomenology as a means to reveal the nature and significance of movement and dance. I was the fortunate beneficiary of the work of these scholars and professors, fashioning my own academic and theoretical skills during a time when these accomplished scholars entered such creative periods in their own work. It was their work that enabled me to begin to understand, in an intellectual way, the beautiful mystery and personal meaning of sport that I knew in a bodily and experiential sense and that now seems so far removed from many contemporary views and analyses of sport.

From these studies, I accepted what is referred to as a non-tenure track appointment in a large state university and was joined by two other young female scholars with similar appointments. We were all writing our dissertations and teaching during these years. The context in which we young women began our professional careers was a difficult one at best. We were without female mentors and placed in positions without the possibility of tenure to assure that standards of gender equality were met. The culture was, by law, required to act in accordance with standards of gender equality and gender equity, yet discrimination against women, and others, of course, took more subtle and egregious forms during the Reagan years. An ambitious man, who aspired to be a dean, chaired the department in which we worked. Colleges and universities, both large and small, began to define themselves as research institutions, and the phenomenon known as "publish or perish" became commonplace, even in departments of physical education and sports studies. I experienced my first taste of the "publish or perish" phenomenon, in its most uncivilized form, which was sweeping through all large universities in the U.S. and now pervades even the smallest of liberal arts colleges throughout the country. And while I had been prepared to take my place in such an environment, I did not anticipate the ruthless pursuit of such a goal.

Using a variety of carefully conceived strategies, one by one, the two other women and I were removed from our positions, all within the regulations of the university. In my case, the position was eliminated. The position I held in sport history was merged with one in sport sociology. A male colleague, who occupied the position in sport sociology and whom I helped hire, continued toward tenure, in spite of his questionable research practices. And so in the early spring of 1984, I learned that by the end of August, I would no longer have a position.

An environment blindly fueled by the "publish or perish phenomenon" can be catastrophic and damaging to the life and work of a young scholar. Moreover, it leaves unexamined the idea that substantial and important works cannot be evaluated by some quantification process, just as the lasting effects of teachers upon students are rarely momentarily realized. In the U.S. we now live with what such methods have done to the discipline, research, and teaching as irrelevant articles proliferate in obscure journals and teaching is subordinated to research (Jacoby, 1987).[1] In retrospect, I can now see that, to some extent, I was affected by a movement much more encompassing than I realized.

In the early 1960s, physical education in the United States entered a period of rather radical change. Scholars began to question the academic status of physical education and sought to establish itself as a "legitimate" discipline of scholarly inquiry, apart from its practical application. There was much concern for the need to identify a specific body of knowledge, a theoretical base, and a central academic focus of the discipline. The shift from the pedagogical to the theoretical, from the teaching of sport to the study of sport, and the renaming of physical education as exercise science, biomechanics, kinesiology, sport science, or a combination thereof, had, and continues to have, profound and dramatic effects on research, curriculum, and the training of teachers and researchers of sport and physical education.

In the context of a pragmatic shift in the function of universities and colleges and accompanying the rapid growth of professional and educational sport, physical education shifted its focus away from the educational importance of physical education to the service of elite athletic performance and commercialized sport. Such changes bespeak an elitism that often goes unquestioned in much of the scholarship devoted to American sport and physical education. With such changes, the dominant focus of the discipline became more natural scientific, and exercise physiology and biomechanics came to dominate departments of physical education. These changes have had serious consequences for those scholars in the social scientific and humanistic study of sport. Within this context, the subdiscipline of sport philosophy began to be marginalized in the 1980s, as courses devoted to philosophic matters began to be excluded from curricula in sports studies. It was not long thereafter that sport history and sport sociology began to suffer a similar fate. Ph.D. programs in these subjects and positions related to the teaching of these subjects began a decline that has continued in most colleges and universities in the U.S. In the place of such studies, sports management programs, devoted to the preparation of workers for commercialized (as opposed to educational) sports programs, began to develop. Such were the years of an academic discipline that began to divide itself into scholar-researcher/teacher-practitioner, between theory and practice, and between a professional/disciplinary focus, creating an academic fault line that has continued to fragment the discipline.

Such a development in physical education seems even more disturbing and purposeless in the context of rapidly changing lifestyles and consequent health-related problems in the American culture. At a time during which physical education programs were badly needed in schools across the country and astonishing levels of obesity began to appear, physical education programs were in sharp decline at all levels of education,[2] and the discipline developed in the service of elite athletic performance and commercialized exercise programs. As such notable thinkers as George Santanya (1972) and Johan Huizinga (1949) noted, the play element was in serious decline, having begun its demise with the industrial revolution. Moreover, when the insights and analyses of scholars in the social sciences and humanities were most needed, departments of exercise science and sports studies shunned their intellectual contributions to the discipline.

Oddly enough the subject of my dissertation (Bandy, 1982) that examined the academic development of physical education in the United States hinted at such a development, but I failed to realize that it foreshadowed the rapid changes that were to come within the discipline in the years that followed and that such changes would, in fact, impact significantly on my life and work. My reaction to the situation was one of great pain, vacillating between rage and despair. I could not imagine that I could or would continue to work in an educational system that devalued teaching to such an extent and evaluated research in irrational and potentially destructive ways. At the time, jobs in the cultural study of sport became increasingly difficult to find. So in both an intellectual and a practical sense, I simply had nowhere to go. Nor could I feel that the elimination of my position was purely a matter of economics or organizational restructuring. It was personal and political, and such thoughts continue to surface as I see others suffer similar fates in their academic careers. As all feminists know, the personal is political and the political is personal.

My experience was not, however, without a beautiful edge and a promising turn. While I held the university position, feminism came into higher education, and the university where I was teaching established the first program in women's studies in the country. There I met my first feminists and joined them in colloquia and seminars. As women's participation in sport was also dramatically increasing, I began to find a fruitful and personally satisfying focus for my work.

I took solace in travel some months after my position was eliminated, traveling for several months from Tokyo to Kyoto to Hong Kong to Bombay to Agra, on to Cairo and Luxor, and then farther west to Athens, Zurich, Berlin, and Munich. It was then from Budapest along the Danube to Vienna and then to Paris. From there I attended my first international conferences in London and Glasgow and returned home to California. From such international contacts and experiences, I realized the isolation in which Americans live and the dangers of such a life. I began to feel rather provincial and uneducated. I had an uncertain yearning that my country and culture could not fulfill.

In January 1986, I fled my profession, my culture, and my country having suffered a fate not uncommon among young female scholars in colleges and universities in the United States at the time. Paris became my home for two years. I lived in small rooms in different parts of the city, slept on the floor, studied French at the Sorbonne with young people half my age, took jobs that few academics would consider, and rode on the metro with laborers on their way to work before dawn. I read great literature, much of which had been written by others who had also sought refuge in Paris, learned about art in some of the greatest museums of the world, and healed my soul in the city with a soul. From Paris I took a much-needed sense and appreciation of beauty, and, equally as important, I discarded the American notion that a human being is defined by her work.

In cafés, small rooms, and parks, I read the works of Edith Wharton, F. Scott Fitzgerald, Ernest Hemingway, Marcel Proust, Gertrude Stein, Colette, James Joyce, and countless others whose lives had been infused with the gifts of Paris and the French. It was in Paris that I came to be enamored with the incomparable Suzanne Lenglen whose life and achievements continue to engage me. I left the sitting rooms of Wharton's old New York and moved into the interior spaces of women's minds of the great Marguerite Duras. I circled around the bodies of Camille Claudel and Auguste Rodin and was drawn through modernity by *The Sleeping Muse* of the great Constantin Brancusi, whose work rivals, in my view, the portrayal of beauty by the ancients. Picasso, Braque, Leger, and Munch showed me ways of seeing that took me away from Monet, Cassat, and Renoir, and allowed me to step through the open, swirling, and pained bodies of Francis Bacon. Line, form, and color began to interest me. Words, formed by culture and history, seeped through into my language.

Paris yields herself to no one, and this is so in an inexplicable way that I find at once disturbing and satisfying, urgent and latent. I came to discover that cities have a gender and a dominant color, later to find out that Mary McCarthy, who wrote so beautifully about Florence, felt the same. Paris is female, gray, and an admixture of burgundy and aubergine.

I would be forever drawn to Paris with her sultry, sensual, and unrelenting beauty and freed by her from the constraints and inadequacies of my own culture.

In Paris, I finished my first book, *Coroebus Triumphs: An Alliance of Sport and the Arts* (Bandy, 1988), an edited collection of papers from the first meeting of the Sport Literature Association. Otherwise, I could not write, only reading and keeping diaries for several years to come. Matters of the heart took me back to my country where I returned to academia as a teacher and director of a small program of physical education at an international university in southern California. I welcomed the return to teaching and advised student athletes from many different countries. However, I found administrative work rather unsatisfying, and after five-and-one-half years the university canceled its intercollegiate athletic program. Soon thereafter, the physical education program was cancelled. I stayed at the university for some months thereafter and could have remained as the director of the liberal arts program, however, the work was not related to sport and I had no passion for it.

This time it was death, rather than culture, that beckoned me. My family began to die, and my partner was terminally ill. And so I left southern California to return to the south. Again, I found myself on the outside of academia and jobless. In a small, provincial town in Appalachia, I tried to find a position in university, only to be asked by the head of a department of physical education and exercise science if I had retired. This comment was followed by one in which I was informed that within a 60 mile radius of the university, there were several people with PhDs who were looking for work. At the time, I was only 45 years old, had studied in one of the best graduate programs in the country, with one of the most accomplished scholars in the discipline, had published, and had worked and studied abroad. However, my career path was not traditional and unexplainable to many who had followed more traditional paths. Eventually I was hired by the university, and in 1993 I began to write again, after five years of silence.

From this provincial place, I returned each summer to Europe and spent my summers in Paris. I began to work with sport literature with the idea that women's creative writings about sport had not been widely studied. Moreover, sport literature had a decidedly American slant, and I felt that a more international perspective was needed.

I yearned to return to Europe, and after repeated attempts, I won a position as a Fulbright scholar to the Hungarian University of Physical Education, a position that was extended for two years. I soon discarded the notion of international for the idea of transnational, one nurtured in Central Europe, where scholars are skeptical about the notion of the modern nation state and the ill effects and exploitative nature of globalization and internationalization that are associated with the market economy. After five-and-one-half years of work, I completed, with a scholar from literature, *Crossing Boundaries: An International Anthology of Women's Experiences in Sport* (Bandy & Darden, 1999). My editor told me that "transnational" was not an acceptable title. It had to be "international"; otherwise book sales would be limited because readers would not know what the word "transnational" meant. Hesitatingly, I accepted his ideas.

I remained in Budapest for five years, working in an institution that had trained coaches and teachers for 75 years and retained the traditions and methods of training teachers that were similar to those with which I had been educated. In this way, I felt at home among teachers and scholars who had not divided the discipline into a hierarchically ordered one of researchers and teachers, and who required students to hold to the traditions of the social sciences and humanities. Entailed in the Hungarian sense of sport were deep cultural traditions that revealed an appreciation of sport that seemed to me to be no longer present in my country. Even so, whispers and traces of the Americanization of higher education and the market economy could be felt in physical education from my first days there in 1997. Already, discussions of the "impact factor," a Hungarian version of the "publish or perish" phenomenon, were ever present and looming in the lives of young scholars. New programs in sport management were also beginning to develop in the university to meet the needs of a developing market economy.

It was again in feminist circles where I forged new ideas about my work. In Budapest, I furthered my education in feminism through an association with the Department of Gender Studies at the Central European University, where I also taught. There I shaped new ideas about feminist thought that were refined by a feminism that was challenging the hegemonic North American and Western European versions of feminism. Accomplished feminist scholars from all over the world grace this department, and such a cross-section and mixture of feminisms requires a reconsideration of many basic assumptions and preliminary notions upon which one's own ideas and scholarship rests, if one has been steeped in American feminism. Of course, such changes can be wrought through the literature, but not so deeply as when confronted by scholars from other parts of the world who rightfully object to the imposition of Western feminism upon their own experiences and who often prefer the French to the American feminism. Such experiences have led me to consider the overwhelming influence of North American feminism upon feminist scholarship in sport throughout North America and Western Europe and the need to reflect upon the benefits of a reconsideration of our approach to feminism as Jennifer Hargreaves (2000) has apparently done in her recent book, *Heroines of Sport: The Politics of Difference and Identity.*

As spring now arrives hesitatingly and belatedly to the east coast of Jutland, I find myself in yet another cultural and sporting milieu. Again language can be part of the challenges of living and working in another culture. In this case it is simply the word "sport." The Danish word *idræt* has no obvious, contemporary corollary in English. The English word "compete," derived from the French *competere*, which means to struggle together entailing notions of being together and desire, is the word that comes closest to connotations of *idræt*. Even so, to compete, in the contemporary American sense, has lost its sense of a common or shared struggle. *Idræt* has a more all-encompassing definition, perhaps to denote an activity that has not been so affected by modernization and professionalization in sport. As I have come to understand, the concept is derived from *id*, which means to struggle and *dræt* which refers to the idea of honor. Such notions come from the medieval Nordic, and, in its contemporary form, *idræt* is often used to designate a purer form of sport. Perhaps it harkens back to former times when the notions of sport encompassed Nordic ideas similar to the Greek notions of *agon*, the contest or the struggle, and *arete*, skill or excellence. Even so, it likely differs from these Greek notions.[3]

The move to Scandinavia has provoked yet another turn in my mind about my work and perhaps about the direction that research in the discipline should go. I have been certain for some time now that the focus on sport in the discipline has precluded information about the physically recreative and sporting practices of peoples who lived in times and cultures other than the ancient Greek and the modern era. Of particular interest are the marginalized and excluded peoples; most importantly for my concerns are the sporting and physically recreative practices of women.[4] Equally as important, the more or less exclusive focus on sport has marginalized and excluded the significant and necessary contributions of the social sciences and humanities to the discipline of sport and physical culture. For some time, I have begun to refocus my research and teaching on physical and body culture, a more encompassing term, which enables far more engaging work, especially as the research pertains to women. The notion of *idræt* has further pointed me toward these reconsiderations.

Such thoughts provoke new approaches to feminist analyses. From my transnational experiences, I am searching for a new way to move beyond the limitations of my own cultural experience and subdisciplinary/interdisciplinary perspectives, as well as the limitations of postmodern thought, which have always been troubling for a variety of reasons, not the least of which is its view of the body and the impossibility of an ecstatic, erotic, and chaotic body (Pronger, 1998). I have now begun to engage the notion of transdisciplinarity as a both a concept (or structure) and a methodology. The idea is to circle around and through ideas about physical and body culture; to reject the linear and the associative in search of connections woven from seemingly vacuous spaces.

This approach will, I hope, overcome the difficulties of binary logic and mind-body oppositions, which have plagued us for centuries. Following the work of the Romanian quantum physicist Basarab Nicolescu, as expressed in his *Manifesto of Transdisciplinarity*, transdisciplinarity "concerns that which is at once between the disciplines, across the different disciplines, and beyond all disciplines" (Nicolescu, 2002, p. 44). The aim is the unity of knowledge together with our being. "Its goal is to understand the present world, of which one of the imperatives is the unity of knowledge" (Nicolescu, 2002, p. 44). In addition to offering a different way of thinking exclusively in terms of binary logic, Nicolescu argues that reality exists on several levels at once. Unlike multidisciplinarity and interdisciplinarity, transdisciplinarity enables us to explore several levels at once from the perspectives of multiple disciplines simultaneously.[5] According to others, a transdisciplinary vision offers an active, open concept of nature and the human being, a vision that transcends the individual fields of the exact sciences, the humanities, and the social sciences. It encourages them to become reconciled with one another and with art, literature, poetry, and spiritual experiences (Brenner, 2003).[6]

For those of us who are interested in feminist perspectives of sport and physical culture I find such an approach encouraging. As Brian Pronger (1998) suggests in his insightful and important essay, "Post-Sport: Transgressing Boundaries in Physical Culture," postmodern strategy must stand in a more fundamental opposition to the modern, which it has not done. It has not freed the body nor successfully enabled us to transgress the spheres of boundary projects of modernity such as manhood and womanhood in sport and even sport itself, which Pronger maintains is a boundary project. I suggest that the notion of transdisciplinarity offers timely insights that may move us away from the passive, socially constructed, and culturally inscribed body that inhabits our research and controls our bodily experiences. Such a view across disciplines with multiple and simultaneous perspectives and levels of reality may enliven our work, revive the body, and enable us to make sense of our own transnational experiences and feminisms. The question, of course, is how to do this.

Upon deeper reflection about these experiences of living and working abroad, I always return to the insights of the great writers who treat the theme of isolation and the concept and role of the outsider in their works. I am remindful of what my compatriot Thomas Wolfe (1940) wrote in *You Can't Go Home Again*; going away always changes a person and in the attempt to return, one finds oneself a stranger in ones' country even in one's hometown and in the company of friends and family. Similarly, Colin Wilson's (1956) analysis in his classic work, *The Outsider*, which explores the role of the outsider in literature, is also instructive. The problem is that the outsider lives in another world, another reality, and, as a result, the self is a divided self, one that is experienced in both worlds. The problem then is the division and fragmentation of the self. Ultimately, this division provokes the quest of the outsider: to go in search of a reconnection, of a genuine identity, of a "way back" to a harmonious and undivided self. Equally as daunting are the words of Rainer Maria Rilke (1989) in his poem *Autumn Day*:

> Lord: it is time. The huge summer has gone by.
> Now overlap the sundials with your shadows,
> and on the meadows let the wind go free.

> Command the fruits to swell on tree and vine;
> grant them a few more warm transparent days,
> urge them on to fulfillment then, and press
> the final sweetness into the heavy wine.

> Whoever has no house now, will never have one.
> Whoever is alone will stay alone,
> will sit, read, write long letters through the evening,
> and wander on the boulevards, up and down,
> restlessly, while the dry leaves are blowing.

The outsider may indeed be the insider and the insider may be the outsider; in fact there may be no inside and outside. Body and skin and air merge. Movement takes us to places and moments that exist between cultures and times, realities that swirl in white places and dance through the mystery of the ages.

NOTES

1. An interesting cultural analysis of these general tendencies in the 1950s in the American culture is provided by Jacoby, R. (1987). *The last intellectuals: American culture in the age of academe.* New York: Basic Books.

2. Such declines and trends in physical education have also been noted in an international context. For further reading, refer to Hardman, K. (1995). Present trends in the state and status of physical education: a global context. *International Journal of Physical Education, 32,* 17–25.

3. I am indebted here to my colleagues, Olav Ballisager and Thora Oskarsdottir, for these insights into the origins and meanings of *idræt*.

4. Work of this nature has already been done. Refer to the analysis of colonial sport, which points in this direction, moving beyond the strict definitions of sport in Struna, N. (1996). *People of prowess: sport, leisure, and labor in early Anglo-America.* Chicago: University of Illinois Press, 1996.

5. Refer to Karen-Claire Voss's Review Essay of Basarab Nicolescu's Manifesto of *Transdisciplinarity.* Retrieved March 21, 2003, from http:///www.esoteric.msu.edu/Reviews/NicolescuReview.htm.

6. Refer to "A Broader View of Transdisciplinarity. " Retrieved March 21, 2003, from http://www.transdisciplinarity.net/statemnt.htm.

REFERENCES

Bandy, S. J. (1982). *The historical development of American physical education as a disciplined form of scholarly inquiry.* Unpublished Ph.D. dissertation, Arizona State University.

Bandy, S. J. (1988). *Coroebus triumphs: An alliance of sport and the arts.* San Diego, CA: San Diego State University Press.

Bandy, S. J., & Darden, A. S. (1999). *Crossing boundaries: An international anthology of women's experiences in sport.* Champaign, IL: Human Kinetics.

Brenner, J. E. (2003). A broader view of transdisciplinarity. Retrieved March 21, 2003, from http://www.transdisciplinarity.net/statemnt.htm.

Hardman, K. (1995). Present trends in the state and status of physical education: A global context. *International Journal of Physical Education, 32,* 17–25.

Hargreaves, J. (2000). *Heroines of sport: The politics of difference and identity.* London: Routledge.

Huizinga, J. (1949). *Homo ludens: A study of the play element in culture.* London: Routledge & Kegan Paul.

Jacoby, R. (1987). *The last intellectuals: American culture in the age of academe.* New York: Basic Books.

Kleinman, S. (1972). The significance of human movement: A phenomenological approach. In E. W. Gerber & W. J. Morgan (Eds.), *Sport and the body: A philosophical symposium* (pp. 175–178). Philadelphia: Lea & Febiger.

Metheny, E. (1968). *Movement and meaning.* London: McGraw-Hill.

Nicolescu, B. (2002). *Manifesto of transdisciplinarity.* Albany: State University of New York Press.

Osterhoudt, R. G. (1979). The term 'sport': Some thoughts on a proper name. In E. W. Gerber & W. J. Morgan (Eds.), *Sport and the body: A philosophical symposium* (pp. 4–10). Philadelphia: Lea & Febiger.

Pronger, B. (1998). Post-sport: Transgressing boundaries in physical culture. In G. Rail, (Ed.). *Sport and postmodern times* (pp. 277–298). Albany: State University of New York Press.

Rilke, R. M. (1989). Autumn day. In S. Mitchell (Ed.), *The selected poetry of Rainer Maria Rilke* (p. 11). New York: Vintage International.

Santayana, G. (1972). Philosophy on the bleachers. In E. W. Gerber & W. J. Morgan (Eds.), *Sport and the body: A philosophical symposium* (pp. 230–234). Philadelphia: Lea & Febiger.

Slusher, H. (1967). *Man, sport and existence: A critical analysis.* Philadelphia: Lea & Febiger.

Struna, N. (1996). *People of prowess: Sport, leisure, and labor in early Anglo-America.* Chicago: University of Illinois Press.

Voss, K-C. (2003). Review essay of Basarab Nicolescu's *Manifesto of transdisciplinarity.* Retrived March 21, 2003, from http:///www.esoteric.msu.edu/Reviews/NicolescuReview.htm.

Wilson, C. (1956). *The Outsider.* London: V. Gallancz.

Wolfe, T. (1940). *You can't go home again.* New York: Harper & Brothers.

Zeigler, E. (1968). *Problems in the history and philosophy of physical education and sport.* Englewood Cliffs, NJ: Prentice-Hall.

Chapter 11

A Collection of Fortuitous Encounters

Shona M. Thompson

I have a collection of birds. Not live ones but artistic models and images of them. It was more an accidental than deliberate collection, beginning with a tiny, china nuthatch given to me a long time ago by an ornithologist with whom I shared an apartment, as a memento of his British homeland. Then one day years later I looked around my home in New Zealand and noticed, to my surprise, that there were birds everywhere—carved, moulded, painted, sketched, printed, and stitched—gifts from friends and lovers and souvenirs of my own travels.

I have also accumulated a collection of encounters with Canada. Again, it seems more accidental than deliberate although it began with my decision to study there in the early 1970s. Then, when I sat down to write this chapter, I was similarly surprised to realize how frequently my journey as a feminist, sport sociologist kept coming back to one common theme—inspirational visits to Canadian institutions, fortuitous meetings with Canadian academics, associations with Canadian colleagues. These have shaped my journey and my work in various ways, as the following story will tell.

My story, however, is set in four different countries. It is not presented in an orderly time line but instead moves through these countries describing how my academic life developed and what influenced its direction. The story begins, appropriately I think, in Finland at a conference where I met Arja Laitinen and where I presented an analysis of New Zealand women's relationships to men's rugby. It then shifts back to New

Zealand to provide some background to that analysis and explains my interest in the topic. Next it moves to Canada, following the path I took to find and develop a feminist perspective from which to view the topic and, on an earlier visit, to the time when I was first introduced to the sociology of sport. It then jumps to Australia to describe the research that followed from my focus on men's rugby. Along the way I thread in some of the joys, trials, and tribulations I have experienced working as an academic within the university system.

JYVÄSKYLÄ, FINLAND

I met Arja Laitinen only once, in Finland in 1987 at the Jyväskylä International Congress on Movement and Sport in Women's Life. Her presentation at that congress about the obstacles she had experienced doing feminist research, and her bravery in voicing them within her own institution surrounded by the very men she criticized, was a profoundly moving and memorable moment from which I drew strength and commitment to my own feminist scholarship. I presented my first overtly feminist paper at that congress and affirmations of it were also memorable, such as having the editor of *IRSS* approach me afterward and invite me to submit it for publication in his journal, and having Ann Hall say to me at the banquet that evening, "I liked your paper, Shona."

To get to Jyväskylä in Finland from Dunedin in New Zealand, where I was living at the time, meant flying almost as far as it is possible around the globe without beginning to return. International long-distance travel was not new to me but when the Jyväskylä Congress was initially publicized it seemed way beyond my reach. As it happened, a profeminist male colleague was responsible for my getting there. Incensed by an announcement that the Bank of New Zealand was yet again sponsoring men's rugby, Bruce had marched into the university branch of that bank and had taken the manager to task on his organization's sexist sponsorship practices. Bruce came to my office afterward and our conversation went something like this:

> *Bruce*: You know that conference about women and sport that's coming up soon?
> *Shona*: The one in Finland? Yes.
> *Bruce*: Do you want to go?
> *Shona*: Well, yes, I'd love to, but . . . What are you suggesting?
> *Bruce*: Well, the Bank of New Zealand will sponsor you.
> *Shona*: What? No! You're kidding? How come?
> *Bruce*: I've just come from the manager's office. I told him that his bank's sponsorship of rugby was sexist.
> *Shona*: You did?! Wow! What happened?

Bruce: Well, he said I had a point and asked me what I thought he should do about it! It put me on the spot really. I was so surprised my mind went blank. So I told him about the international conference on women and sport and suggested his bank sponsor someone to it. It shouldn't be me; it shouldn't be any male, so I suggested you. He wants you to go talk to him about it.

So I did. The so-called sponsorship the bank manager offered was to loan me the fare to attend the conference at the extortionate interest rate of 20%, which was about 1.5% less than the standard borrowing rate in New Zealand at the time. Big deal! But, being flattered by the offer of any support at all, I accepted. It took me two years to fully pay back that loan but I still consider it was worth every cent. The congress was a milestone for me, where I began to find my own research voice and to realize I had something to say based on experiences from my own culture that could be of interest to others. More importantly, it gave me affirmation to stand confidently as a feminist sport sociologist, providing me with a legitimate framework for future work and a much-needed theoretical "identity" with which to claim a space within the university environment where I was then employed.

DUNEDIN, NEW ZEALAND

The paper I presented at the congress in Jyväskylä was completed while I was a lecturer at the University of Otago in Dunedin. It was titled "Challenging the hegemony: Women's opposition to rugby and the reproduction of a capitalist patriarchy." It had been a long time in the making—in some respects, a lifetime.

Its main focus was the male dominated sport of rugby union, which is much heralded as my country's national sport even though such a classification is both arrogant and androcentric. The extent to which rugby has been, and still is, associated with constructions of hegemonic masculinity and gendered power relations in New Zealand has been well documented (Fougere, 1989; James & Saville Smith, 1999; Phillips, 1986) and cannot be overstated.

While growing up, rugby had not actually been a big part of my life. I lived on a sheep farm in rural New Zealand, in a family where my father, my two brothers, numerous aunts, uncles, and cousins all played field hockey (although we found no need for the "field" bit). The most highly profiled and sanctioned sports in the country, however, were strongly gender marked—rugby for men and netball for women (Thompson, 2002). Netball was the only winter sport offered to girls at the primary school I attended so I was forced to play but found it far too physically restricted to be enjoyable. It was not until I was 12 years old and at high school that I had the opportunity to play organized field hockey. From then on I played it every season for the next 12 years.

My brothers also faced gender-based restrictions. Although they were able to play field hockey at primary school, when they moved on to their all-boys high school they were forced to play rugby for their first two years, presumably to "make men" of them before they were allowed to return to what was considered then to be the more effete sport of field hockey. It was the norm for rugby to be compulsory for boys in New Zealand high schools.

Girls did not play rugby then. As a young teenager I spent a brief time idolizing visiting international male players but mostly I was disinterested in the game. By the time I was 30, however, this disinterest had turned to embarrassment, frustration, rage, and despair as I witnessed my country being plunged into international disgrace and internal social turmoil because of the New Zealand Rugby Union's insistence on regular competition against Apartheid South Africa.

The long history of tension surrounding New Zealand's sporting exchanges with South Africa has been well analyzed and documented (Nauright & Black, 1995; Richards, 2001; Thompson, 1975). These tensions reached a crescendo in 1981 when the Springboks, South Africa's representative male rugby team, arrived in New Zealand for a tour of 14 games played over eight weeks. This tour contravened the Gleneagles Agreement signed by Commonwealth Heads of Governments, including our own, designed to stop all sporting contacts with South Africa and prevent further boycotts of major sporting events such as occurred at the 1976 Olympics in Montreal.

Within New Zealand, opposition to the 1981 tour was massive and became increasingly mobilized as the tour progressed. Equally vociferous were the stalwart rugby/tour supporters and the resulting clashes were enormous. The consequences reverberated throughout New Zealand society and left it deeply scarred (Fougere, 1981; Richards, 2001; Shears & Gidley, 1981). One of the many divisions was gender based. Women had joined the protest movement in large numbers, frequently opposing the men in their families. Maori women were particularly high profile as leaders. It was clearly recognized at the time that, as well as protesting against racism, women were expressing their long-held frustrations with the particular mix of white-supremist, patriarchal power that was vested in the sport of rugby and strongly intertwined with New Zealand politics and economics (Aitken & Noonan, 1981; Coney, 1981; Dann, 1982; Hall, 1981). Out of this frustration had grown an organization calling itself Women Against Rugby (WAR). Its rallying cry was for women to stop doing the (mostly domestic) labor traditionally done supporting rugby—laundry, providing food, fostering sons playing the game, accommodating husbands' participation. Considering the significance of this sport to the social fabric of the country, it was a profoundly political stance for women to take although at the time I did not fully appreciate this. It was several years before I understood the extent to which second-wave feminism had powered the protest.

Even though I was involved in the protest movement and felt passionately about its cause, I did not have much of an analysis beyond thinking that something particularly nasty was happening within my country, that rugby was to blame, and women knew it. At my workplace, as was so often the case, "The Tour" was such a potentially volatile and divisive topic of conversation that few dared raise it. Besides, gendered power relations were being played out in other ways.

I had been hired at Otago University's School of Physical Education (OUSPE) in 1978 to teach Recreation and Leisure Studies and Outdoor Education. In the meantime a new dean had been appointed who was hell-bent on turning this 40-plus year old school for the training of New Zealand's physical educators into a faculty of kinesiologists pumping out research publications. Someone had changed the rules of the game and different players were preferred. Most of my female colleagues and I were in insecure positions. Realizing we were all feeling aggrieved and vulnerable we formed a support group, calling ourselves the Unofficial Women's Committee when we were refused recognition within the official committee structure. Nevertheless, our ranks declined rapidly (Peart, 1986). Two senior women beat a hasty retreat and retired early, as did some men. These were people who had dedicated their lives to the physical education profession, who were well trained, highly competent and respected teachers, pioneers in tertiary physical education in New Zealand. I watched too many of them end their careers feeling worthless, overlooked, and discarded, and vowed I would not stay in mine so long that I finished it with similar sorrows.

Meanwhile I was struggling to stay in it at all! I scrambled for credibility and ways to achieve the things now more overtly expected of me, such as research publications and conference presentations. Male colleagues encouraged me and assisted with two strongly positivist studies, which were published (Thompson 1981a, 1985) but of which I did not feel particularly proud. I wanted to be able to say things that were more critical and woman-centred but did not know how to do so within the limitations of academic acceptability.

I knew that all was not well in the world of sport but I struggled to know how to express it. My unease had come partly from the social tensions leading up to the 1981 Springbok Rugby Tour, and partly from my developing comprehension of sexism in New Zealand society. I rejected the theory, popular at the time, that sport was merely a reflection of society and recall arguing this point with a colleague who was steadfastly guarding his territory as the only "legitimate" sport sociologist in the faculty. To me there seemed to be a much more dialectic relationship between sport and society, a conclusion that had mainly come from my observations of rugby. I knew some of what went on in men's rugby circles. I understood that these were sites where New Zealand men learned and practiced doing masculinity, with its associated misogynist and homophobic values. I also knew that men moved from those circles, taking the values and practices they had learned there, into positions of social, economic and political power. In my view this was no mere "reflection." My not yet well-developed arguments, however, were dismissed as being both ignorant and poor sociology. It was before I could call on the work of Lois Bryson (1983), Tim Curry (1991), or Varda Burstyn (1999) to help me articulate my claims.

My first public attempt at a critique of sport was to warn women of its horrors, for which I was severely criticized for implying that women should leave it well alone. It was at the Women and Recreation Conference in Wellington in 1981 where I presented a paper titled "Women in Sport – Is this what we want?" In it I emotively described cases of violence, child abuse, and cheating in sport, and crudely attempted to debunk the notion that sport participation was "character building" (Thompson, 1981b). I quoted Libby Darlison asking, "to what extent should women be attempting to determine an ideology of their own in sport? Is not pursuing the male paradigm . . . admitting a stroke at the stigma of femininity and the legitimacy of that male eminence that coined the standards" (Darlison, 1980, p. 38), although I understood neither the analysis nor the vocabulary to fully comprehend what she meant in describing sport as a male paradigm.

Libby, an Australian, had been invited as a keynote speaker to this conference in New Zealand, being well recognized at the time as one of the very few feminist sport sociologists in the region. In her address she called for feminists and sportswomen to talk to each other, emphasizing that these two groups of women were viewed as being mutually exclusive, not fully understanding the barriers to women's equality in sport and recreation on one hand, or appreciating its potential for women's liberation on the other (Darlison, 1981). Libby chaired the session in which I presented my paper and obviously recognized the struggle I was having in trying to contextualize and theorize my concerns about sport. She saw the answer. Her comments to me afterward went something along the lines of, "Good work, Girl, but go get yourself some feminism!"

EDMONTON, CANADA

I found feminism at the University of Alberta while visiting there on sabbatical leave in 1984. This was not my first time at the University of

Alberta but I shall describe my earlier visit in more detail later. In 1984 I enrolled in a course called Feminism in Canada taught in the Canadian Studies Department by Susan Jackel. It was the first course at the University of Alberta to have the word feminism in its title and was filled to capacity for precisely that reason. We women read such works as those by Mary Daly, Geraldine Finn, Heidi Hartmann, Nellie McClung, Mary O'Brien, Dorothy Smith, and many others. We had long, impassioned debates about women's standpoint, institutionalized sexism, abortion, and feminist ethics, often continuing these discussions in the nearby bar long beyond the official class time. Suddenly so much made sense to me; it felt like coming home.

With clarity afforded by distance (both geographical and temporal) and my new-found theoretical tools, I began to develop a feminist analysis of the 1981 Springbok Rugby Tour of New Zealand, initially as an essay for a course tutored by Catherine Bray who gave us Williams (1978) to read and impressed us with the concept of hegemony. These beginnings eventually became the paper I presented at the Congress in Jyväskylä and was subsequently published (Thompson, 1988; 1994). It focused on New Zealand women's involvement in the protest against the "tour," presenting reasons for why we were there and arguing that a collective feminist consciousness fueled our opposition to the patriarchal relations of power within New Zealand that rugby both symbolized and perpetuated. I also argued that our protests were a legitimate challenge to the current hegemony and I wrote optimistically that a new social order was in the making, one in which men's rugby would no longer reign supreme. What a silly notion. Suffice to say this did not come about (Jackson, 1995; Thompson, 2000).

My first time in Canada had been nine years earlier, in 1973. I had gone there as a 22-year-old with a Trained Teacher's certificate, two years' experience teaching primary school and a huge thirst for adventure. It was my particular version of the great Kiwi OE[1], a traditional ritual whereby generations of young New Zealanders have felt compelled to abandon this small group of islands in the far southern Pacific Ocean and seek "overseas experience." I had been accepted into the University of Alberta's Faculty of Physical Education with advanced credit and during the next three years completed the requirements for its BPE and MA degrees.

On reflection it was probably the biggest adventure of my life. Certainly one of the most profound. I visited the campus again in autumn 2002. Wandering nostalgically around, reveling in vistas of blue spruce trees and mountain ash turning yellow, feeling crispness in the air and wondering if I still retained the ability to smell a snowfall coming, I felt overwhelmingly amazed by what I had done almost 30 years earlier. On a beginner teacher's salary I had saved enough in two years to fund it entirely myself. I had left New Zealand for the very first time, on an airplane journey that required five stopovers, to travel alone to a country on the other side of the world where I knew not a soul, to enroll for a university qualification unheard of in my country at the time, and to the absolute bewilderment of everyone I knew except one encouraging, male lecturer at the teacher's college I attended who had done similar by traveling to study at the University of Oregon. And all simply because I thought it would be fun, which, of course, it was.

I had toyed with the idea of majoring in dance but the lure of the Canadian outdoors was greater and outdoor education became my main focus. It also took me away from field hockey because weekend games clashed with outdoor field trips. I plunged into new adventures such as canoeing, rock climbing, orienteering, cross-country skiing, ice fishing, and camping in spruce-bough bivouacs in subzero temperatures, eventually finding myself in the incongruous situation as a graduate assistant being expected to teach Canadian students how to snowshoe. Another great adventure was the compulsory, final year course, PEd 449 Sociology of Sport. To coin a cliché, it blew my mind. It was only the sixth year a course considering the social aspects of sport had been taught at the University of Alberta and was one of the earliest anywhere. I found it utterly fascinating, mostly because its focus was a world almost completely foreign to me. I had landed in the midst of highly organized, professionalized, commercialized, and televized sport at least 20 years before we saw anything like it in New Zealand and was drawn to the nascent critical edge that sociology gave to comprehending this amazing phenomenon.

I had not intended to stay in Edmonton beyond completing the BPE (there was still so much more of the world to see) but I was enjoying myself too much to leave so I enrolled in the graduate program. Part of my MA degree included two courses in which I did projects about sportswomen and 'tomboys.' One was "Psycho-social Aspects of Women in Sport" taught by Ann Hall. This was 1975, a time that Ann herself describes as being devoid of understanding "that sporting practises are historically produced, socially constructed and culturally defined to serve the interests and needs of powerful groups in society" (Hall, 1996, p. 6). There was very little feminist literature to read and we were not couching our analyses within a framework that could be described as gender relations (Birrell, 1988). Nevertheless, we were trying hard to grapple with issues within sport that spoke about women's experiences.

My project was based on interviews with a few prominent female sports players amongst my PE student associates. It described how they had all considered themselves tomboys when they were young but that most were now uneasy with the term and attempting to "grow out" of it. I did not have the words to articulate it as such then but their attempts would now be described as doing gender in hyper-feminine ways (Cox & Thompson, 2000). At the time, analyses of tomboyism as a phenomenon were greatly influenced by Money and Ehrhart's (1972) work. They described girls with preferences for the outdoors and active athletics as tomboys and linked them with fetal androgenization caused by progestinic drugs prescribed in the 1950s to pregnant women with a history of habitual miscarriage.

In a second course, Research Methods, students were required to prepare an application for a Canada Council Research Grant. Building on my work for the previous course and taking my lead from Money and Ehrhart (1972), I proposed a study in which I would identify a group of self-professed tomboys, record their sporting histories, and analyze their mothers' medical records to determine whether or not they had been prescribed progestinic drug during the pregnancy that produced these tomboy daughters (ethical or privacy issues were apparently not serious concerns back then). Presumably my intention was to investigate a possible cause and effect.

After presenting this hypothetically proposed research to the class, I recall being asked why I was not planning to actually do the project. I replied that my thesis research in outdoor education was already well advanced, which was true but also a good excuse. I was by then feeling most uncomfortable about studying tomboyism within the theoretical framework I had proposed. If one was to accept a label such as "tomboy," I knew I had been one and was proud of it. Pursuing a line of inquiry, therefore, which presupposed that physically active and confident girls were the outcome of medical aberration or misadventure, did not sit easily alongside my developing comprehension that women's biology had been repeatedly used to blame, explain, or excuse our disadvantage, especially by those in the medical profession. The obvious outcome of thoroughly critiquing the theoretical foundations of my proposed research, as I should have done, would have been to discard the idea and choose, at least another framework and method, if not another topic altogether. How could I admit this, however, to the professor engaged in grading my work as presented? Besides, I had written to my mother to ask her if I had been a progestin-androgenized baby. It figured, I thought. She had had miscarriages; I knew she had been medicated for this during at least one pregnancy; I was born in the 1950s. But her subsequent communication ignored my question and this unusual silence was disturbing. Did she take it as blame? Did my curiosity touch, in her, possible feelings of guilt about how I was not "doing gender" in expected ways, or instead, about my older sister's very problematic congenital hip displasia? I could not bring myself to raise the subject with her again.

I look back at it now and find that my MA thesis ignored gender. It also ignored class, race, or anything related to structures or power relations. While I considered it to be sociological, its concepts were much more closely aligned with psychology. I had wanted to capture the special dynamics that occur amongst a group of people who share an exciting and challenging adventure in a beautiful wilderness environment. I tried to do so by measuring self-concept changes and comparing them with the perceptions of others, using Likert scales, T-tests and SPSS with state-of-the-art computer key-punch cards (Thompson, 1975). I found nothing statistically significant, which I put down to the too-short and superficial time period my outdoor expedition groups were in the wilderness environment.

It did not occur to me that the method itself may have been lacking and I tried replicating the research back in New Zealand a few years later. By then I was at OUSPE, where each year we took the entire cohort of Year 2 students to outdoor education camps of 10 days' duration, which, I reasoned, would be a more likely length of time and intensity to find something statistically significant. The project, however, did not get far. For one, I needed help to make sense of the computer-generated statistical results but could not bring myself to ask for it because to do so would have exposed me as being the impostor in academe that I considered myself to be. So the data remained unanalyzed. But secondly, Paradise Camp where we took the students had, by then, become an extremely special place. It is set amongst native beech forest at one end of Lake Wakatipu in the South Island, beneath rugged mountain ranges and between the glacial Dart and Rees Rivers. The teaching staff would spend almost the entire summer month of February there, living predominantly under canvas, without electricity and sharing wonderful, sometimes life-changing experiences with our students. Any attempt to quantify this experience, using some arbitrary and abstracted measure, seemed to me to be a huge violation of the immense beauty of the place, the emotional response it usually evoked and the intangible developmental processes occurring. Positivist research methods proved grossly inadequate but, within the scientific traditions of physical education, I had not the vision, the tools nor the support to develop a workable alternative. It was delightful, therefore, two decades later to read Geoff Ockwell's (2001) master's thesis in which he had used narrative inquiry to reflexively explore his own and others' sense of place related to that magnificent environment. Geoff had been an undergraduate student at Paradise Camp at about the time I was foisting Likert Scales on them!

As Hall noted (1996, p. 7), we are products of our time. The point here, I think, is that the issues of interest to me and the questions I was asking during the 1970s and early 1980s could not be adequately dealt with using the theories or methods of the day, which were the traditional research tools employed within physical education. I did not feel at all comfortable with the research process until much later, when I had the opportunity and skills to use qualitative methods, which came alongside feminism.

PERTH, AUSTRALIA

I jump now to 1989. I left OUSPE at the beginning of that year, by which time I was the only female, full-time member of the academic staff. We had been 50% when I had arrived there 10 years earlier and, as the percentage rapidly tumbled, the decision-makers of the university paid only lip-service to addressing the problematic imbalance. A more entrenched "old boys' club" would have been hard to find. Coming to the conclusion that my impotence in the faculty was a consequence of not having a PhD, I ambivalently succumbed to the pressure to do one. Probably closer to the truth, I was dragged to Australia, weakly protesting, by my partner, Bob, who was determined to rescue us both from an academic environment in which I had become so jaded that the only future I could see for myself was to move to Central Otago and farm goats. Being drained of energy, however, it was easier to go along with his vision of our dual academic careers. He accepted a research fellowship at the University of Western Australia in Perth, where he had done his PhD a few years previously, and I enrolled as a student in women's studies within the department of sociology at Murdoch University in the same city.

This was not an environment, however, into which I fitted smoothly. Those around me did not seem to know how to respond to someone with a strange and somewhat suspicious academic background in physical education, and who wanted to study something as distasteful, in their eyes, as sport. Credibility was an endless struggle, achieved because my work was based in feminism but always conditional on my saying the correct thing. Besides, I was a New Zealander in Australia and rivalry abounds between these two neighbouring countries.

I arrived knowing only that I wanted to study something about women's relationship to sport through the participation of their family members. This interest had come directly from what I had observed during the 1981 Springbok Rugby Tour and my attempts to understand this through writing the "Challenging the Hegemony" paper. The shift needed to turn that interest into a research question within a workable theoretical framework came to me when I was, once again, back in Canada. This time it was 1988 and I was traveling on a Canadian Studies Faculty Enrichment Award granted through the Canadian High Commission. At a leisure studies research seminar at Dalhousie University in Halifax, I presented my work about New Zealand women's opposition to the Springbok Rugby Tour. Susan Shaw and her colleagues in the department at the time were intrigued by my focus on the domestic labor that New Zealand women had traditionally done for their husbands' sport and the way this had been strategically withdrawn as a form of protest. "You know," Sue said at lunch afterward, "it's like being married to the sport. It reminds me of Janet Finch's work about women being married to their husbands' work. You might find her book interesting, Shona."

I did. Sue loaned me her copy of *Married to the Job. Wives Incorporation in Men's Work* (Finch, 1983) in which Finch reported research about women married to men who were doctors, clergymen, politicians, and railway operators to show how this work both structured the women's lives and elicited their contribution to it. I saw clear parallels between Finch's analysis of women being married to men's jobs and women's experiences of being married to their husbands' sport, even when it was played as leisure. I wanted, therefore, to investigate how it was that women were incorporated into men's sport in this way, but I also wanted to extend the question further and consider children's sport and its demand on mothers.

I chose tennis as my focus for several reasons, not the least being that it is widely played in Australia and arguably the most culturally important of the mass participation sports. I interviewed 46 women in three, often overlapping, groups: mothers of junior players, wives/partners of male players and women who were veteran players, themselves, thus longterm members of the widely available, local tennis clubs. Overall, I found that this sport could have a profound impact on the everyday lives of the women involved and could be particularly demanding of them. I situated my analysis of this within a discussion of the material and ideological conditions of these women's lives. I drew on Michele Barrett's (1988) socialist feminist analysis and highlighting how these conditions were organized by heterosexual gender relations, driven by ideologies of wifehood and motherhood, which were both reflected in and constructed by sport.

The thesis was subsequently published as a book (Thompson, 1999). I have noticed that libraries and bookstores seem unsure of how to categorize it. Is it sociology, sport science, women's studies or family studies? My first royalties check, for US$1.47, remains uncashed and pinned above my desk, providing a comical conversation piece and keeping me humble.

I am fortunate enough to be able to say I thoroughly enjoyed doing my PhD, which I have come to learn is not a common experience. With a scholarship and Bob's full support I was able to be a full-time student for much of the time and had very few other roles to juggle. It was a luxurious indulgence, a time out, made even more enjoyable by living in the charming township of Fremantle and sail-racing every Saturday afternoon on a gracious old ferro-cement sloop, with a crew of mostly women, a skipper who never yelled at us, and for the weekly fee of a cheap bottle of Australia's fine Methode Champagnoise.

As a researcher, however, what both fascinated and challenged me throughout the entire process was my relationship with the women I interviewed and my location in their tennis culture. It meant endlessly addressing issues related to identity, credibility, and voice.

I had a lot in common with these women, in that the majority were white, Anglo-Saxon, middle-class, and around my age, but there was one key disjuncture. I have deliberately rejected the institution of marriage and have remained childless by choice. To be honest I had not, up to this point, reflected on any possibly associated reasons why, therefore, my research interest has been to critique the ideologies of wifehood and motherhood as they are played out through sport. But the women I interviewed were obviously curious about this and invariably asked about my familial circumstances. I was always honest (if not expansive) in my reply. A moment of heavy silence usually interrupted the flow of conversation after I said I did not have children. I am used to this uncomfortable pause. It stands in place of the question from people who are afraid to ask if my childlessness is by choice but are assuming it is not. In the context of these interviews, however, especially those with the mothers of junior tennis players, I felt unable to fill that silence with an explanation about how I had chosen to reject the lifestyle of motherhood that I was now prevailing on them to describe to me. The irony of the situation would have served only to create distance between us, which, as a researcher, I was guarding against. I suspect many thought my focus on the demands of motherhood was some sort of compensatory therapy I needed to act out and they were graciously indulging me. It always remained an awkward, unaired tension.

Another area that challenged me on issues of credibility related to my location as an outsider to tennis. Early in the process I had applied to the Australian Sports Commission National Sports Research Centre (ASCNSRC) for a financial grant. My first application was unsuccessful but one of the anonymous reviewers had suggested it would be worthwhile in a future conceptualization of the study to include data from participant observations. Considering that particular application proposed research focusing exclusively on mothers, I had, by then, received enough of the sort of comments about my research to suspect that the suggestion was motivated by the reviewer's belief that the "naïve" researcher (i.e., myself) needed to see "ugly" parents in action and thus the "real" story about sport mothers that I would only see if I sat on the sidelines. My thesis critiqued this perception of women in sport and I did sit on the sidelines to give weight to my critique. Nevertheless it was an attractive suggestion that I could legitimately include the membership fee to a tennis club into the budget of a future grant application and view the research environment as a player. At the time, the average annual membership fee to a tennis club in Perth was around AUS$200. There was a large tennis club very near where I was living; all its courts were grass and beautifully maintained; I can play tennis reasonably well; Bob was keen to join me; it would have been a quintessential West Australian experience of the type I usually welcomed when living in a different country. Why, then, did I not do so?

I argued in my thesis, and still stand by it, that remaining outside tennis and fully disclosing my interest as a researcher was the more honorable and worthwhile position for me to take. However, I had to admit that the more I learned about the tennis culture in Western Australia the more I realized how difficult it would have been for me to become a fully immersed insider.

To begin with, I heard stories about how it could take several years before new tennis club members were fully accepted into the social fabric of the club, unless they were exceptionally good players. I was not an exceptionally good player. I heard that some groups could be cliquey, especially if the members had been playing together for decades as had most of the women I interviewed. But what discouraged me most was the type of labor demanded of women in tennis clubs, and how their experiences of tennis were constructed in very classed, gendered, and hyper-heterosexual ways.

I could not have passively taken my turn on the roster to serve tea for the men, for example, knowing they were never expected to reciprocate. I could not have gone with my partner to the club's fund-raising social activities, performed my (and only ever my) expected role of taking "a plate" of home cooking to share, and comfortably watched my identity there be constructed as the other (read lesser) half of a heterosexual couple. I cringed at the thought of having to wear a little white skirt; I wondered how I would explain, at Mid-week Ladies competitions, not having to rush away afterward to pick up children or prepare a family meal, knowing all along that these many deviations from "normal" women tennis-players' behavior would have further added to the length of time taken for me to be accepted enough for the exercise to have achieved its purpose, whatever that may have been.

In an early draft of my thesis, where I discussed the limitations of being an "outsider" to tennis culture, I had included a comment about not joining a tennis club but had not elaborated. My New Zealander colleague, Lynne Star, who carefully read my drafts, wrote in the margin, "Wimp! Go on, say it. They would have thought you were weird!" She was right; they would have. As my research progressed and I got to know the tennis culture better, I felt increasingly more alienated from it. This raised important issues about feminist praxis and the efficacy of bringing about positive changes for people who are marginalized and silenced (Kirby & McKenna, 1989). I had presented a strong case about the invisibility, marginalization, and exploitation of women in tennis in Western Australia but had avoided being in a position to do much about it.

Overall, I would have to say that my research was not well received in Australia. I will not go so far as to say it was a conspiracy but many things transpired that tempted me to think so. For example, a paper based on my research was rejected by the Australian committee hosting the 1993

Congress of the International Association for Sport and Physical Education for Girls and Women (IASPEGW). A research report funded by the ASCN-SRC was "lost" in that organization for two years before my regular inquiries eventually precipitated it being printed. Three separate attempts to have articles about my research published in the local, *West Tennis* newsletter were thwarted by two different editors. By comparison, presentations of the research in both New Zealand and Canada received quite substantial media interest (e.g., Long, 1994; Walch, 2000; 'Research airs sport's dirty washing,' 2000), all of which is interesting, considering it is about Australian women and Australian sport. I put considerable effort into communicating my results directly back to the women in Western Australian whom I had interviewed but much beyond that was made difficult by the fact that, on completion of the project, I returned to New Zealand.

AUCKLAND, NEW ZEALAND

I went back to New Zealand in 1994, to a position as senior lecturer in the Department of Leisure Studies at the University of Waikato. It was a shock. I had left New Zealand as a junior academic, silenced and overlooked. I came back to face the dauntingly high expectations placed on someone appointed to a senior position, with young, confident, articulate, and ever-challenging colleagues. Where, I wondered, had been the gentle middle years to prepare me for this? Six months later Bob also returned, to head a new Department of Sport and Exercise Science at the University of Auckland. We commuted between the two cities for three years before I, too, joined that department.

Bob is Canadian, a graduate of the University of Alberta, a biomechanist. We met in New Zealand at Otago University where we were both lecturers of equal status in the School of Physical Education. Nineteen years later he was my boss! The university administration found the situation more problematic than we did, however, taking 10 weeks to determine my contract and, without once consulting me, redefined the position so that it became split between two faculties and I was line managed by someone else. Even though this arrangement was unusual, cumbersome, and confusing I was told it was in my best interest.

Within the Department of Sport and Exercise Science I am also different in other ways. I am the only sociologist and the only arts person in a department of kinesiologists in a faculty of science. I am the only qualitative researcher and the only person conversant with feminist literature. I have become the pedantic person who is expected to ask "why (always) male subjects" when graduate students present their research proposals. I am the only New Zealand–born academic in the department (60% of my colleagues are Canadian) and find that I am increasingly directing my feminist consciousness toward issues of race and the interests of our Maori students.

Being different is tiring. So too is the realization that, while young students consider feminism irrelevant, sexism still surrounds them. The struggle is unrelenting. I was reminded of this most recently when I sent a book proposal to a local publishing company. The book collects together some excellent research that has been done in various New Zealand universities about New Zealand women and sport. It has 14 contributors and addresses issues such as identity, sexuality, ethnicity, racism and agism. Its coeditor, Camilla Obel, and I are excited about the quality of the work and about it being a timely first for this country. The acquisitions editor of the publishing company rejected it, however, because, in his words, "only half the student population would read it" and thus it would not be commercially viable. Commercial viability, here, equals biographies of male rugby and cricket players released just prior to Christmas.

Having now been associated with academia for more than three decades, it seems that crises of credibility and confidence can happen more, not less, frequently with longevity and age. My dearest colleague at OUSPE was a woman named Frances Cruickshank, a graduate of Dunfermline College in Scotland, a member of our Unofficial Women's Committee and one who had retired early, feeling passed by. She would regularly tell me I was too hard on myself. I wrote the following not long after her death from cancer in 1994 and share it here because I believe it speaks about both the joys and pains of women in academe.

FRANCES'S MESSAGE

Your message to me, my dear, I recalled today
from the last time you spoke,
my hand holding yours
lying inert, sallow
on hospital sheets
attached to a body
quietly
frustratingly
failing you
at long long last.

It was well past midnight,
Helen had been,
bubbly, chatty,
showing us how to disbelieve
your wretched form and making plans
for your next drive down The Peninsular together,

describing in detail the people
she would introduce you to,
once there.
And I was telling you about my radio interview,
how badly it had gone, I thought,
what a fool I had felt but
with an aside about, perhaps,
being hard on myself.

You squeezed my hand,
fleetingly, almost a twitch
but too firm to be involuntary
and I knew you had heard
agreed
understood
and given me, in your final semi-conscious hours,
one last message to send me back
to a world without you.

So I sit here today
in that world of academe where I most need your wisdom
and think about how I have done it again
and again
since that long sweet night,
but this time I recall
the significance of your squeeze,
your parting advice,
and resolve to heed
your deliberate message
more often.

This chapter was not easy to write. I worried about the boundaries of what could or should not be said and who would be my readers. Who could possibly be interested? I worried that it would turn out to be too self-indulgent or too sycophantic. I procrastinated, finding excuses in teaching workloads and concerns for the care of an elderly parent, until I found myself once again in Canada on another sabbatical leave and with no further excuses. There, suddenly, the writing flowed.[2] So fast and fluid that initially it surprised me, until I realized the significance of where I was—back in the place that had always nurtured my intellectual journey. It was, apparently, the very right place in which to reflect on that journey and the fortuitous encounters that had made it what it is, adding yet another piece to the already abundant collection.

NOTES

1. A kiwi is a flightless bird, native to New Zealand and used as a symbolic icon for the country. In an international context the word also refers to people from New Zealand.

2. I am grateful for the hospitality provided by Janice Morse, Director of the International Institute for Qualitative Methodology at the University of Alberta. Also to Patricia Bates in Edmonton and Sandra Kirby in Winnipeg who housed me while I wrote. Sandi provided many helpful comments, knowing much of the story. We met in 1984 in the Feminism in Canada course I describe.

REFERENCES

Aitken, J., & Noonan, R. (1981). Rugby, racism and riot gear. *Broadsheet*, 94, 16–19.

Barrett, M. (1988). *Women's oppression today. The Marxist/Feminist encounter.* London: Verso.

Bryson, L. (1983). Sport, ritual and the oppression of women. *Australian and New Zealand Journal of Sociology*, 19, 413–426.

Burstyn, V. (1999). *The rites of men: Manhood, politics and the culture of sports.* Toronto: Toronto University Press.

Birrell, S. (1988). Discourses on the gender/sport relationship: From women in sport to gender relations. *Exercise and Sport Sciences Review*, 16, 459–502.

Chapple, G. (1984). *1981: The Tour.* Wellington: A.H. & A.W. Reed.

Coney, S. (1981). Women against the tour. *Broadsheet*, 92, 8–11.

Curry, T. (1991). Fraternal bonding in the locker room: A profeminist analysis of talk about competition and women. *Sociology of Sport Journal*, 8, 119–135.

Cox, B. & Thompson, S. (2000). Multiple bodies: Sportswomen, soccer and sexuality. *International Review for the Sociology of Sport*, 35, 1, 5–20.

Dann, C. (1982). The game is over. *Broadsheet*, 97, 26–28.

Darlison, L. (1980). Women and sport: A sociological analysis. In J. Shallcrass, B. Larkin, & B. Stothart (Eds.), *Recreation reconsidered into the eighties* (pp. 35–38). Auckland: Auckland Regional Authority.

Darlison, L. (1981). The politics of women's sport and recreation – A need to link theory and practice. In A. Welch (Ed.), *Papers and reports from the 1981 conference on women and recreation* (pp. 15–23). Wellington: New Zealand Council for Recreation and Sport.

Finch, J. (1983). *Married to the job: Wives' incorporation in men's work.* London: George Allen & Unwin.

Fougere, G. (1981). Shattered mirror. *Comment*, 14, 12–14.

Fougere, G. (1989). Sport, culture and identity: The case of rugby football. In B. Willmott & D. Novitz (Eds.), *Culture and identity in New Zealand* (pp. 110–122). Wellington: Government Printer.

Hall, M. A. (1996). *Feminism and sporting bodies.* Champaign, Il.: Human Kinetics.

Hall, S. (1981). Dykes against the Tour. *Broadsheet*, 92, 10.

Jackson, S. (1995). New Zealand's big game in crisis: Mediated images of the transformation, reinvention and reassertion of rugby. Paper presented at the NASSS annual meeting, Sacremento, Nov. 1–4.

James, B., & Saville Smith, K. (1999). *Gender, culture & power*. Auckland: Oxford University Press.

Kirby, S., & McKenna, K. (1989). *Experience, research, change. Methods from the margins*. Toronto: Garamond Press.

Long, W. (1994, Aug. 13). Battle of the sexes still leaves women off some courts of sporting action. *Vancouver Sun*, p. H1.

Money, J., & Ehrhart, A. (1972). *Man & woman, boy & girl: The differentiation and dimorphism of gender identity from conception to maturity*. Baltimore: John Hopkins University Press.

Nauright, J., & Black, D. (1995). New Zealand and international sport: The case of All Black-Springbok rugby, sanctions and protest against Apartheid 1959-1992. In J. Nauright (Ed.), *Sport, power and society in New Zealand: Historical and contemporary perspectives* (pp. 67–94). UNSW, Sydney: Australian Society for Sports History Inc.

Ockwell, G. (2001). *Understanding place: A case study*. Unpublished Masters thesis, University of Otago, Dunedin, New Zealand.

Peart, R. (1986, April 4). Women's place in the phys. ed. faculty. Where have all the women gone? *University of Otago Critic*, p.1.

Phillips, J. (1986). *A Man's Country? The image of the Pakeha male: A history*. Auckland: Penguin.

Research airs sport's dirty washing. (2000, April 28). *New Zealand Education Review*, p. 11.

Richards, T. (2001). *Dancing on our bones. New Zealand, South Africa, rugby and racism*. Wellington: Bridget Williams Books.

Shears, R. & Gidley, I. (1981). *Storm out of Africa: The 1981 Springbok tour of New Zealand*. Auckland: Macmillan.

Thompson, R. (1975). *Retreat from Apartheid: New Zealand's sporting contacts with South Africa*. Wellington: Oxford University Press.

Thompson, S. M. (1975). *Self concept changes in self and others in outdoor education field groups*. Unpublished Masters Thesis, University of Alberta, Edmonton, Canada.

Thompson, S. M. (1981a). Physical Education practical "essentials" in New Zealand secondary schools. *New Zealand Journal of Health, Physical Education and Recreation*, 14, 54–58.

Thompson, S. M. (1981b). Women in sport – is this what we want? In A. Welch (Ed.), *Papers and reports from the 1981 conference on women and recreation* (pp. 70–79). Wellington: New Zealand Council for Recreation and Sport.

Thompson, S. M. (1985). Women in sport: Some participation patterns in New Zealand. *Leisure Studies*, 4, 19–24.

Thompson, S. M. (1988). Challenging the hegemony: New Zealand women's opposition to rugby and the reproduction of a capitalist patriarchy. *International Review for the Sociology of Sport*, 23, 205–212.

Thompson, S.M. (1994). Challenging the hegemony: New Zealand women's opposition to rugby and the reproduction of a capitalist patriarchy. In S. Birrell

& C. Cole (Eds.), *Women, sport and culture* (pp. 213–220). Champaign, Il.: Human Kinetics.

Thompson, S. M. (1999). *Mother's taxi. Sport and women's labor.* Albany: State University of New York Press.

Thompson, S. M. (2000). Legacy of the Tour: A continued analysis of New Zealand women's relationship to sport. In G. Patterson (Ed.), *Sport, culture, society* (pp. 79–92). Wellington: Stout Research Centre.

Thompson, S. M. (2002). Women and sport in New Zealand. In I. Hartmann-Tews & G. Pfister (Eds.), *Sport and women. Social issues in international perspective* (pp. 252–265). London: Routledge.

Walsh, R. (2000, March 27). Mothers crucial to sporting success. *NZ Herald*, p. A5.

Williams, R. (1978). *Marxism and literature.* Oxford: Oxford University Press.

Conclusion

Pirkko Markula

In this book, the authors have told about their personal experiences as feminists studying sport. The chapters recount the development of feminist sport studies through the contributors' personal research histories, they include recollections of personal experience when conducting research projects, and they combine the contributors' personal and professional selves into one coherent story. As this book demonstrates, many of these experiences are deeply traumatizing and troublesome as they reflect the social context and power relations of our work. Although the individual steps taken by these feminist sport scholars have now formed a collective path, it is still narrow and windy. This slows the journey down. It is, therefore, important to demonstrate how feminist sport researchers' experiences reflect the social context and power relations of our work—power relations are slow to show a major change. In order to further challenge this context, we need to be brave enough to tell about these experiences although it might mean contesting mainstream academic conventions and power positions.

As demonstrated throughout this book, writing stories about one's experiences as a researcher provides self-reflexive accounts of what it means to be a feminist sport academic. While not always an easy position, it can also be a rewarding experience. Despite many obstacles the first generation of feminist sport researchers have created groundbreaking work, which now supports the feminist theory-building by the current generation. While feminist sport researchers today might share some of the negative aspects, we now have a group of women whose experiences can encourage us to carry on despite disappointment or troublesome academic politics. In addition, the stories in this book demonstrate that it is not the feminist academic's incompetence but the context of our experiences that is to blame for the many struggles in our careers. While we share some of the pain suffered by our foremothers, we can now also share the joy of a well-established strand of feminist theorizing in sport and physical activity. Therefore, to conclude, it can be worthwhile to further account the reasons for sport feminists to embrace writing about personal experiences in the future. These reasons include 1) to highlight the constraints of producing feminist knowledge in the sport sciences, 2) to further discuss topics in women's sport that are otherwise "sensitive" to represent, 3) to provide texts that are accessible to a wide range of audiences interested in issues regarding women's sport. I will briefly discuss each of these issues.

The chapters in this book advocate a closure of the division between the personal and professional to call for fuller accounts of the contexts of women's lives. These reflections effectively capture the contradictions in the life of a critical scholar and challenges the reader to rethink the connection between knowledge construction, lived experience, and the social context of being a woman in an academic research and writing process. These self-reflexive texts can tell about the context for constructing feminist knowledge: how we theorize, how we construct knowledge, who we study, and what topics we choose are the results of our experiences as women academics. Evidently, it is necessary to write about our different selves if we aim for, not only a description of our lives, but collectively wish to advance feminist knowledge on women's physical activity. Furthermore, while experience and emotionality are integral aspects of our lives, it is important to observe that writing about personal experiences does not advocate a leap into writing that is devoid of theory. On the contrary, if we aim, not for mere confessionality, but for collective stories that reveal the experiences of a sociologically constructed category of people in the context of larger sociocultural and historical forces (Richardson, 1997), we must look for a synthesis of theory, personal experience, and political advocacy. In these texts, self-reflexivity is not self-indulgence, but a necessary component of politicizing the construction of feminist theory. The aim here is to deconstruct power relations between feminist academics and "other" women, women researched, and to collapse the traditional authority of scientific inquiry. I agree with Synthia Sydnor (1998) who reminds sport researchers "to open up their title and text pages to their subject/informants:"

> I pointed out that living in the sport world has become too easy for us as scholars, that it is too easy for us to explain away the riddle for sport with our rote critiques and ethnographies of gender, race, class and so on, as we sit among the "Other" in stadia, gymnasia and sport sociology classes. (p. 22)

To create texts that matter, Sydnor argues, the researcher has to become "Other" herself. Opening one's self to critical reflection takes some guts as it is far easier to hide behind an objective text talking about how "Others" are constructed by societal forces.

The contributors for this book have taken up the challenge of openly discussing how their personal lives shape their research projects. Their chapters have revealed aspects of their identities that, while significant in the research process, could not have been discussed in "scientific" research texts. Some have engaged in representing results from "sensitive" research topics such as sexual harassment. Others have described the aftermath of Arja Laitinen's (1987) keynote address that would have otherwise never been recorded in research articles published from the Congress. Therefore, writing about one's personal experience can provide an opportunity to tell what might otherwise be "unsayable" in social science research (Bruce, 2003). As Toni Bruce (2003) argues, such writing "lets researchers take risks and go places that would not be possible in other forms of research" (p. 148).

In addition to revealing the social construction of the feminist research process, and representing issues otherwise left unsaid, feminist sport researchers can reach for a variety of audiences by writing about their personal experiences. This is a goal that services the political objective of feminism to create large-scale social change in women's condition. If we want our excellent theoretical work to have an impact on the world, we need to get people reading it. This does not mean, however, that we should entirely abandon theoretical research accounts in favor of writing about our personal experiences. On the contrary, the academic audience, of course, is also one of our target markets and it is often most appropriate to address this audience through theoretical texts that clearly convey the intended argument. However, this way of writing should not be the only option we have, rather we should celebrate differences in ways of writing much like we celebrate the differences in women's lives, experiences, and conditions.

Finally, the contributions to this book that have experimented with combining personal with theoretical ways of writing undoubtedly enrich the ways we understand women's sporting experiences and the feminist construction of knowledge. They have included recollections of personal experience within our theoretical texts, they have recounted personal research histories, and they have aimed to reflect on their personal and professional selves in autoethnographic texts. Together these chapters construct a collective story that—based on a synthesis of theory, personal experience, and political advocacy—reveals the experiences of the first generation of feminist sport scholars in the larger context of sociocultural and historical forces (Richardson, 1997). This was also one of the main goals of Arja Laitinen's research. Our intention, therefore, is that this book, by continuing Arja's legacy as a feminist sport researcher, provides one avenue toward the goal of collective social action in sport. As such, these stories, we hope, provide further encouragement for sharing joy amongst all feminist sport researchers.

REFERENCES

Bruce, T. (2003). Pass. In J. Denison & P. Markula (Eds.), *Moving writing: Crafting movement for sport research* (pp. 133–150). New York: Peter Lang.

Kohn, N., & Sydnor, S. (1998). "How do you warm-up for a stretch class?": Sub/in/di/verting hegemonic shoves toward sport. In G. Rail (Ed.), *Sport and postmodern times* (pp. 21–32). Albany: State University of New York Press.

Richardson, L. (1997). *Fields of play: Constructing an academic life.* New Brunswick, NJ: Rutgers University Press.

Contributors

Susan J. Bandy earned a BA in literature and physical education at Berry College (1970), an MEd in physical education at the University of Georgia (1972), and a PhD in sport studies at Arizona State University (1982). She taught at San Diego State University, United States International University, and East Tennessee State University. She was also a Fulbright Scholar to the Hungarian University of Physical Education 1997–1999, a visiting professor in the Faculty of Physical Education and Sport Science, Semmelweis University, Budapest 1999–2003, and a visiting professor in the Department of Gender Studies at that Central European University 2000–2003. At present she is a faculty member in the Department of Sport Science of Aarhus University in Denmark. Her expertise is in the cultural study of sport with particular emphasis on sport literature, the participation of women in sport, and gender and the body. She has edited two books: *Coroebus Triumphs: The Alliance of Sport and the Arts* and *Crossing Boundaries: An International Anthology of Women's Experiences in Sport* and one monograph devoted to women, sport, and literature, a special issue of *Aethlon: The Journal of Sport Literature*. Her most recent book is *The Viking Tradition: 100 Years of Sport at Berry College.*

Celia Brackenridge, PhD, MA, BEd (Hons) Cantab, MILAM, AcSS, runs her own research-based consultancy company, specializing in child protection and gender equity issues in sport and leisure. Celia previously worked at Sheffield Hallam and Gloucestershire Universities and is currently an honorary visiting professor in the Centre for Applied Childhood Studies at Huddersfield University. She is an accredited BASES researcher, a World Class Adviser for the *UK Sports Institute* and was the first Chair of the UK *Women's Sports Foundation.*

Joan L. Duda is a Professor of Sports Psychology in the School of Sport and Exercise Sciences at the University of Birmingham in the United Kingdom and an Adjunct Professor in the Department of Psychological Sciences at Purdue University in the USA. She completed her BA (1977) in Psychology (minor in Women's Studies) at Rutgers University, her MS degree (1978) at Purdue University, and PhD (1981) at the University of Illinois at Urbana-Champaign. Dr. Duda is Past-President of the Association for the Advancement of Applied Sport Psychology and is currently on the Scientific Committee of the European Congress of Sport Science. She was editor of the *Journal of Applied Sport Psychology* and is on the editorial board of the *Journal of Sport and Exercise Psychology*, the *International Journal of Sport Psychology*, and the *Psychology of Sport and Exercise Journal*.

Dr. Duda has authored/coauthored more than 150 scientific publications and book chapters focused on the topic of motivation in the physical domain and the psychological aspects of sport and exercise behavior and has presented more than 220 papers at professional meetings. She is the editor of the book *Advances in Sport and Exercise Psychology Measurement* (1998). She is certified as a consultant by the Association for the Advancement of Applied Sport Psychology. Her hobbies include music, playing club tennis, and traveling.

Kari Fasting is a full professor at the Department of Social Science of the Norwegian University of Sport and Physical Education in Oslo, Norway, where she teaches sociology of sport and research methods. She became the first elected chair of this institution and served as the rector from 1989 to 1994. She is past president of the International Sociology of Sport Association, and is currently the vice-president of the executive board of Women's Sport International. She has published widely on different aspects related to women, exercise and sport. During the last years her focus of research has been on sexual harassment and abuse in sport.

M. Ann Hall is a Professor Emeritus in the Faculty of Physical Education and Recreation at the University of Alberta, Edmonton, Canada where she taught for more than 30 years. Her most recent book is *The Girl and the Game: A History of Women's Sport in Canada* (Peterborough, ON: Broadview Press, 2002).

Ulla Kosonen, Licenciate in Sport Sciences and PhD in Social Sciences, is currently a researcher of Jyväskylän Katulähetys (a third-sector organization). She has published books and articles about body experiences, school memories, and experiences of middle aged women.

Sabine Kröner born 1935, (Professorin, Dr.phil) is Professor Emerita, Faculty of Sport Sciences, University of Münster, Germany. She is an author of numerous research articles and books on gender/women, sport/sport science.

Pirkko Markula is currently with the Department of Education at the University of Bath, United Kingdom. She earned her PhD at University of Illinois at Urbana-Champaign and since then has worked in the United States, New Zealand, and the United Kingdom. She is currently involved in ethnographic research on mindful fitness practices from poststructuralist feminist perspective. She is a coauthor, with Jim Denison, of *Moving Writing: Crafting Movement in Sport Research* (Peter Lang).

Carole A. Oglesby (PhD, PhD) is professor emeritus at Temple University following 40 years in the professoriate. Carole Oglesby is now Kinesiology Chairperson at California State University, Northridge. She has been major professor for 49 successful doctoral students. President of Women Sport International and past member of the International Working Group for women and sport, Carole has edited *Women and Sport: From Myth to Reality*, 1978 and *The Encyclopedia of Women and Sport in America*, 1998. She was a member of the Board of Directors of the U.S. Olympic Committee 1992–1996, on the Olympic Committee Registry of Sport Psychology since 1994 and Chef de Mission of the USA World University Games Winter team in Czechoslovakia, 1987. Awards include the National Association of Girls and Women in Sport Honor Fellow, Association of Intercollegiate Athletics for Women Award of Merit, Women's Sports Foundation USA Billie Jean King Contribution Award, American Alliance of Health, Physical Education, Recreation and Dance Honor Award, R. Tait McKinzie Award and C.D. Henry Award for contributions to African-American professional advancement and the ICSSPE Phillip Noel-Baker Research Award 2001; participated in Amateur Softball Association championship tournaments in 1972, 1973, and 1975 and coached two teams from two different universities to the College World Series in the 1970s.

Gertrud Pfister, a Professor, University Copenhagen, obtained PhD in history at the University of Regensburg in 1976; PhD in sociology at Ruhr-Universität Bochum in 1980. 1981–2001 she was a professor for sport history at the Free University in Berlin; since 2001 she has been professor at the Institute of Exercise and Sport Sciences, University of Copenhagen. Since 2004 she has served as president of the International Sport Sociology Association; 1983–2001 President of the International Society for the History of Physical Education and Sport, since 1996 vicepresident of the German Gymnastic Federation; and since 1993 Head of the Scientific Committee of the International Association for Physical Education and Sport for Girls and Women. She has been a visiting professor at universities in Finland, Canada, Brazil, and Chile and has published several books and more than 200 articles. Her main area of research is gender and sport. She loves all kinds of sport activities, namely skiing, tennis, and long-distance running.

Nancy Theberge is a professor at the University of Waterloo, where she holds a joint appointment in the departments of Kinesiology and Sociology. She has published widely in the sociology of sport and the sociology of the body and is the author of *Higher Goals: Women's Ice Hockey and the Politics of Gender* (State University of New York Press, 2000), winner of the North American Society for the Sociology of Sport Outstanding Book Award in 2001. She served as the Editor of the *Sociology of Sport Journal* from 2002 to 2004.

Shona M. Thompson is currently Head of Department and a Senior Lecturer in Sport and Exercise Science at The University of Auckland. She is a New Zealander who has lived and studied in both Canada (BPE and MA, University of Alberta) and Australia, where she did a PhD in Women's Studies in the Department of Sociology at Murdoch University. This research has been published in the book, *Mother's Taxi. Sport and Women's Labor* (SUNY, 1999). For fun, she renovates old houses and still enjoys the outdoors. Her latest venture has been establishing an olive grove.

Index

Robert E. Rinehard and Synthia Sydnor (eds.), *To the Extreme: Alternative Sports, Inside and Out*

Eric Anderson, *In the Game: Gay Athletes and the Cult of Masculinity*

Pirkko Markula (ed.), *Feminist Sport Studies: Sharing Experiences of Joy and Pain*